T0139170

Series: Cyber Ecosystem and Security

Cloud Security

Concepts, Applications and Perspectives

Editor

Brij B Gupta

Department of Computer Engineering
NIT Kurukshetra, India

CRC Press
Taylor & Francis Group
Boca Raton   London   New York

CRC Press is an imprint of the
Taylor & Francis Group, an **informa** business

A SCIENCE PUBLISHERS BOOK

First edition published 2021
by CRC Press
6000 Broken Sound Parkway NW, Suite 300, Boca Raton, FL 33487-2742

and by CRC Press
2 Park Square, Milton Park, Abingdon, Oxon, OX14 4RN

Library of Congress Cataloging-in-Publication Data

Names: Gupta, Brij, 1982- editor.
Title: Cloud security : concepts, applications and perspectives / editor,
    Brij B Gupta, Department of Computer Engineering NIT Kurukshetra,
    India.
Description: First edition. | Boca Raton : CRC Press, 2021. | Includes
    bibliographical references and index. | Summary: "Cloud Computing has
    proven itself as an extraordinary computing paradigm by providing
    rapidly deployable and scalable Information Technology (IT) solutions
    with reduced infrastructure costs. However, there are numerous
    challenges associated with this technology that require a complete
    understanding in order to be prevented. Cloud Security: Concepts,
    Applications and Perspectives discusses the state-of-the-art techniques
    and methodologies, and covers wide range of examples and illustrations
    to effectively show the principles, algorithms, applications and
    practices of security in Cloud Computing. It also provides valuable
    insights into the security and privacy aspects in Cloud"-- Provided by
    publisher.
Identifiers: LCCN 2020048922 | ISBN 9780367407155 (hardcover)
Subjects: LCSH: Cloud computing--Security measures. | Data protection.
Classification: LCC TK5105.59 .C576 2021 | DDC 005.8--dc23
LC record available at https://lccn.loc.gov/2020048922

ISBN: 978-0-367-40715-5 (hbk)
ISBN: 978-0-367-72296-8 (pbk)
ISBN: 978-0-367-82155-5 (ebk)

Typeset in Times New Roman
by Radiant Productions

Dedicated to my family and friends for their constant support during the course of this book

—B B Gupta

Preface

Nowadays, Cloud Computing facilities are becoming an obvious part of the modern Information and Communication Technology (ICT) systems. Cloud Computing services have proven to be of significant importance, and promote quickly deployable and scalable Information Technology (IT) solutions with reduced infrastructure costs. However, utilization of Cloud also raises different issues related to security, privacy, latency, governance, and so forth, that keep Cloud Computing arrangements from turning into the predominant option for mission critical frameworks. Now the demand is to identify the challenging areas and to apply appropriate security mechanisms to address them. *Cloud Security: Concepts, Applications and Perspectives* is a comprehensive book of substantial technical details for introducing the state-of-the-art research and development on various approaches for security and privacy of Cloud services, novel attacks on Cloud services, Cloud forensics, novel defenses for Cloud service attacks, and Cloud security analysis. It discusses the present techniques and methodologies, and presents a wide range of examples and illustrations to effectively show the concepts, applications and perspectives of security in Cloud Computing. Highly informative subject matter of this book will prepare readers for exercising better protection in terms of understanding the motivation of the attackers and how to deal with them to mitigate the situation in a better manner. In addition, the book covers future research directions in the domain.

This book is suitable for professionals in the field, researchers and students who are looking forward to carry out research in the field of computer and cloud security, faculty members across the universities, and software developers who are seeking to carrying out software development in the field. Specifically, this book contains discussion on the following topics:

- Secured IoT devices management in Cloud-Fog Environment using Blockchain

- Integrating Cloud and Health Informatics: Approaches, Applications and Challenges

- A Flow Based Anomaly Detection System for Slow DDoS Attack on HTTP

Acknowledgement

Many people have contributed greatly to this book on Cloud Security: Concepts, Applications and Perspectives. We, the editors, would like to acknowledge all of them for their valuable help and generous ideas in improving the quality of this book. With our feelings of gratitude, we would like to introduce them in turn. The first mention is the authors and reviewers of each chapter of this book. Without their outstanding expertise, constructive reviews and devoted effort, this comprehensive book would become something without contents. The second mention is the Science Publisher, CRC Press, Taylor and Francis editors, especially Vijay Primlani and his team for their constant encouragement, continuous assistance and untiring support. Without their technical support, this book would not be completed. The third mention is the editor's family for being the source of continuous love, unconditional support and prayers not only for this work, but throughout our life. Last but far from least, we express our heartfelt thanks to the Almighty for bestowing over us the courage to face the complexities of life and complete this work.

June, 2020   Brij B Gupta

Contents

1

Secured IoT Device Management in Cloud-Fog Environment using Blockchain

Asutosh Kumar Biswal,[3] Sourav Kanti Addya,[1] Bibhudatta Sahoo[2],*
and Ashok Kumar Turuk[2]

1.1 Introduction

The integration of Internet of Things (IoT) with cloud and fog computing makes people's lives simpler. The term IoT implies the interconnection of various physical objects or "things", such as laptops, mobile phones, etc. These devices are also termed as IoT nodes. By this time, there are billions to trillions of IoT devices communicating for different purposes and producing a huge amount of data. Cloud plays an important role in processing and analyzing these huge amounts of data. In order to process and analyze the data, we need the help of cloud. Cloud gives us the option of renting storage infrastructure and computing services [1]. For any minimum computation requirements, data packet travel from the IoT devices to cloud is always costly in terms of network latency, immediate devices response time, etc. Therefore, to bring cloud services closer to the end-users, such as IoT nodes, a new layer called 'Fog' was introduced a few years back [2]. Figure 1.1 depicts the logical relation between IoT, fog and cloud.

[1] Assistant Professor, Department of Computer Science and Engineering, National Institute of Technology Karnataka ↗, Surathkal, Mangalore-575025.
[2] Department of Computer Science and Engineering, National Institute of Technology Rourkela, Sundargarh, Odisha, India - 769008.
[3] Cloud Computing Research Lab, Department of Computer Science and Engineering National Institute of Technology Rourkela India.
* Corresponding author: bibhudatta.sahoo@gmail.com

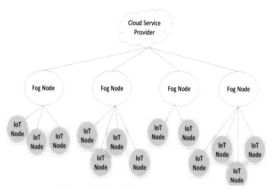

Figure 1.1: IoT-fog-cloud network.

As the usage of IoT devices is increasing in different application areas of daily life, threats to IoT nodes are also increasing. Currently, transferring data securely is a major challenge, in IoT-fog-cloud platform [3]. It affects the network by compromising IoT node(s) in the network, slowing down the communication speed, tampering with the data by malicious node, etc. [4]. In order to prevent these issues, a secure key-based combinatorial BIBD model and a blockchain-based solution is adopted. With respect to the BIBD model parameters, we shaped distinctive user groups consisting of a fixed number of IoT devices under fog nodes.

The blockchain is essentially an append-only data structure that records all the activities in transactions and creates an immutable and distributed ledger of blocks when all participants in the peer-to-peer network agree without requiring trust on a central authority. In blockchain network, nodes do not trust each other because it has the ability to tolerate Byzantine failure. Each block in blockchain is packed with many transactions and consists of a time-stamp or nonce, senders and receivers keys, ids, communication message, device registration date, resources and those required for authentication with a link to its predecessor via a cryptographic pointer, which forms a blockchain. The blockchain starts expanding from the genesis block, which is usually hard coded and does not have any references to the previous block. After this, whenever the transactions start, they are collected in blocks, which are found by the special nodes of the network (miners) in a certain time period (ten minutes for bitcoin blockchain). To mine a valid block, the miners have to follow different consensus techniques, like Bitcoins Proof-of-Work (PoW), Proof-of-Stake (PoS), Proof-of-Authority (PoA), etc. After reaching a consensus, the block is broadcast to other nodes in the network for validation. If all the nodes find that the block is a valid one, then it is added to the blockchain. The concept of blockchain is shown in Figure 1.2.

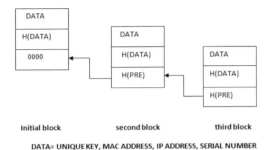

Figure 1.2: Blockchain working principle.

1.1.1 Our Contribution

The contribution of the paper is two folds:

i. Firstly, a key-based communication model using Balanced Incomplete Block Design (BIBD) to secure communication among the IoT devices in a same user group and gateway node selection technique to communicate between two user groups.

ii. Secondly, if one or more IoT nodes are compromised after deployment of the network, then in order to identify the compromised node(s), a blockchain-based solution has been proposed. Here, we adopted bitcoin's proof of work for the same.

The rest of the chapter is organized as follows: Section 1.2 explains the literature that we have reviewed, section 1.3 discusses the proposed model, section 1.4 discusses the performance evaluation of our proposed model, and finally in section 1.5, we draw the conclusion and highlight the future work.

Table 1.1: Notations used.

Notation	Description	Notation	Description
P	Total number of fog nodes	b	Number of blocks or IoT nodes
S	Total number of symbols	r	Repetition of each symbol
V	Total number of symbols selected	k	Length of Key
Λ	Length of repetition	S_{fp}	Symbol set for *pth* fog node
w, x	*jth* key of *ith* fog node	y, z	*nth* key of *mth* fog node
$f_p key_b$	*bth* node of *pth* fog node	Ugi	*ith* user group under fog node

1.2 Related Work

In this section, we review the work reported in the literature. With the growing popularity of IoT, it has become a major component of our daily life. The authors discuss energy efficiency, network flexibility and scalability of IoT nodes in [5]. However, most of the interactions at the backend are achieved using the cloud. Though cloud provides extensive computational resources and storage capacity, it suffers from higher latency. This issue has been resolved using a new paradigm called fog-Computing [3]. A lot of work has been done on the security of cloud-IoT networks, as discussed in [6]. One of the major issues is key distribution [7]. The authors in [8], proposed a mathematical model for secure-key generation and distribution with the help of cloud service providers. The gateway node efficiently connects two similar or dissimilar networks, but its deployment is done during the design time [9]. However, devices can be selected as a gateway on the basis of reachability-information, constraints, and policies, as shown in [10]. They can also be selected on the basis of bandwidth, overload, and velocity, as shown in [11]. The introduction of Vehicular Ad-hoc Network (VANET) requires dynamic selection of gateway nodes to provide information and connection to high-velocity vehicles. The gateway nodes are selected dynamically using clustered and non-clustered strategies [12]. The same can be extended to IoT-fog-cloud architecture in order to leverage network load and service time, thereby simultaneously improving responsiveness and resource visibility [13].

Recently, the emerging blockchain has developed a lot of techniques to overcome the IoT security challenges, as shown in [15]. One of the major issues is attribute compromise or authentication problem, which is addressed in [16]. The decentralization concept of blockchain eliminates third parties, as shown in [17], which also overcomes the deletion issues by replicating from the nearest IoT devices because a copy of the database is available with every node.

In this paper, we focus on finding a gateway node from a set of IoT nodes with the assumption that all devices are 100% capable of becoming a gateway node. The selection is based on a maximum number of connections a node has with different user groups. Since key distribution is expensive and one-time only, the efficiency of the network is greatly affected if any node is compromised. In fact, the effect is deleterious if the gateway node is compromised. In order to identify the IoT node which has been compromised, we append a blockchain-based solution to the BIBD model which enables us to determine the compromised node.

1.3 Proposed Model

In this section, we first formally define an overall working mechanism in two folds. Firstly, we discuss the key generation procedure and gateway selection in IoT-cloud networks and secondly, we discuss security model using blockchain if any node or gateway node is compromised.

1.3.1 BIBD Key Generation and Gateway Selection

In our proposed model, we consider a 3-tier architecture that includes cloud, fog and IoT nodes, as depicted in Figure 1.1. A group of interrelated IoT nodes connected to nearer fog devices. To securely communicate in any user group, a secure key from a key pool will be distributed among the nodes. The responsibility of this distribution can take place at fog layer with the concern of cloud service provider (CSP). The key pool is a combination of different sub-keys. For example, one group may contain (1, 2, 3..., 9), and the other may have (A, B, C..., Z). Now the keys are combined from two groups with a combinatorial model known as BIBD. The model will generate keys like A12, B2A (combination of two groups) which are of three bytes [18]. Since the key management and distribution requires more cost in terms of time, we assume the distribution can take place in the time of deployment of the IoT nodes by assuming the channel to be a secure one. After the distribution of the keys, the IoT nodes will establish a link among themselves with the common key they have. Let us assume the centralized cloud service provider C contains a set of symbols defined as $S_{CSP} = \{S_1, S_2, S_3..., S_s\}$. Let there be a number of fog nodes where $F = \{f_1, f_2, f_3, ..., f_p\}$ and each fog node consists of IoT devices denoted as $I = \{i_1, i_2, i_3, ..., i_b\}$ where b is a predefined parameter.

In order to provide communication between cloud, fog and IoT nodes, the cloud service provider uses the BIBD model to generate unique keys. The BIBD model consists of 5 parameters (v, k, λ, b, r) where v denotes total number of Symbols selected, k is the length of Key, λ is length of repetition, r is repetition of each symbol and b is the number of blocks which is same as number of IoT nodes [14]. In the BIBD model, the parameters b and r are dependent on other three parameters and not every combination of v, k, λ can give BIBD key. The equation which interconnects the parameters are:

$$bk = vr \qquad (1.1)$$

$$(v - 1) = r (k - 1) \qquad (1.2)$$

The CSP will select the symbols for different fog groups from S_{CSP}. For example, $S_{f1} \in S_{CSP}$ for fog group 1, $S_{f2} \subseteq S_{CSP}$ for group 2 ... $S_{fp} \subseteq S_{CSP}$ for group p in such a way that

$$S_{f1} \cap S_{f2} \ldots \cap S_{fp} \neq \Phi \qquad (1.3)$$

now the parameters for fog node to generate keys using BIBD model are $(S_{fp} v, S_{fp} k, S_{fp} \lambda, S_f b, S_{fp} r)$. For instance, the parameters for fog node 1 will be $(S_{f1} v, S_{f1} k, S_{f1} \lambda, S_{f1} b, S_{f1} r)$.

Since the symbol pool has been distributed to fog nodes and using BIBD approach, it will generate a set of unique keys represented as $f_p key = \{f_p key_1,$

$f_p key_2, f_p key_3, \ldots, f_p key_b\}$ in which a key is a composition of k symbols. Links between the nodes are established with the common sub-key they have and the BIBD model is designed in such a way that each node is connected to every other node, as shown in Figure 1.3:

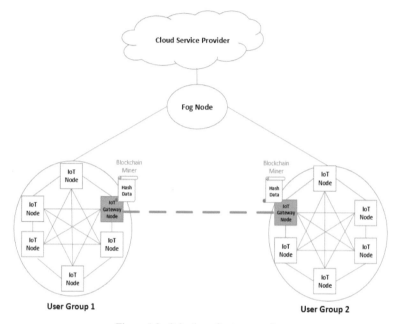

Figure 1.3: Selection of gateway node.

In order to find the gateway node, we have to communicate between different nodes under different fog node. The IoT nodes in one group communicate with IoT nodes of other groups if they have any common sub-keys and these are the potential candidates for the gateway node. In general

$$f_w key_x \cap f_y key_z \neq \Phi \tag{1.4}$$

for each node, we count such intersections. The node which gives the maximum value is selected as a gateway node. This process is depicted in Figure 1.3 and the algorithm 2 is as described. We select a node as gateway node which is capable of monitoring all the transaction in the user group while communicating with other nodes. In this paper, we execute key generation and key distribution process only once, i.e., CSP distributes the key to each IoT node with the help of fog nodes. Then we establish a link between the nodes with the common key they have and find the IoT node that is connected to the maximum number of other IoT nodes, which monitors all the internal and external traffic, data communication within and between the different user groups.

1.3.2 Secure using Blockchain

The keys distributed to IoT nodes under one user group are $f_p key = \{f_p key_1, f_p key_2, f_p key_3 \ldots, f_p key_b\}$. The difference between $f_p key_1$ and $f_p key_2$ may be a one or two symbols, for example, one IoT node may have A12 and another one may have 1B2, in which one symbol is different, so by applying any crypt-analysis technique (brute force) one can spoof the key. Once the key is compromised, the efficiency of the network is hampered. In order to authenticate and protect the IoT device, a cryptographic, verifiable and publicly viewable solution, popularly known as blockchain, is proposed. Algorithm 3 describes the steps of the proposed security. In the blockchain platform, the data of each device is hashed, and a unique hash value is generated. The attribute of IoT device includes unique key distributed by cloud service provider (CSP) ($f_p key_b$), MAC Id (*Mb*), IP address (*IPb*), device number (*Db*), time of installation (*Tb*) and a nonce (*Nb*). So, the attribute set is

$$Ab = (Fpkeyb, Mb, IPb, Db, Tb, Nb).$$

The unique hash for each device can be found as per the difficulty level, which is easy to verify and expensive to compute. The hash value is calculated by applying SHA-256 as per the following equation.

$$H(Ab) = Sha\_256(Fpkeyb, Mb, IPb, Db, Tb, Nb).$$

The generated hash contains the number of zeros as per the difficulty level followed by digest digits or characters which is of length 64 digit. For example, if the difficulty level is set to 4 then the valid hash is shown as in Figure 1.4.

000042ef6d8bfa302ced8fc9f51ece397750a3407430ae870de1c26f078aaaa9

Figure 1.4: Hash value.

Algorithm 1: Gateway Selection

Input: $S = \{S_1, S_2, S_3, \ldots, S_s\}$
Output: Gateway Node
1 CSP(C) selects symbol from S_{csp} for *Ugi* and *Ugj* such that

$$Sugi \cap Sugj \; Ç \; \Phi$$

Generate keys

$$Ki, i = 1, 2, \ldots nb$$

using BIBD model for n numbers of *Ug* and *b* number of blocks in each *Ug*
Distribute *Ki* to

$$bni, n = 0, 1, 2\ldots$$

   for *(i = 0; i < n; i + +)* **do**
2   **for** *(j = 0; j < n; j + +)* **do**
3   Gateway Node Selection (*Ugi, Ugj*); //Algorithm **2**

The hash value of all the IoT nodes is calculated and stored in the block. When a key is compromised or one node spoofs another node, we get a different hash value or a matched hash value in the worst case with respect to the recorded hash block. If any discrepancy is found with respect to the hash values, then we can get back to the initial values and restore the node details, which means there is no chance of a compromise.

Algorithm 2: Gateway Node Selection

Input: (*Ugi, Ugj*)
Output: Gateway Node
1   **for** *each Ki in Ugi* **do**
2   count <—0
3   **for** *each Kj in Ugj* **do**
4   if(ki ∩ *kj ≠ null*)
5   count = count+1;
6   Gateway node = max(count).

1.4 Performance and Evaluation

Algorithm 3: Security Algorithm Using Blockchain

Input: (*Ai, Gateway node, Difficulty level*)
Output: Device Compromised Or Not Compromised
1 Make Gateway node as miners of blockchain network.
2 Find

$$H(Ab) = Sha\_256(Fpkeyb, Mb, IPb, Db, Tb, Nb).$$

3 If H(Ab) starts with('Difficulty-level')
4 Broadcast through the network add to the block
5 End
6 Compromised-Ab=Randomly compromise attribute of any device.
7 Find

$$H(CAb) = Sha\_256(Compromised - Ab)$$

8 If H(Ab) not equal to H(CAb) then
9 Device is compromised
10 else
11 Not compromised
12 end If

1.4.1 Simulation Setup

The proposed model was implemented using JMP tool [19] and python 3.0 in a desktop system with Intel (R) Core (TM) i7-7700K CPU processor with 4.20 GHz and 32 GB memory. BIBD key generation is done using JMP tool and imported into python for key distribution and gateway selection. For simulation purposes, we have created 40 variables, each represents one IoT node and settled 10 IoT nodes in one user group as per the BIBD model parameter ($v = 6$, $k = 3$, $\lambda = 2$) which gives $b = 10$ (each block treated as one IoT node) and $r = 5$, as shown in Table 1.2. The deployment of IoT nodes is shown in Figure 1.5.

The four different users are marked with different shapes. The generated keys are distributed to all the nodes and communication links are established with the nodes which have one or more common keys. A gateway node is selected from the IoT node which has the maximum connections with all other nodes. The gateway device for the four user groups is 8, 18, 27 and 31. After selection of the gateway node, the efficiency of the network is found in terms of resiliency by compromising 5%, 10%, 15% nodes randomly, which follows Poisson distribution as shown in the Table 1.3. Resiliency is measured in order to observe how the IoT-cloud-fog environment will cope with the changes when any of the devices is compromised. It is observed that when a node is compromised the resiliency of the network is affected, which is high when the gateway device is compromised so the security of the gateway device is more important. The resiliency of the network (in our simulation 4 user groups are considered) is evaluated as per equation 1.5.

Table 1.2: BIBD Key generation and distribution.

Node Number	BIBD Key	Node Number	BIBD Key
1	132	11	165
2	2B3	12	5C6
3	A1B	13	D1C
4	12C	14	15B
5	BA2	15	CD5
6	2CA	16	5BD
7	CA3	17	BD6
8	BC1	18	6CB
9	3BC	19	CB1
10	A31	20	D61
User Group 1 Sug1 ={1, 3, 2, A, B, C}		User Group 2 Sug2 ={1, 5, 6, B, C, D}	
links from Ug1 to Ug2 [5, 5, 8, 8, 5, 5, 5, 10, 8, 5]			

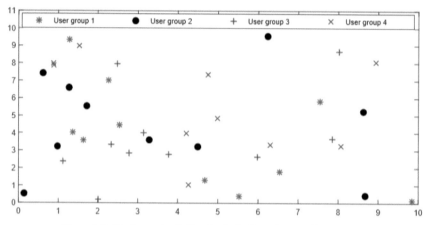

Figure 1.5: Deployment of IoT nodes in the Cartesian coordinate system.

Table 1.3: Simulation results.

5% fail		10% fail		15% fail	
Node Number	**Resiliency**	**Node Number**	**Resiliency**	**Node Number**	**Resiliency**
7, 22	3.6553	22, 9, 26, 29	7.0496	25, 35, 21, 39, 36, 22	11.7493
0, 10	3.0026	0, 19, 29, 32	7.9634	22, 39, 7, 14, 8, 1	12.7937
15, 9	4.6997	1, 38, 15, 36	8.8772	26, 13, 7, 22, 35, 39	13.4464
13, 5	5.7441	37, 5, 9, 10	10.5744	5, 8, 39, 6, 37, 16	14.6214
35, 8	6.1357	9, 8, 3, 33	11.6187	13, 6, 10, 27, 8, 25	17.2323
18, 31	6.5274	10, 31, 27, 18	12.0104	18, 13, 10, 26, 31, 7	18.0156

Since the deployment of our model is static because key pre-distribution is unique and expensive and we are not dealing with any cryptographic key techniques, like public key and private key concept, one can find the BIBD key using brute force method; if 2–3 parameters of the model are known, attackers can easily hack the MAC address and IP address. To overcome these issues a blockchain-based solution is adopted.

$$\text{Resiliency} = \frac{Number\ of\ links\ compromised}{Total\ number\ of\ communication\ links} \qquad (1.5)$$

In the following Subsections, we evaluated the following: In Subsection 1.4.2, we evaluated the issues that the proposed model might have to face and a detailed analysis of what can be done to overcome it after any node is compromised using blockchain. In Subsection 1.4.3, we analyzed the security aspects of the blockchain and the consequences if the uniqueness of the keys is compromised.

1.4.2 Solution using Blockchain

In each user group, the selected gateway nodes are the miners of the blockchain peer-to-peer network. The miners will mine, validate all the device information and update in a distributed ledger which will be updated at the miners of the different user group. The information of the first user group is kept in genesis block and the information of the second user group is kept in the second block, with a link to the genesis block. Similarly, all the group information is linked into the blockchain network. The genesis block and all other blocks will become part of the blockchain when these are successfully mined and validated by the miners. The most expensive part of blockchain technique is proof-of-work, which depends upon the difficulty level, which is set to 4 (for easy simulation) in our implementation. This means that if any hash value starts with 4 zeros then it is valid, which is expensive to calculate and easy to verify. To ensure more protection to the IoT gateway nodes, the difficulty level is set to 5 (for IoT gateway of user group 1), 6 (for IoT gateway of user group 2), and 7 and 8 to the rest of the user groups. The proof-of-work hash values for four IoT nodes are shown in Figure 1.6. It can be observed from Figure 1.6 that for each IoT node the calculated hash value starts with four zeros which denote the difficulty level of hash value. From the implementation point of view, we keep the number of zeros at the beginning of the hash to four, which indicates moderate difficulty. In the proposed model, the hash values of all the nodes are calculated using BIBD-generated unique key, MAC address, IP address and device-id associated with a node. If valid, this copy is then broadcasted to all the miners. If all miners are agreed and validate the block, then the copy is updated in the distributed ledger at the gateway nodes of all the user groups or all the miners of blockchain network.

Index	Type	Size	Value
0	str	1	0000c01a542192ed5da8a288cef1b49ffa3539af635a47e126bce7d8c7ab1be3
1	str	1	00005d59cc4e52043ef4d3fbae8a5171ca714ccea76f40a82316958d9357d32c
2	str	1	000003c8564f33849c3f05ad45a39316aac68d9c964c40bf8a3e27506d893678
3	str	1	00001870f5c3fb2287996f0faea281354679714721097fcf167cf10bf04a8ae4

Figure 1.6: Proof of work.

1.4.3 Security Analysis

The security of blockchain mainly lies on the difficulty level and computational power. Higher difficulty level consequently increases the complexity of calculation in terms of time and resource utilization. If any parameter of the device is changed, the hash value will be changed because of its uniqueness. We have compromised a random device attribute and observed that the hash values are different even if the attacker is following the same proof-of-work. The compromised proof-of-work for the first device is shown in Figure 1.7. It can be observed from Figure 1.7 that the hash value has four leading zeros, but the remaining hash characters are changed. After a broadcast, the hash values will produce a mismatch at the miners and, hence, it can be concluded that one IoT node has been compromised. The compromised node is placed inside a rectangle to mark the difference, as shown in Figure 1.8. Similarly, any changes or new hash values are found with respect to the proof-of-work of IoT gateway devices and we can directly tell which gateway device is compromised within very little time.

Figure 1.7: Compromised proof of work.

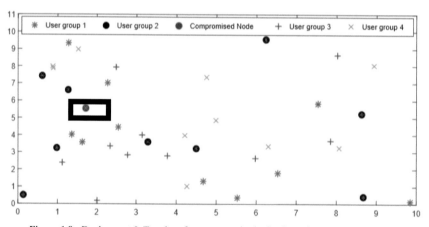

Figure 1.8: Deployment IoT nodes after compromise in the Cartesian coordinate system.

1.5 Conclusion

In this paper, we have emphasized the need of the blockchain to solve key compromise problem. Using the BIBD model, the keys are generated and efficiency of the network is evaluated. It is observed that, when a node, mainly a gateway node, fails or is compromised, the productivity of the system, which is determined in terms of resiliency, is very high and no more correspondence is workable for the compromised device since the deployment is static. To overcome this problem, we deployed a blockchain-based solution to protect the compromised node, which is not achievable using the BIBD model. This technique helps in making the system more secure and trustworthy due to the decentralization, cryptographic verification and mining techniques of blockchain.

In future, we will work on compressing the miners database and will use a blockchain-based authentication schema during the deployment time of the IoT networks.

Key Terminology & Definitions

Blockchain – A blockchain is a tamper-proof, incorruptible distributed database that maintains a continuously growing ordered list of records called blocks. The blocks are validated by the miner nodes in the peer-to-peer network. All the confirmed and validated blocks are linked and chained from the beginning of the chain to the most current block. The confirmation of blocks happens when the network comes to a consensus with the help of different consensus algorithms, like proof of work, proof of stack, proof of authority and many more.

Internet of Things – It is composed of two words: internet and thing, where internet is a global wide area network that uses the internet suite to deliver communication, while things can be defined as any physical devices embedded with sensors, actuators and software to collect and transmit data. The combination of these two concepts brings a lot of opportunity and benefit in social, individual and industrial application with improved efficiency. Some well-known IoT devices include smart phones, laptops, tablets, digital cameras and wearables. The major applications are big data analysis, smart city, smart markets, smart healthcare and many more.

Bitcoin – Bitcoin is a digital currency, which means it only exists electronically. It is not attached to any central authority or regulatory body but uses peer to peer technology in the network. Exchanges are confirmed by chosen organize hubs, known as miners, through cryptography and recorded in an open distributed record known as blockchain. The miners use a consensus algorithm, i.e., proof of work, to validate the block.

References

[1] Emeakaroha, V. C., Cafferkey, N., Healy, P. and Morrison, J. P. 2015. A cloud-based IoT data gathering and processing platform. pp. 50–57. *In*: International Conference on Future Internet of Things and Cloud, Aug 2015.

[2] Fu, J., Liu, Y., Chao, H. C., Bhargava, B. and Zhang, Z. 2018. Secure data storage and searching for industrial IoT by integrating fog computing and cloud computing. Journal IEEE Transactions on Industrial Informatics, 4(1–4): 28.

[3] Yousefpour, A., Ishigaki, G., Gour, R. and Jue, J. P. 2018. On reducing IoT service delay via fog offloading. Journal IEEE Internet of Things Journal, 998–1010.
[4] Huang, X. and Ansari, N. 2017. Secure multi-party data communications in cloud augmented IoT environment. pp. 1–6. *In*: IEEE International Conference on Communications (ICC), May 2017.
[5] Elhammouti, H., Sabir, E., Benjillali, M., Echabbi, L. and Tembine, H. 2017. Self organized connected objects: rethinking QoS provisioning for IoT services. Journal IEEE Communications Magazine, 41–47.
[6] Singh, J., Pasquier, T., Bacon, J., Ko, H. and Eyers, D. 2016. Twenty security considerations for cloud-supported internet of things. Journal IEEE Internet of Things Journal, 269–284.
[7] El Hajjar, A. 2016. Securing the Internet of things devices using pre-distributed keys. pp. 198–200. *In*: IEEE International Conference on Cloud Engineering Workshop (IC2EW), April 2016.
[8] Moharana, S. R., Jha, V. K., Satpathy, A., Addya, S. K., Turuk, A. K. and Majhi, B. 2017. Secure key-distribution in IoT cloud networks. pp. 197–202. *In*: Third International Conference on Sensing, Signal Processing and Security (ICSSS), May 2017.
[9] Zhong, C. L., Zhu, Z. and Huang, R. G. 2015. Study on the IOT architecture and gateway technology. pp. 196–199. *In*: 14th International Symposium on Distributed Computing and Applications for Business Engineering and Science (DCABES), Aug 2015.
[10] Beijar, N., Novo, O., JimÃ©nez, J. and Melen, J. 2015. Gateway selection in capillary networks. pp. 90–97. *In*: 5th International Conference on the Internet of Things (IOT), Oct 2015.
[11] Idrissi, A., Retal, S., Rehioui, H. and Laghrissi, A. 2015. Gateway selection in vehicular ad-hoc network. pp. 1–5. *In*: 5th International Conference on Information Communication Technology and Accessibility (ICTA), Dec 2015.
[12] Alawi, M., Sundararajan, E., Alsaqour, R. and Ismail, M. 2017. Gateway selection techniques in heterogeneous vehicular network: Review and challenges. pp. 1–6. *In*: 6th International Conference on Electrical Engineering and Informatics (ICEEI), Nov 2017.
[13] Lee, W., Nam, K., Roh, H. G. and Kim, S. H. 2016. A gateway based fog computing architecture for wireless sensors and actuator networks. pp. 210–213. *In*: 18th International Conference on Advanced Communication Technology (ICACT), Jan 2016.
[14] Addya Sourav Kanti and Ashok Kumar Turuk. 2010. A technique for communication of distance node on key pre-distribution in wireless sensor networks. *In*: ACEEE.
[15] Minhaj Ahmad Khan and Khaled Salah. 2018. IoT security: Review, blockchain solutions, and open challenges. Journal Future Generation Computer Systems, 395–411.
[16] Yu, R., Wang, J., Xu, T., Gao, J., An, Y., Zhang, G. and Yu, M. 2017. Authentication with block-chain algorithm and text encryption protocol in calculation of social network. Journal IEEE Access, 24944–24951.
[17] Xu, C., Wang, K. and Guo, M. 2017. Intelligent resource management in blockchain based cloud datacenters. Journal IEEE Cloud Computing, 50–59.
[18] Ruj Sushmita and Roy Bimal. 2010. Key predistribution using combinatorial designs for grid-group deployment scheme in wireless sensor networks. Journal ACM Trans. Sen. Netw., 4(1–4): 28.
[19] JMPÂ®, Version 12. SAS Institute Inc., Cary, NC, 1989–2007.

2

Integrating Cloud and Health Informatics

Approaches, Applications and Challenges

Sheshang M Ajwalia,[1,*] *Anu Mary Chacko*[2] and *Madhu Kumar S D*[2]

2.1 Introduction

School of Informatics at the University of Edinburgh defines Informatics as "the study of the structure, behaviour, and interactions of natural and engineered computational systems". According to the United States National Library of Medicine (NLM), Health Informatics is "the interdisciplinary study of the design, development, adoption and application of IT-based innovations in healthcare services delivery, management and planning". HI System Architectures (HISA) deals with the resources, devices, and methods required to optimize the acquisition, storage, retrieval, and use of information in health by collaborating with various healthcare organizations.

HI comprises clinical informatics and clinical research informatics. Clinical informatics focuses on public and personal health outcomes. It deals with the procurement, customization, development, implementation, management, evaluation, and continuous improvement of clinical information systems, HI tools, and Clinical Decision Support Systems (CDSS) according

[1] Morgan Stanley, Mumbai, India.
[2] Department of Computer Science and Engineering, National Institute of Technology Calicut, India.
  Emails: anu.chacko@nitc.ac.in; madhu@nitc.ac.in
* Corresponding author: sidajwalia@gmail.com

to the information and knowledge needs of healthcare professionals and patients. While clinical research informatics improves the quality of clinical research, it handles problems of the integrated data repository, data sharing platforms for clinical data study and common data standards.

The rest of the paper is organized as follows: some of the relevant existing works in HISAs are reviewed in section 2.2, discussion on reviewed literature is presented in section 2.3, in section 2.4, the existing work in the area is classified by some identified parameters, section 2.5 presents our findings and lists the potential research areas and the challenges in the cloud-based HIS, and section 2.6 summarizes this review.

2.2 Related Works

Scalable and Collaborative Infrastructure for a Learning Healthcare System (SCILHS) [1]: SCILHS was developed by the researchers at Harvard Medical School as *Clinical Data Research Network (CDRN)* and supported by *Patient-Centered Outcomes Research Institute (PCORI)*. *The Learning Healthcare System (LHS)* is the base concept used in this architecture to generate and apply the best evidence for the collaborative healthcare choices of each patient and provider and to drive the process of research and analytics as a natural outgrowth of patient care.

SCILHS aimed to create a quarriable semantic data model nationwide, and ten health organizations were part of it, initially collaborating with data of 8 million patients. SCILHS architecture was built on the top of the network of organizations that already had a common clinical and translational research IT and regulatory framework.

SCILHS architecture was built with the help of open-source, free, and modular components. The data collected by Electronic Health Records (EHRs) from participating organizations is stored in a research-based, shared, freely accessible health data warehouse which is known as a *sidecar*. This sidecar approach for data storage allows real-time querying of the data collaborated between heterogeneous institutions. *i2b2 (Informatics for Integrating Biology and Bedside)* is the open-source analytic platform for EHR. *SHARINE (SHAred health Research Information NEtwork)* is used to query sidecar i2b2 nodes in the real-time collaboratively. *SMART (Substitutable Medical Applications, Reusable Technologies)* is the App Store, created specifically for this architecture to allow any developer to develop *SHARINE/i2b2* compatible applications.

mySCILHS is the patient-centric platform based on *Patient-Powered Research Networks (PPRNs)*. This API exposes the structured clinical summary data for each participating patient.

In phase 2, SCILHS is turned to the *Accessible Research Commons for Health (ARCH)* [2]. ARCH deals with the effectiveness of treatment and developing personalized medicines. Collaborators simply have to select and apply disease-specific filters and input the patient data to get outcomes [3].

Shared Pathology Informatics Network (SPIN) [4]: Another famous public health HI architecture is SPIN-based NHIN, developed to support *National Health Information System (NHIN)* by researchers at Harvard-MIT Division of Health Sciences and Technology, and the Laboratory of Computer Science, Massachusetts General Hospital. The SPIN architecture supports distributed data storage to protect privacy, institutional autonomy to promote participation, various levels of invigilation access and self-scaling architecture to encourage regional collaboration into the nationwide system.

In this peer-to-peer architecture, each participating peer site is given the freedom to have local databases that can define their own privacy policy along with HIPAA compliance. Some of the peers behave as super-nodes and create a tree structure. Data is stored at peer after ETL processes like Anonymization, Re-Identification, Auto coding. Original identity is stored in a separate site, *codebook*, with unique anonymization identifier. There are three levels of accesses, namely (1) Routine Analysis—real-time analysis of anonymized patient data, (2) Alarm Investigation—more detailed investigation of aberrant patient records only with increased permission to anonymized details, and (3) Emergency Investigation—the role with broad investigative powers with the identification of patient data. Query thrown by investigator first checks with the trusted agency about the worthy-ness of the investigator. On verification, from supernode the query is distributed to all the peers, according to peer policy, data is accessed, and the aggregated result is returned to the investigator via supernode. Architecture is self-scaling, allowing any participant to leave the community without leaving data trails behind (loosely coupled) and allowing new organizations to join the system as new peers attached to some super-node (bottom-up approach).

Healthcare Software-as-a-Service Platform (HSP) [5]: Korean researchers Sooyoung Yoo et al. proposed HSP that offers a fixed set of applications that are suitable for small and mid-sized hospitals or individual organizations. As a Cloud-based CDSS, HSP can provide rule-based services for medications, alert registration services, and knowledge services. Other than CDSS, it also provides essential functional services like order entry management, patient management, and appointment management.

Architecture adopted is a multi-tenancy model with a shared database with separate schemas for each tenant through a single application. Each tenant has the freedom to host their data on a local server or cloud. HSP is implemented as a multi-layered architecture. HSP uses SOA framework for exposing business processes as web services and to interact with external systems. This framework takes care of security and privacy and provides authentication and authorization, access control, encryption, and backup at various levels of the framework like PC, network, application, system and database. Authors propose to provide high usability and faster accessibility to the offered services by providing multi-platform mobile services created with the help of Mobile Enterprise Application Platform (MEAP). The architecture also proposes to useHL7 *InfoButton standard* and *decision support service standard* to achieve interoperability with heterogeneous legacy systems for context-aware knowledge retrieval services.

CYCLONE [6]: Health informatics research involves data-intensive scientific application workflows. This workflow can run more efficiently on the cloud as it offers advantages of scalability and load balancing. The problem of inter-cloud or federated cloud management is tackled in the development of CYCLONE, which provides an automated federated cloud platform for life science researchers to deploy their workflow tools securely and efficiently. The major component in CYCLONE is *Slipstream*, which provides a uniform interface for most major cloud providers and primary open-source cloud distributions. As an automation tool, developers define recipes to convert base machines into the components of the needs. By interconnecting such components of the requirements, a complete cloud application can be built. Each component is a set of recipes, namely pre-install, package-installs, post-install, deployment, and reporting. CYCLONE also has an App Store similar to SCILHS.

CYCLONE aims at security infrastructure with the provision of the set of ready-to-use components. Most focused areas are federated identity management, federated authorization management, and secure end-to-end data transfers.

The architecture reviewed till now focuses more on clinical research, the rest of the section looks at tools for public and personal health. It evaluates HI tools developed for better patient care through real-time monitoring and providing continuous care. Point of care devices, mobile sensors and agents are essential components of these architectures.

The Australian research about the Mobile Cloud for Assistive Healthcare (MoCAsH) [7]: This Architecture is made up of mobile data sensing and collecting sensors. Mobile devices auto-switch the network for real-time monitoring. The primary data analysis and processing can be done on the client-side only to reduce the load on the cloud. Non-persistent client-cloud connection keeps the power consumption lower. This system uses context-aware cloud middleware to evaluate the dynamically captured patient's condition based on the age, mental condition, time zones, environment and geolocation of the patient. A repository of context data and rules in cloud middleware helps in evaluating the new inputs and delivering the decisions. Federated clouds keep the system real-time and mobile. It deploys grid architecture as the private cloud for data storage with security and SOA architecture to provide services to the end devices.

Cloud-based MCC-centric Ubiquitous Healthcare System [8]: Taiwan researchers Chen-Shie Ho and Kuo-Cheng Chiang proposed this model. Medical call centre (MCC) behaves like a call transferring service and interface between patients and hospitals. It attends calls from patients and diverts it to the respective doctor or healthcare institute. From context-aware mobile sensors and home appliances, the signals are processed in MCC, and for any vital signs, the doctor and patient are notified for further action. Healthcare cloud consists of multiple *s-clouds (service clouds)*, each specific to a particular healthcare service.

In the experiment, three copies of the same hospital information system were executed on three s-clouds distributed over three stations of the Taipei metro system. When the patient moves between these stations, information is pushed to the patient's mobile device. During the time, if some signs are updated, data analysis will be done on the back end of s-cloud and updates will be distributed to all three copies. Results are also sent back to the patient in the moving situation.

Intelligent Agent Framework [9]: Framework proposed by Hasan Omar Al-Sakran is based on the intelligent agents and Case-Based Reasoning (CBR) for providing interoperability between already existing agents. The framework creates an interface agent for creating proper interaction between agents. Each agent contains a knowledge base and set of rules. Mobile agents communicate with each other directly, achieve goals and adapt to the changing environment. Mobile agents require common language applications to communicate with each other and across heterogeneous networks. CBR generates advice on a particular problem by analyzing solutions to previously solved problems and builds intelligent systems for disease diagnostics and prognosis. The new case is added in the case repository for future. This model is weak in the aspect of security during data movements among agents and from outsiders.

In the present time, the HISs with sensors and real-time monitoring is more prevalent. Gupta et al. [10] proposed IoT based architecture to analyze the human's physical activities for the onset of disease. BodyEdge [11] is based on edge computing-based IoT human-centric applications.

Data Standards: Communication between various devices, platforms and autonomous systems becomes tough if each participant involved in communication uses different data standards. Uniformity is required for interoperability.

Third revision to the HL7 [12] is introduced as Fast Healthcare Interoperability Resources (FHIR) [13] and is making HL7 standards easy to implement, making founded on popular web standards like XML, JSON, OAuth, and a human-readable serialization format for ease of use by developers. It added standards for evidence-based medicine, Translational research, and data capture into the existing pool of HL7 standards. Object Management Group (OMG) has developed and is working on Industrial IoT (IIoT) standards [14]. It standardizes Data Distribution Service (DSS) protocol for network interoperability of connected devices, the standard for threat information sharing known as Thread Modelling, Unified Component Model (UCM) for providing common middleware for different embedded systems, and Interaction Flow Modeling Language (IFML) for expressing content and control behaviour of front-end of applications. HIMSS Electronic Health Record Association (EHRA) [15] makes efforts to create interoperable EHRs in clinics, personal use, and mobile care settings. Regarding medical imaging, Digital Imaging and Communications in Medicine (DICOM) [16] is the standard for the communication and management of medical imaging information and related data. CDISC [17] standardizes the data formats to organize, plan, collect and analyze, specifically aiming at the clinical research process.

2.3 Analysis of the Existing Work

Shared data repository of SCILHS requires the participating institutions to have the common data standards and regulatory IT framework. Institute not matching those standards either does not qualify to join the network or needs to create one extra layer. Comparatively, SPIN-based NHIN is good as it uses peer databases that allow participants to have their own privacy policies and access levels. Also, this data storage structure provides institutional autonomy. However, as this architecture allows for individual policies, interoperability between participants is the issue [18]. SCILHS uses the *Kimball's Star Schema* for storage over each peer node, but being a highly denormalized database schema, it turns out to be a purpose-specific schema and works only for the simpler queries. So, expansion or flexing of the architecture over the research areas other than implemented or the complex analytics may become required. However, on the plus side, the inclusion of the Learning Healthcare System (LHS) is beneficial for the most accurate analysis, as it continuously learns from the recent data fed to the analytics.

In NHIN work, due to geospatial anonymization, clustering algorithms can give less accuracy than expected. Also, the tree structure of the system implies a single point of failure as the breakdown of the super-node can make peer nodes unreachable. De-Identification of patient data results in multiple entries for the same patient if entries are done at different locations.

The Taiwan model proposes creating an MCC component for working of architecture while an agent-based framework uses all the existing devices and agents and has intercommunication. Taiwan model and MoCAsH are working on the base of context-aware intelligence, but the agent framework proposes CBR. This agent-based framework does not take an idea of lower energy consumption into consideration, as opposed to the other two models.

Interoperability between HISs can be ensured only if systems follow standards in data storage and communication. HSP uses the *InfoButton standard and decision support service standard* for context-aware knowledge retrieval services. HL7 data exchange standards are the most common HL7 standards being used for the uniform data exchange.

Not all reviewed work is implemented at full scale. Research networks like SCILHS and SPIN-based NHIN are very well implemented and are used at a nationwide level for a long span of years, and later upgraded with new functionalities or replaced with another HIS. While some works were prototyped over short time-span or tested on particular demographic areas to validate the proposed idea, like CYCLONE, Taiwan ubiquitous model and Intelligent agents' framework. HSP and MoCAsH are only proposed models.

All the reviewed works have architectures according to personal characteristics. Figure 2.1 shows the basic components of any HIS.

Users enter the information from the front, and interactive ends (data-sources). These front-end nodes can be individually connected to the database or can have a complex internal network, as in the case of SPIN. If all the

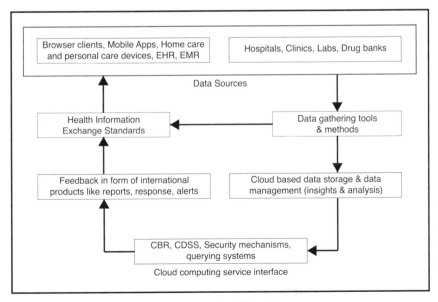

Figure 2.1: Generalized HIS architecture.

participants in the network are not using similar information exchange standards, interoperability standards like HL7 are used to translate and exchange the information. Gathered data is sent to the database. Database arrangements can be multi-tenant, shared or localized. Computing interface has a collection of business logic, security mechanisms, and querying mechanisms. Database and computing interface may be maintained over a single or federated cloud. The computing interface sends results to the clients after translating them into client-specific formats.

2.4 Classification of Existing HIS

The reviewed work can be categorized and classified according to the various matrices. Table 2.1 classifies the HIS according to the purpose of the system. Table 2.2 identifies the core architecture concept used in the HIS. Table 2.3 classifies the reviewed HIS according to whether HIS is a research informatics system or public health informatics system. Table 2.4 shows whether the HIS architecture was developed within a single cloud or required multiple cloud services. Lastly, Table 2.5 classifies the HIS by the deployment stage of the HIS, based on whether it is implemented or not.

Table 2.1: Classification by usage.

Usage	HIS Architectures
Research Network	SCILHS, SPIN-based NHIN, CYCLONE
Clinical Decision Support System	HSP, SPIN-based NHIN
Real-time Monitoring	MoCAsH, Taiwan Ubiquitous Model, Intelligent Agent Framework
EHR System	HSP

Table 2.2: Classification by base HIS architectures.

Base Architecture	HIS Using the Base Architecture
Distributed	Scalable & SCILHS, SPIN-based NHIN
SaaS	HSP
SOA	HSP, MoCAsH
Agent-based	MoCAsH, Intelligent Agent Framework, MoCAsH, Taiwan Ubiquitous Model

Table 2.3: Classification of HIS architectures by informatics zone.

Category of Informatic Zone	Architectures in that Category
Clinical Research	SCILHS, SPIN-based NHIN, CYCLONE
Public Health	HSP, Intelligent Agent Framework, MoCAsH, Taiwan Ubiquitous Model

Table 2.4: Classification by cloud usage.

Type of Cloud	HISA Using Such Cloud
Single Cloud	SCILHS, SPIN-based NHIN, HSP, Intelligent Agent Framework
Multi/Federated/Heterogeneous/InterCloud	HSP CYCLONE, MoCAsH, Taiwan Ubiquitous Model

Table 2.5: Classification by deployment status.

Deployment Status	HIS Architectures
Distributed	Scalable & SCILHS, SPIN-based NHIN
SaaS	HSP
SOA	HSP, MoCAsH
Agent-based	MoCAsH, Intelligent Agent Framework, MoCAsH, Taiwan Ubiquitous Model

All the research works studied are assessed on selected parameters and are listed in Table 2.6. The table summarizes the features of these research projects and also highlights the weaknesses in each of them.

In the next section, we elaborate on the challenges in this field which are open research issues.

Table 2.6: An assessment of HIS architectures.

Model	Support Cloud Data Storage?	Support Security and Privacy?	Usage of Data Standards?	Support for Mobility Management?	Availability of Apps or Services?
SCILHS	Yes	N.R.	Yes	No	Yes
SPIN	Yes	Strong	N.R.	No	N.R.
CYCLONE	Yes	Strong	N.R.	No	Yes
HSP	Yes	Strong	Yes	No	Yes
MoCAsH	Yes	Weak	Yes	Yes	No
Taiwan Model	Yes	N.R.	N.R.	Yes	Yes
Intelligent Agent Framework	Yes	No	Yes	Partial	No

N.R.: Not Reported

2.5 Challenges in Cloud-based Health Informatics

After reviewing the works in the area of cloud-based HI, we have identified the building blocks of the cloud-based HIS. There are plenty of challenges in each of these domains, inviting the attention of researchers. A few of the challenges identified in this survey are given below:

- **Cloud-based Data Storage and Data Security**

  It can be distributed or centralized, shared, peer, or private as per the requirement of the system. In small organizations, centralized database approach works well as it has lower security costs, however, in organizations with multiple participants, high traffic creates bottleneck problems, so distributed databases are recommended. Distributed databases require more efforts to ensure data integrity and security. Shared databases make it easier for participants to communicate between themselves but it does so by putting the security and privacy of individual participants at risk. Peer-to-peer databases consider this aspect and give institutional autonomy and flexible security policies. Peer-to-peer databases require a hub or supernode in the network to handle the communication and querying between peer nodes. This single hub or central supernode for communication comes at the price of the single node failure problem.

  A virtual private database (VPD) is a concept introduced by Oracle in Oracle8i and a feature of Oracle Database 11g Enterprise Edition [19]. Using a peer to peer database with a peer-specific schema and VPD access roles for database-level security is a hot area for research.

- **Security and Privacy**

  These parameters touch multiple aspects. Numerous sources and formats of data imply the necessity of data validation processes, like ETL. Access authorization is a necessary security step as healthcare data is some of the most sensitive personal data. De-Identification of patient data can be achieved by removal of certain attributes from the information. Geographical anonymization of patient identity is in trend. But de-identifying the individual's results in the reduction of accuracy in research informatics. Making a balanced security approach is highly important work. Re-Identification of anonymized data is necessary when an investigator with higher-level access roles needs the identity of a particular data point. On the contrary, re-identification is unwanted and risky when an initiative like Semantic Web identifies the encoded entry with the linkage of some other public datasets. Removing the critical attributes or aggregating the data points over bins can be one solution to it. ML and AI can help in identifying critical attributes. Government policy compliance, and failure and handling of hardware-level breaches are also big concerns here.

  Before sharing the patient data for research, consent from an individual is necessary. *Dynamic consent* [20] is a comparatively new concept which talks about providing individuals with necessary information about the platforms when their data will be used. New tools and technologies that help in automatically enabling sharing preferences over the range of clinical databases need to be developed. *Safe Havens* [21] is a new term referring to the authorized environments for centrally stored data. Tools and technologies which help in maintaining the confidentiality of data within heaven and enforce the data access controls are to be developed.

- **Data Standards for Uniform Data Exchange**

  Involving more than one participant in the HI system, use of IoT devices, storage, and sharing of healthcare and clinical data strongly requires the ease of inter-communication in order to overcome the problem of heterogeneity. HL7 is the most prominent and consumed set of standards in the market.

  While standards are made for interoperability between devices, data formats and participants, making these all standards themselves interoperable and inter-communicating, so that differences in standards do not become the reason for the inefficiency of HI System, is an exciting task to do. Another issue to look upon is, how to make these standards compatible with each country's health care regulation policy, so that the countries can pick up the use of these standards without compromising their regulations.

- **Query Building, Distributing and Result-Aggregation Tools**

  Cloud-based query manipulation is the most crucial part of any large Health Informatics System. Many open-source protocols and query management tools are available, and a developer can create their proprietary tools also. Considering that the end-user communicates and stores data in a human-understandable form, NLP tools would be an appropriate choice to make the querying more user-friendly. Improvement in this area can reduce the efforts of converting incoming raw healthcare data into query-processing compatible formats.

- **Mobility Management**

  Mainly focusing on real-time monitoring systems, personal health, and assistive health management, continuous updates of the patients' health signals are important. Tracking the patient's vital health signals, gestures and postures, mood, and also the environmental and geographical situations at the same time. It involves the use of sensors, wearables, mobile apps, and IoT devices.

  Their continuous tracking emphasizes very efficient mobility management, as the components will be active 24*7. Use of minimal energy is another issue to focus on. Globe is parted into and covered by the number of network divisions. Lossless maintenance of data and signals over the switch of the network is the most crucial aspect to take care of.

- **App Store**

HIS can become more popular if it provides a range of Apps to deploy based on the use case. There is a big opportunity for the use of handheld devices, such as mobile phones, and the development of mobile services in the form of Apps running on them.

- **Learning System**

Healthcare is an industry where there are a lot of changes and advances happening rapidly. The use of learning systems to continuously learn from the data collected will be a good strategy in improving research and health care.

A learning health care system is one in which science, informatics, incentives, and culture are aligned for continuous improvement and innovation, with best practices seamlessly embedded in the healthcare process, patients and families actively participating in all elements, and new knowledge captured as an integral by-product of the care experience [22].

- **Federated Cloud Management**

Healthcare solutions span across different organizations, offering a vast pool of services and use cases. Each service has its resource requirements and computing environment. Considering the heterogeneity of participant systems and their requirements, multi-cloud, federated cloud, and inter-cloud architectures are suggested as they allow the use of the best features from each cloud service provider. Each cloud platform provides state-of-the-art security measures, but equally, robust security and networking protocols are needed for data transfers between the clouds. This is another potential area to work on.

2.6 Conclusion

Cloud Computing and Data Analytics brought a revolution in the healthcare sector in terms of the way that health data was being stored, shared and processed through HISs. Factors that influence the quality of HIS include autonomous participation, active monitoring, data privacy and security, and heterogeneity of participants. The inclusion of multiple healthcare organizations into a single HIS makes the research network very efficient.

For public and personal healthcare, active monitoring is much-required. The aimed usage of the system defines the specific subset of components and functionalities that will go into the architecture.

References

[1] Mandl, K. D. et al. 2014. Scalable collaborative infrastructure for a learning healthcare system (SCILHS): architecture. Journal of the American Medical Informatics Association, 21: 615–620.

[2] Accessible Research Common for Health, arch-commons.org/. Last Accessed 10 September 2018.

[3] Mandl, K. D. et al. 2017. Biases introduced by filtering electronic health records for patients with complete data. Journal of the American Medical Informatics Association, 24: 1134–1141.

[4] McMurry, Andrew J. et al. 2007. A self-scaling distributed information architecture for public health, research and clinical care. Journal of the American Medical Informatics Association, 14: 527–533.

[5] Sooyoung Yoo et al. 2015. Architecture design of healthcare software-as-a-service platform for cloud-based clinical decision support service. Healthcare Informatics Research, 21(2): 102–110.

[6] Yuri Demchenko et al. 2016. CYCLONE: A platform for data-intensive scientific applications in heterogeneous multi-cloud/multi-provider environment. *In*: IEEE International Conference on Cloud Engineering Workshop, Berlin, Germany.

[7] Doan B. Hoang and Lingfeng Chen. 2010. Mobile cloud for assistive healthcare (MoCAsH). *In*: IEEE International Conference on Cloud Engineering Workshop, Hangzhou, China.

[8] Chen-Shie Ho and Kuo-Cheng Chiang. 2010. Towards ubiquitous healthcare by integrating active monitoring and intelligent cloud. *In*: 5th Int. Conference on Computer Sciences and Convergence Information Technology, Seoul, South Korea.

[9] Hassan Omar Al-Sakran. 2015. Framework architecture for improving healthcare information systems using agent technology. International Journal of Managing Information Technology (IJMIT), 14(1): 17–31.

[10] Gupta, P. K. et al. 2017. A novel and secure IoT based cloud-centric architecture to perform predictive analysis of users' activities in sustainable health centres, Multimedia Tools and Applications, 76: 18489–18512.

[11] Pasquale Pace et al. 2018. An edge-based architecture to support efficient applications for healthcare industry 4.0. In IEEE Transactions on Industrial Informatics, 15: 481–489.

[12] Health Level 7 International, www.hl7.org/. Last Accessed 10 September 2018.

[13] Abdelali Boussadi and Eric Zapletal. 2017. A FHIR layer implemented over i2b2. BMC Medical Informatics and Decision Making.

[14] Industrial IoT Standards, www.omg.org/hot-topics/iot-standards.htm Last Accessed 10 October 2018.

[15] HIMSS EHR Association, www.ehra.org/ Last Accessed: 10 October, 2018.

[16] DICOM PS3.1 2018d – Introduction and Overview, dicom.nema.org/medical/dicom/current/output/chtml/part01/chapter_1.html. Last Accessed: 10 October 2018.

[17] Clinical Data Interchange Standards Consortium, www.cdisc.org/standards. Last Accessed 10 October 2018.

[18] Coustasse, A. et al. 2016. The feasibility of the nationwide health information network. The Health Care Manager, 35(2): 103–112.

[19] Virtual Private Database, www.oracle.com/technetwork/database/security/index-088277.html. Last Accessed 10 September 2018.

[20] Williams, H. et al. 2015. Dynamic consent: a solution to improve patient confidence and trust in use of EMR. JMIR Medical Informatics, 3(1).

[21] Information: To share or not to share? The Information Governance Review,https://assets.publishing.service.gov.uk/government/uploads/system/uploads/attachment_data/file/192572/2900774_InfoGovernance_accv2.pdf. Last Accessed 10 October 2018.

[22] Roundtable on Value & Science-Driven Health Care. 2012. The Roundtable. Institute of Medicine, Washington, DC.

3

A Flow-Based Anomaly Detection System for Slow DDoS Attack on HTTP

Muraleedharan N[1],* and Janet B[2]

3.1 Introduction

Nowadays, due to the proliferation and popularity of Internet, services from communication, transport, health-care, financial and banking, education sectors, etc., are remotely accessed through the network. As more and more critical services are Internet enabled, ensuring the availability of these services to the genuine user is one of the mandatory requirements for the service providers. However, adversaries such as hackers, competitors and enemies try to disrupt or disable these services to the intended users through Denial of Service attack (DoS).

DoS can be defined as an attack on the availability of resources which prevents the authorized access to a system resource by delaying of system operations and functions. The DoS attack from which the attack traffic originates from multiple attackers is known as Distributed Denial of Service (DDoS). Based on the volume of traffic and transmission rate, the DDoS attack can be broadly classified in to High rate DDoS (HDDoS) and Slow DDoS (SDDoS). The HDDoS targets layers three and four of the ISO/OSI model where it generates an enormous number of bogus requests for accessing the

[1] Centre for Development of Advanced Computing (C-DAC), Bangalore, India.
[2] National Institute of Technology (NIT), Tiruchirappalli, Tamil Nadu, India.
  Email: janet@nitt.edu
* Corresponding author: murali@cdac.in

resources located at the server. During this attack, as the number of requests is very high, it may increase the traffic volume and bandwidth usage of the network. The complexity of this attack has evolved to generate more than one Terabits/second (Morales, 2018).

As the network bandwidth and system resources have increased, the attackers need to generate massive volume of traffic to deny a service using volumetric DDoS attack. However, in order to generate huge volume of attack traffic, more resources are required. To avoid huge resource allocation for DDoS traffic generation, the attackers use slow DDoS attack.

The slow DDoS attacks generally target the application layer in which the attacker sends bogus requests to the server impersonating as a legitimate request. In SDDoS, the attackers send requests in very low rate. In order to process these requests, the server needs to hold the resources for a longer time period, which subsequently blocks the access for a legitimate user. The SDDoS attack traffic volume is similar to the legitimate network traffic. Hence, compared to the HDDoS attack, it is difficult to identify the SDDoS attack by analyzing the network traffic volume. Unlike the HDDoS attack, application layer DDoS targets the server resources, such as memory, maximum concurrent connections, etc. Table 3.1 shows the difference between Normal traffic, HDDoS and SDDoS in terms of traffic volume, transmission time and resource usage.

Table 3.1: Categorization of traffic in to Normal, SDDoS and HDDoS.

Traffic Volume	Transmission Time	Resource Usage	Traffic Type
Low	Low	Low	Normal
Low	Low	High	SDDoS
Low	High	Low	Normal
Low	High	High	SDDoS
High	Low	Low	Normal
High	Low	High	HDDoS
High	High	Low	Normal
High	High	High	HDDoS

In this chapter, we are proposing an anomaly-based slow DDoS monitoring and detection system using network flow data. The novelty of our approach is the usage of inactive flows details for identifying the Slow DDoS attack. This approach has the following advantages:

- As the slow DDoS attack takes more time to complete the attacks, data for a longer time period is required for analysis and detection. Compared to the packet level traffic, network flow data have lesser volume, which can provide a faster response.

- Slow DDoS detection approaches which use host level parameters, such as number of interrupts, context switch, number of TCP sockets, etc., are required to have host level access to collect these parameters. Hence, it will be difficult to use the same approach to collect host level parameter for different OS environment. However, since we are using network-based parameters available in the flow data in the proposed system, the collection and analysis of flow data can be done using host and Operating System (OS) independent techniques. So, the proposed method can be used to detect slow DDoS attack independent to OS and host level parameters.
- As the flow data derived from the packet header, the slow DDoS attack which uses encrypted traffic, such as HTTPS, can be monitored and analyzed.

The main contributions of this paper are

- Analysis of the impact of inactive flow for slow DDoS detection.
- Monitoring and accurate detection of slow HTTP DDoS using network flow data.
- Usage of host and OS independent parameters for slow DDoS attack identification.

The remaining part of this paper is organized as follows: Section 3.2 explains the background of slow DoS and related work. The proposed system details are explained in section 3.3, result obtained and result analysis is described in section 3.4. Conclusion and future work are explained in the last section.

3.2 Background and Related Work

A classification of DDoS attack based on the traffic volume is shown in Figure 3.1. As shown in the figure, the DDoS can be broadly classified as High Traffic volume DDoS and Low volume DDoS or slow DDoS attack. The details of each category are described below.

High Volume DDoS

The high-volume DDoS sends a huge number of requests to the victim. Usually, the attack traffics are generated using network and transport layer protocols. Different types of high-volume DDoS are explained below.

Flood

In a flooding attack, the attacker sends a huge amount of network traffic in order to exhaust the victim's network bandwidth. The flooding attack traffic

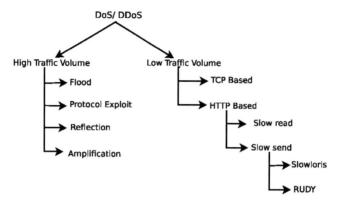

Figure 3.1: Classification of DDoS attack.

can be generated using different protocols, such as TCP, UDP, ICMP, DNS, etc. In this attack, the attacker targets the entire network where the victim exists.

Protocol Exploit

In this attack, the attackers exploit the vulnerabilities of network protocols. For example, using TCP SYN attack, the attacker sends SYN packets to the victim server with spoofed source addresses of unreachable hosts. Upon receiving this request, the victim replies with a SYN/ACK packet which goes to the spoofed IP and never gets a response. The attacker opens many active connections in order to saturate the server's resources (Peng et al., 2007).

Reflection Based

A reflector is any IP host that will return a packet for the received packet (Paxson, 2001). In reflector-based DDoS attack, the attackers send packets to the reflector servers with a source IP address set to their victim's IP. By receiving this request, the reflector replies back to the victim machine which overwhelms the victim machines network bandwidth.

Amplification

In amplification attack, the attacker crafts a request to generate a larger response. In this attack, the volume of traffic received by the victim is substantially greater than the volume of traffic sent by the attacker. To make it more effective, attackers select the protocol which provides larger response size for smaller request (Rossow, 2014). To generate very high rate of attack traffic, combination of reflectors and amplification techniques are used by the attacker. Figure 3.2 shows the pictorial representation of reflective amplification DDoS (Paxson, 2001).

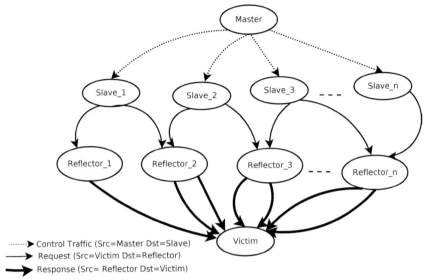

Figure 3.2: Illustration of reflective amplification DDoS.

Slow HTTP DDoS

Hyper Text Transfer Protocol (HTTP) is one of the prominent application layer protocols used in the Internet. The web servers and clients are using this protocol for their communication. The popularity and wide usage of HTTP protocol in the Internet attracted the attackers to target it for different types of attacks, including DoS and DDoS attack. Some of the application layer DDoS targeted on HTTP is explained below.

Slowloris Attack

The web server follows client-server architecture where the clients send requests and the server responds. Once the server receives the request, it allocates resources to process it. Some of the web servers are designed to process the request only after receiving the entire request content from the client. If the server has not received the entire request content, it waits to receive it from the client. The attackers make use of this property of the vulnerable web servers to send many partial requests to the server. As the server needs to wait for the remaining part of the request, it cannot release the allocated resources for the partial requests. To handle the indefinite waiting for the request content, web servers have to be configured with a time-out value. This enables the web server to wait only for the specified time (time out) to receive the message, after which it closes the connection and release the resources.

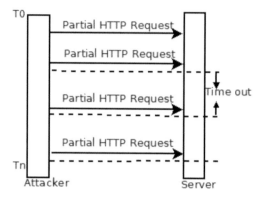

Figure 3.3: Illustration of slowloris attack.

In slowloris attack, the attacker sends multiple partial requests to the server. Since it is a partial request, the web server needs to wait up to the configured timeout to release the connection. But to force the web server to continue to wait, the attacker will send the next part of the request just before the time-out. The pictorial representation of slowloris attack is depicted in Figure 3.3.

RUDY Attack

R U Dead Yet (RUDY) is another application layer DoS attack targeting the web servers. In this attack, the attacker tries to submit a form using HTTP POST request (Najafabadi et al., 2016). Through 'content length' filed in the POST request, the attacker informs the server that it needs to send huge content (for example 'X' bytes). Later, it starts to submit the form data by breaking it in very small packet size (X/Y where Y ≈ X). Figure 3.4 shows the RUDY slow DoS attack scenario (Muraleedharan and Janet, 2017).

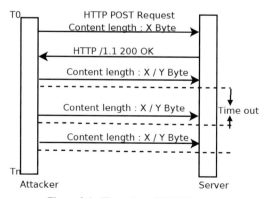

Figure 3.4: Illustration of RUDY attack.

Slow Read

As shown in Figure 3.5, during slow read attack, the attacker will send a valid HTTP request to the server and read the response in very slow rate. To read the content in very slow rate, the attacker informs the web server that the buffer space is not available to receive the content from the server. To indicate the non-availability of the buffer, a TCP packet with zero window size is sent to the server. Upon receiving the client's packet with zero window size, the server assumes that the client does not have buffer to hold the content and waits to send it. This forces the server to keeps the connection opened for long period of time (Park et al., 2014).

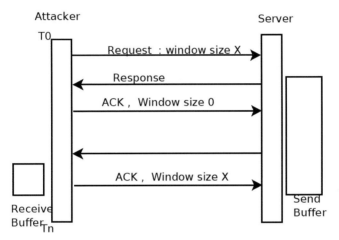

Figure 3.5: Illustration of slow read attack.

Related Work

Compared to layer three or four DDoS attack, the slow DoS attack sends legitimate packets at a slow rate. Therefore, it is difficult to distinguish slow DDoS from normal traffic. Researchers have studied different aspects of the Slow DoS/DDoS attack targeting on HTTP servers. A detailed survey and research challenges on application layer DoS attack on HTTP server is presented in (Singh et al., 2017). Tripathi et al. (Tripathi et al., 2016) studied the vulnerabilities and possibilities of HTTP-based DoS attack on popular web servers.

An analysis of slow read attack and some of the countermeasures are described in (Park et al., 2014). Different studies on HTTP-based slow DoS attacks are explained in (Jazi et al., 2017; Ni et al., 2013) and (Maciá-Fernández et al., 2010).

Table 3.2 shows the summary of slow DoS detection approaches. To detect slow DoS attack, host level parameters, such as number of interrupts, context switch, number of TCP sockets, etc., are used (Aqil et al., 2015). However, host level access is required in order to collect and analyze these parameters.

To address the limitation of host level parameters for slow DoS/ DDoS detection, techniques which use network parameters are introduced. A network traffic analysis of HTTP-based slow DoS attack and impact of different network level parameters is explained in (Muraleedharan and Janet, 2017). Najafabadi et al. (Najafabadi et al., 2016) used different network parameters to detect RUDY attack using machine learning approach. Zhou et al. (Zhou et al., 2017) propose a method based on the distribution difference of the packet size to distinguish low-rate DDoS attack. Flow level data are used for identifying network-based anomaly detection and attack analysis. A flow level detection of different network anomalies is explained in (Galtsev and Sukhov, 2011). Kemp et al. (Kemp et al., 2018) used netflow-based machine learning techniques to detect slow read attack on web servers at the application layer. In their approach, they used the features from netflow data as the input for machine learning. As the slow DoS attack targets the timeout values of the application servers, we focus on the inactive time and flow expire reason for our analysis.

Table 3.2: Summary of slow DoS/DDoS detection approaches.

Approach	Input Used	Parameters	References
Host-based	Host level parameters	Number of interrupts, context switch, number of TCP sockets, etc.	(Aqil et al., 2015)
Packet-based	Network packet parameters	Window Size, Inter packet arrival time, number of connections, duration	(Najafabadi et al., 2016), (Muraleedharan and Janet, 2017), (Hirakawa et al., 2016)
Flow-Based	Flow level parameters	Packet size distribution, connection definition features	(Zhou et al., 2017), (Kemp et al., 2018)

3.3 Proposed System

The details of the proposed anomaly-based slow DDoS monitoring and detection system using network flow data system are described below.

Architecture

Figure 3.6 shows the overall architecture of the proposed anomaly-based slow DDoS detection system. As shown in the architecture, this system takes network packets as the input and, after analysis, generates slow DDoS events

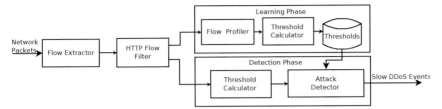

Figure 3.6: Proposed slow DDoS detection system architecture.

for identified attacks. The proposed anomaly-based system works in two phases, named as 'Learning Phase' (LP) and 'Detection Phase' (DP). In the learning phase, the system collects and profiles the inputs in order to understand the normal behavior of HTTP communication. The basic assumption of the learning phase is that the data used for learning contains no slow DDoS attack in it. After the LP, the system derives threshold values for the identified flow level parameters.

In detection phase, the system collects the identified flow level parameters and analyzes them in order to derive the threshold values and compare them with the threshold derived during LP. If it finds any deviation in the threshold values, then it generates the slow DDoS attack events.

To process the inputs, it uses different components, known as flow extractor, HTTP flow filter, flow profiler, threshold calculator and attack detector. The detail of each component is described below.

Flow Extractor

The flow extractor component takes network packets as the inputs and groups them into network flow data. The reasons for using flow data and detail of flow extractor component is described below.

Traditionally, network packet level data has been used for traffic monitoring and analysis. But due to the deployment of high-end network infrastructure, the traffic rate and volume has increased into multiple folds. It creates a challenge in the packet level monitoring and analysis of network traffic. Moreover, the collection and analysis of all the packets in the high-speed network requires an enormous amount of storage, networking and computing resources. To overcome this challenge, flow level data are used for traffic monitoring and analysis.

Network flow is defined as a unidirectional sequence of packets traveling from a source to a destination for a specific time period. Flow level data are derived from network packets by grouping the packets using five-tuple (Source IP, Destination IP, Source Port, Destination Port and protocol) fields. These five fields are also known as 'Flow Key'. In addition to the flow key, flow level data also consists of the connection level summary information, such as aggregated packet count, number of bytes transferred, duration, TCP flag values, etc. (Hofstede et al., 2014). The format of 'Flow Key' and 'Flow Records' are shown below

FlowKey = {SrcIP, DstIP, SrcPort, DstPort, Protocol}

FlowRecords = {FlowKey, Timestamp, duration, Pkts, Bytes, flag values, etc.}

The reasons for using flow level data for our anomaly detection system are:

Firstly, compared to the packet level information, the volume of flow data is less. Secondly, as the data volume is less, more data can be collected, stored and analyzed. This helps to detect slow attacks which last more time. Thirdly, as it is derived from the packet header, this dataset can be generated even from the encrypted traffic, which is the major requirement for today's web application traffic monitoring and analysis.

As flow level data are configured to send periodically for monitoring and analysis, long lasting connections details are divided into multiple flows using the active timer. Similarly, inactive connection details are divided in to multiple flows using the inactive timer. Figure 3.7 shows the details of flow data generation process from the network packets.

As shown in the figure, the 'Flow 1' (F1) consists of 14 packets and 'Flow 2' (F2) is derived from 7 packets. Flow 3 (F3) and flow 4 (F4) consists of five and four packets, respectively. Since the packets are frequently transferring in F1, the flow records of F1 can be sent after the configured active time value. The time delay between two consecutive packets in a flow is considered as inactive time, which is represented between packets 'P2' and 'P3' in Flow 2.

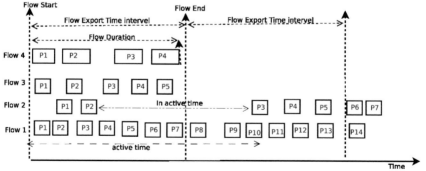

Figure 3.7: Illustration of flow generation process using packets.

HTTP Flow Filter

As we are focusing on the slow DDoS detection on HTTP, we need to filter out the HTTP flows from other flow records for further analysis. The 'HTTP flow filter' is used to take the flow records generated by the Flow extractor and segregate HTTP flows using the 'Protocol' and 'Port number' field in the 'Flow Key'. As the HTTP uses TCP as the transport layer protocol for its communication, first, it selects all the TCP flows using the protocol field. Later, the source port or destination ports of the selected TCP flows compared with the standard communication ports of HTTP (80) or HTTPS (443). If the flow records port numbers are matched with any of these port numbers, then it is considered as a HTTP flow and passed on for further process.

Flow Profiler

The flow profiler takes HTTP flow records and analyzes them in order to derive the normalcy of HTTP traffic parameters for slow DDoS detection. To define the normalcy of HTTP traffic, the flow profiler takes two inputs. Firstly, the number of iterations needed to define the normalcy and, secondly, the number of flows required in the iteration. Depending on the traffic rate in the network and web server, these two parameters can vary. The number of iterations needed for deriving the normal threshold can be defined as 'x' and the number of flows required in the iteration can be defined as 'n'. During the learning, the system collects and groups 'n' number of flows. From this group, it computes the number of 'inactive-flow' to derive the ratio of 'inactive flow' with total flows. Similarly, the ratio of inactive flow to total flow is calculated for all the 'x' iterations.

Threshold Calculator

The threshold calculator derives the learning time threshold value of the anomaly detector using the number of inactive flows in the iteration. We are calculating the Inactive flow ratio in each iteration (IFR) using equation (3.1). The average inactive flow ratio for the entire learning period is ($TIFR_{avg}$) derived using equation (3.2) and threshold value (T) is derived using equation (3.3).

$$IFR = \frac{Fi}{Ft}; \text{ where Fi is the inactive flows and Ft is the total flows} \qquad (3.1)$$

$$TIFR_{avg} = (\sum_{i=1}^{x} IFR)/x; \text{ where } x \text{ is the number of iterations} \qquad (3.2)$$

$$T = TIFR_{avg} + 3 * TIFR_{std}; \text{ where } TIFR_{avg} \text{ and } TIFR_{std} \text{ is the average and standard deviation of total inactive flow respectively in the learning period.} \qquad (3.3)$$

As shown in the equation (3.3), the threshold value is fixed as $TIFR_{avg}$ + 3 * $TIFR_{std}$. The main reason for setting $TIFR_{avg}$ + 3 * $TIFR_{std}$ as the threshold is to reduce the false positive rate. As the profile threshold is higher than the average number of inactive flow ratio, as the attacker delays the connection during the slow HTTP DDoS, it may generate a greater number of inactive flows. However, due to the genuine reason, such as a client that is connected in a low bandwidth network, it may generate inactive flow. To avoid these types of events, we are setting higher threshold values during the learning period. One drawback of setting higher threshold values is that it may not able to detect some of the slow DDoS events if the number of inactive flows is below the threshold value.

During the detection phase, the threshold detector component takes the 'n' number of flows and calculates the inactive flow ratio as per equation (3.1).

Attack Detector

Once the normalcy of HTTP traffic is profiled and a threshold is derived in the learning period, the slow DDoS detector can carry out the attack detection in the detection period. The attack detector collects 'n' flows to derive the inactive to total flow ratio. Further, the derived value is compared against the learning time threshold value. If the calculated threshold value is higher than the learning time thresholds, then it generates an alert to indicate the slow DDoS attack.

Data Set and Tools Used

To verify the effectiveness of the identified techniques, we have used '2017-SUEE-data-set'. This data set contains incoming and outgoing traffic of the web server of the Student Union for Electrical Engineering at Ulm University (2017-suee-data-set., 2017). The summary of the collected data set is shown in Table 3.3.

The SUEE dataset consists of the normal and attack traffic and is available as network packet dump (pcap) format. Hence, as a per-processing step, we converted it into flow level data using the 'joy' tool (Joy, 2018). The details of this conversion and the tools used are explained below.

Table 3.3: Summary of dataset used.

Dataset	Duration	No. of Hosts	No. of Packets
SUEE1	24 Hours	1,634	2,089,436
SUEE8	8 Days	8,286	19,301,217

Packet to Flow Conversion

We have used 'joy' tool (Joy, 2018) to generate flow data from network packet dump. Joy is an open source software suite for collecting and analyzing network data and for generating flow records (Anderson, 2016). This tool can be used for monitoring and analysis of the real-time network as well as offline network traffic stored in 'pcap' format.

To avoid the indefinite wait of flow data for monitoring and analysis, timeout values for active and inactive flows were defined. Based on this, a flow record is derived and exported for analysis whenever the inter arrival time of two consecutive packets in the flow exceeds the configured inactive time. By default, the flow inactive timeout period and active timeout period are configured as ten seconds and thirty seconds, respectively. By this configuration, a flow record will be created if a flow is inactive for ten seconds, or if it is active for thirty seconds. The 'expire type' column in the flow record generated by 'Joy' tool is used to indicate the reason for flow expiry where 'i' denotes an inactive expiration, and 'a' denotes an active expiration of the flow. Table 3.4 shows the fields available in the 'joy' flow record.

Table 3.4: Summary of flow data fields used for analysis.

Flow Field	Description	Derived From
sa	Source IP Address	IP header
da	Destination IP Address	IP header
pr	Transport layer Protocol Number	IP header
sp	Source Port	TCP or UDP header
dp	Destination Port	TCP or UDP header
bytes out	Number of bytes transferred from source to destination	Any protocol
num pkts out	Number of packets sent from source to destination	Any protocol
Time_start	Start time	Any protocol
Time_end	End time seconds since epoch	Any protocol
packets	Array of packet lengths, directions and times	Any protocol
bytes in	Number of incoming bytes to source address	Bi-directional flow
Num_pkts_in	Number of incoming packets to source address	Bi-directional flow
expire_type	Reason for flow expiry	'i' for inactive and 'a' for active expiration

3.4 Result and Result Analysis

The results obtained from the 'SUEE1' and 'SUEE8' dataset and analysis of the results are explained below.

Result

As the 'SUEE' dataset is in packet dump (pcap) format, it was converted to flow data for our analysis. Using the SUEE1 data set, we generated 60,190 flows to train the system to understand the normalcy. To train the system, we grouped 5,000 flows and counted the number of inactive flows in it. We have used 12 iterations during the learning to deriving the threshold value. The details about results obtained and its analysis are explained below.

Active Vs Inactive Flow

After deriving the flow data from the network packets, we segregated it into 'active' and 'inactive' flows using the 'expire type' fields in the flow data. The number of active flows and inactive flows observed during the normal traffic are summarized in Table 3.5.

Figure 3.8 shows the histogram plot of active flows observed during normal traffic and slow DDoS attack. Each value in the histogram shows the number of active flows in the group of 5000 flows. In the 'x' axis, the first 12 values are related to the normal traffic flows and remaining values are related to the slow DDoS traffic. The 'y' axis shows the number of flows. As we have selected 5,000 flows for our analysis in a group, the max value of 'y' is fixed as 5,000.

Table 3.5: Active flow and inactive flow in normal traffic.

Iteration	Active Flows	Inactive Flows	Inactive Flow Ratio
1	4,143	857	0.1714
2	5,000	0	0
3	4,962	38	0.0076
4	4,962	38	0.0076
5	4,967	33	0.0066
6	4,994	6	0.0012
7	4,970	30	0.006
8	4,967	33	0.0066
9	4,971	29	0.0058
10	5,000	0	0
11	4,973	27	0.0054
12	4,972	28	0.0054

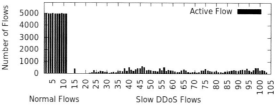

Figure 3.8: Active flows during normal traffic and slow DDoS attack.

Result Analysis

The results obtained from active flow against inactive flow analysis reveals that, during the slow DDoS attack, the number of inactive flows is exorbitantly high compared to the normal HTTP traffic. From the Table 3.5, we can observe that, among 5,000 flows observed in iteration, the maximum number of inactive flows generated was 857 (around 17 percentage of the total flows) in the first iteration. Among the remaining iterations, the number of inactive flows was less than forty, which is less than 0.8 percent of the total. To set the threshold value, we calculated the average and standard deviation of the inactive flow ratio using the normal flow data. The average value of the inactive flow ratio is 0.0208, the standard deviation is 0.0468 and the derived threshold value is 0.1614. This indicates that, in the analyzed flow dataset, if the inactive flows are more than 16 percent, then it can be considered as slow DDoS. From the inactive flow ratio in the slow DDoS dataset, we can observe that the number of inactive flows was increased and it has at least 88 percent of the total flows. From the result, we can conclude that the number of inactive flows is one of the prominent parameters for detecting slow DDoS attack traffic.

The reason for generating more inactive flows during slow DDoS attack is explained below. As the inactive timeout of the flow is configured as ten seconds in the SUEE dataset, if packets are not received within ten seconds, it generates a flow record with 'expire type' as 'i'. During the slow DDoS attack, the attacker sends the request in very slow rate. Hence, the delay between two packets is more than ten seconds during the attack time, generating inactive flow. So, as a first level analysis, we can count the number of inactive flows and if it is high then further analysis can be carried out using other inter- and intra-flow level parameters.

Inactive flows can exist in the normal traffic as well. However, during the normal traffic, the possibility of generating a very high rate of inactive flow from multiple clients can be considered as an anomaly. As the flow level parameters are configurable, the inactive time also can be configured by the administrator. Hence, this detection method may not be able to detect all the slow DDoS if the inactive timer is configured as higher than the inter arrival time of the attack packets. Similarly, this approach may generate false positive alerts if the inactive timer is configured with very small value.

3.5 Conclusion and Future Work

An anomaly detection system for slow HTTP DDoS using network flow data was described in this paper. This work mainly focused on the time-based flow level parameter for slow DDoS detection and a detailed analysis on the impact of inactive flow in slow DDoS is carried out. The attack detection capability of the proposed system is evaluated using the SUEE dataset. From the obtained results, we observed that the flow level parameters can be used for the detection and analysis of the slow DDoS attack targeted to HTTP servers. For the faster segregation of slow DDoS traffic from benign traffic, inactive flow details can be used. Compared to packet level data, flow data have lesser volume which helps to analyze the data and detect the attack more rapidly. Moreover, the computational complexity of the proposed method is also less. In the future, we are planning to evaluate and benchmark this approach with other slow DDoS datasets and further to incorporate different inter flow parameters in order to improve the detection accuracy.

References

2017-suee-data-set. 2017. 2017-suee-data-set. Retrieved from https://github.com/vs-uulm/2017-SUEE-data-set.

Anderson, D. M. 2016. Understanding network traffic through Intraflow data. FloCon2016.

Aqil, A., Atya, A. O., Jaeger, T., Krishnamurthy, S. V., Levitt, K., McDaniel, P. D. et al. 2015. Detection of stealthy tcp-based dos attacks. Military Communications Conference, MILCOM 2015–2015 IEEE, pp. 348–353.

Galtsev, A. A. and Sukhov, A. M. 2011. Network attack detection at flow level. pp. 326–334. *In*: Smart Spaces and Next Generation Wired/Wireless Networking. Springer.

Hirakawa, T., Ogura, K., Bista, B. B. and Takata, T. 2016. A defense method against distributed slow HTTP DoS attack. Network-Based Information Systems (NBiS), 2016 19th International Conference on, pp. 152–158.

Hofstede, R., Čeleda, P., Trammell, B., Drago, I., Sadre, R., Sperotto, A. et al. 2014. Flow monitoring explained: From packet capture to data analysis with netflow and ipfix. IEEE Communications Surveys & Tutorials, 16: 2037–2064.

Jazi, H. H., Gonzalez, H., Stakhanova, N. and Ghorbani, A. A. 2017. Detecting HTTP-based application layer DoS attacks on web servers in the presence of sampling. Computer Networks, 121: 25–36.

Joy. 2018, January. Joy—a package for capturing and analyzing network data features. Retrieved from https://github.com/cisco/joy/blob/master/doc/using-joy-05.pdf.

Kemp, C., Calvert, C. and Khoshgoftaar, T. 2018. Utilizing netflow data to detect slow read attacks. 2018 IEEE International Conference on Information Reuse and Integration (IRI), pp. 108–116.

Maciá-Fernández, G., Rodríguez-Gómez, R. A. and Díaz-Verdejo, J. E. 2010. Defense techniques for low-rate DoS attacks against application servers. Computer Networks, 54: 2711–2727.

Morales, C. 2018, March 1.1 Terabit DDoS Attacks Become a Reality; Reflecting on Five Years of Reflections. Retrieved May 8, 2020, from https://www.netscout.com/blog/asert/1-terabit-ddos-attacks-become-reality-reflecting-five-years.

Muraleedharan, N. and Janet, B. 2017. Behaviour analysis of HTTP based slow denial of service attack. Wireless Communications, Signal Processing and Networking (WiSPNET), 2017 International Conference on, pp. 1851–1856.

Najafabadi, M. M., Khoshgoftaar, T. M., Napolitano, A. and Wheelus, C. 2016. RUDY attack: detection at the network level and its important features. FLAIRS Conference, pp. 288–293.

Ni, T., Gu, X., Wang, H. and Li, Y. 2013. Real-time detection of application-layer DDoS attack using time series analysis. Journal of Control Science and Engineering, 4.

Park, J., Iwai, K., Tanak, H. and Kurokawa, T. 2014. Analysis of slow read DoS attack and countermeasures. The International Conference on Cyber-Crime Investigation and Cyber Security (ICCICS2014), pp. 37–49.

Paxson, V. 2001. An analysis of using reflectors for distributed denial-of-service attacks. ACM SIGCOMM Computer Communication Review, 31: 38–47.

Peng, T., Leckie, C. and Ramamohanarao, K. 2007. Survey of network-based defense mechanisms countering the DoS and DDoS problems. ACM Computing Surveys (CSUR), 39: 3.

Rossow, C. 2014. Amplification Hell: Revisiting Network Protocols for DDoS Abuse. NDSS.

Singh, K., Singh, P. and Kumar, K. 2017. Application layer HTTP-GET flood DDoS attacks: Research landscape and challenges. Computers & Security, 65: 344–372.

Tripathi, N., Hubballi, N. and Singh, Y. 2016. How secure are web servers? An empirical study of slow HTTP DoS attacks and detection. Availability, Reliability and Security (ARES), 2016 11th International Conference on, pp. 454–463.

Zhou, L., Liao, M., Yuan, C. and Zhang, H. 2017. Low-rate DDoS attack detection using expectation of packet size. Security and Communication Networks.

4

Explicating Fog Computing
Key Research Challenges and Solutions

John Paul Martin,[1] Vipin Singh,[2,]* K Chandrasekaran[2] and A Kandasamy[1]

4.1 Introduction

With the emergence of cloud computing, the end users have been endowed with an infinite pool of resources like computation, storage, and network. Cloud service providers commit to a Service Level Agreement (SLA) which guarantees connectivity, stability, and security of the resources provided to the end users. There has been the induction of billions of IoT devices due to the exposure of Internet-of-Things (IoT). These IoT devices collect data from their environment and send the data to the cloud for further processing. Majority of IoT devices are latency sensitive and require the computing services to be brought closer to the end users. However, since the physical distance between the end users and the cloud servers is huge, it introduces a substantial amount of end-to-end delay, high latency and communication cost. To overcome these issues, CISCO came up with Fog Computing, which serves as a substitution to conventional cloud computing. The idea is to extend cloud computing over to the edge of the network. The proposed Fog computing is distributed, latency sensitive and provides Quality-of-Service (QoS) and location awareness to its end users.

[1] Department of Mathematical and Computational Sciences, National Institute of Technology Karnataka, Surathkal.
[2] Department of Computer Science and Engineering, National Institute of Technology Karnataka, Surathkal.
* Corresponding author: vipin.singh289@gmail.com

4.1.1 Edge Computing and Fog Computing

Edge computing and Fog computing are somewhat similar to each other and both the terms are used exchangeably; also, the main objectives of both of them are the same, that is, to reduce the network and delay congestion. The main distinction between Edge computing and Fog computing lies in how they handle data and process it. Edge computing involves pushing the computational service towards the data sources, which includes sensors, mobile devices, etc. In Edge computing, the main focus is to process the data in fog nodes locally rather than sending the information to the cloud where different components process the data [1]. Meanwhile, in Fog computing, a decision needs to be made regarding whether to process the data at the local level, i.e., Fog layer, or process the information in the cloud. In Fog computing, if the request from a device node cannot be satisfied by the resources present at the Fog layer, only then is the request sent over to the cloud. Thus, edge computing is localized while Fog computing extends the computation resources to the edge of the network.

4.1.2 Load Balancing and Security Issues

Although Fog computing promises lower latency, location awareness, and other benefits as compared to traditional cloud computing, there are still some issues that require attention. Implementing an efficient load balancing technique in Fog is a major issue, along with security and privacy issues. Load balancing refers to the efficient assignment of computing loads to the Fog nodes such that no Fog node is under-utilized. Various load balancing techniques have been proposed by researchers in the past, each having their own merits and demerits. Similarly, providing security to the end users is a huge concern. The heterogeneous devices and the geographically distributed structure of the Fog environments increase the security challenges involved. Despite extensive research in the area, the domain of Fog computing is prone to security attacks. In the following sections, we will investigate the current state-of-the-art works regarding load balancing and security issues in the Fog computing paradigm.

4.1.3 Organisation of the Paper

The remaining portion of the paper is organized in the following manner. Section 4.2 discusses the related work in the load balancing domain of Fog computing. Section 4.3 discusses the various security and privacy issues that prevail in Fog computing. Section 4.4 elaborates the solutions proposed by the researchers for securing the Fog computing domain. Section 4.5 consists of discussion and the open challenges, and finally, section 4.6 concludes the paper.

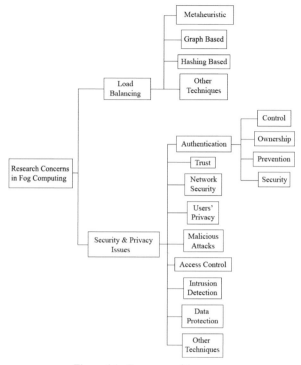

Figure 4.1: Taxonomy of the paper.

4.2 Load Balancing in Fog Computing

Load balancing is a way to assign or distribute workloads among numerous computing units like computers, processing units, network devices, and disk drives. The primary aim of load balancing is to increase the capacity and reliability of applications by decreasing the burden on servers, thus improving the overall performance of the applications. Balancing the load on the servers improves the performance in terms of resource usage, throughput and response time. In the Fog layer, the resources are limited and the workload should be evenly distributed among the servers so that they can be utilized properly. Efficient load balancing leads to the optimal utilization of resources which, in turn, enhances the performance of the servers. Load balancing is performed by using either software-based or hardware-based load balancers.

In the next subsection, we discuss the related work being done to propose better load balancing techniques for the Fog computing domain.

4.2.1 Heuristic Based Load Balancing

He et al. [2] proposed a modified load balancing algorithm that works on the Particle Swarm Optimization (PSO) in the Internet-of-Vehicles. The proposed method makes use of Software Defined Networking in Fog computing to address problems such as position consciousness, high latency, and less mobility support. The proposed algorithm enhances the performance of constrained optimization PSO which is applied over the software-defined Fog networking architecture. Simulation results indicate that the latency performance in the Software Defined Fog/Cloud Net-working architecture can be improved using the suggested algorithm as compared to the conventional Fog architectures. A considerable amount of reduction in the application latency is observed along with an improvement in the QoS factors in the Internet-of-Vehicles.

Table 4.1: List of acronyms.

Acronym	Full Form
IoV	Internet of Vehicles
SDN	Software Defined Networking
ELBS	Energy Aware Load Balancing and Scheduling
EDC	Edge Data Center
BFS	Breadth First Search
SDLB	Scalable and Dynamic Load Balancer
MEC	Mobile Edge Computing
RTES	Real Time Efficient Scheduling
SVT	Server Virtualization Technique
VM	Virtual Machine
SSLB	Self Similarity based Load Balancing
SLA	Service Level Agreement
MITM	Man-In-The-Middle attack
IoT	Internet of Things
IDT/IDS	Intrusion Detection Techniques/Schemes
ABE	Attribute-Based Encryption
CSP	Cloud Service Provider
CP-ABE	Cipher-Text Policy Attribute-Based Encryption
ABS	Attribute-Based Signature
UBP	User Behaviour Pro ling
SBD	Signature-Based Detection
ABD	Anomaly-Based Detection
SPBD	Specification-Based Detection
SPAD	Stateful Protocol Analysis Detection
VPN	Virtual Private Network
DoS/DDoS	Denial of Service/ Distributed Denial of Service
HH	Hyper Heuristic

Wan et al. [3] proposed an energy-aware load balancing technique (ELBS) for smart factories, which takes into account the vitality utilization of devices. Initially, a model is developed to capture the energy-related information corresponding to the smart factories. The model is then used to derive the correlation between the workload and the energy consumed by the equipment. An adapted version of PSO is then employed in order to obtain the optimal solution. Subsequently, a multi-agent system uses the calculated task priority values to balance the load on the equipment. Minimizing the load balancing based energy awareness function by using the PSO algorithm is the primary objective. The proposed ELBS method is mainly focused on complex energy consumption problem in the smart factory and, thus, plays an important role in equipment performance and life cycle improvement.

Chen et al. [4] uses the connected car system to propose a load balancing technique for minimizing the total runtime and deadline misses in Fog computing. Utilization of mobility patterns of vehicles is done and then, accordingly, periodic load balancing is performed at the Fog servers. After that, a task model that resolves the task organization problem at the server level rather than at the device level is formulated. A load balancing optimization problem that solves the above-mentioned problems is formulated.

4.2.2 Graph-based Load Balancing

Ningning et al. [5] proposed a dynamic load balancing method built upon the graph partitioning mechanism. The author adopts cloud atomization technology to turn physical nodes in different levels into virtual machine nodes. The related elements of the system are defined first. Then, the cloud atomization process is carried out on system physical nodes and the physical node graph model is abstracted into a virtual machine node model. The partitioning of virtual machine nodes is administered to achieve load balancing of task allocation. The mechanism is dynamic and according to the situation of the resources of node and network, the load is appropriately balanced.

4.2.3 Hashing-based Load Balancing

Ye Yu et al. [6] proposed a load balancing technique (SDLB) that is dynamic and scalable in nature which satisfies the requirements of mobile edge computing. The core algorithm of the technique uses minimal perfect hashing. Existing load balancing solutions cannot be applied directly to MEC load balancer. Requirements of a MEC-LB are that it should be scalable, software-based, memory efficient, adaptive to MEC changes and portable. The proposed model uses a data structure called POG. POG applies the hypothetical investigations of minimal perfect hashing. It also takes advantage of Software Defined Networking (SDN) along with the support of network dynamics. An evaluation shows that the proposed method is quicker and utilizes less memory than the traditional hash table-based load balancers and is also flexible towards network dynamics.

4.2.4 Other Load-Balancing Techniques

Puthal et al. [7] proposed a load-balancing technique that works in two phases. The first phase involves authentication of EDCs and the second phase involves finding EDCs which are less stacked for task assignment. The suggested methodology combines both authentication and load balancing techniques. It also assesses the performance by substantiating the efficiency and scalability. The cloud initiates the authentication process by using public-key-infrastructure as a measure to provide authentication. Each individual EDC authenticates other EDCs so that no malicious EDC can later participate in the load balancing mechanism.

Verma et al. [8] proposed an algorithm (RTES) for load balancing in the Fog environment, taking into consideration the time constraints on the tasks. The proposed architecture follows the three layer architecture of Fog computing. Initially, the algorithm balances the load amongst the Fog devices. After that, if the client is unable to get the resources from the Fog devices, the request is forwarded to the cloud servers. The main objective of the algorithm is to finish the real tasks well within the deadline. The resource allocation is done in such a way that the virtual machines remain occupied at all times. Data consistency is also maintained while communicating between the VMs of Fog layer and the cloud layer.

Li et al. [9] proposed a Load Balancing strategy (SSLB) for mass Fog computing environments. The authors also propose a scheduling algorithm based on adaptive thresholds to improve the efficiency of the SSLB. When the end users submit applications to the Fog, the applications are first broken down into constituent tasks. These tasks are then assigned to different nodes and queued. Then, after processing each task, the nodes forward the computation results to a node designated as the administrator node. The various research works focussed on load balancing in Fog environments have been summarised in Table 4.2.

4.3 Security and Privacy Issues in Fog Computing

Cloud computing provides access to configurable resources like computation, storage, and software to a variation of end users such as IoT devices. Fog computing provides the functionalities of cloud computing to the edge of the network. Fog computing reduces the distance between the end nodes and the data centers which, in turn, provides lower latency and real-time assessment.

Even though there are various benefits of using Fog computing, there are still several security gaps that need to be filled. Re-searchers are working on these security gaps and many techniques to overcome these security gaps have been proposed. Efforts are being made to create a secure and reliable Fog computing platform. Some of the security issues that are present in the Fog computing paradigm are discussed below:

Table 4.2: Summarization of load balancing approaches.

Paper	Problem Addressed	Description	Proposed Solution	Limitations
[2]	Load-balancing in Internet-of-Vehicles	Integration of FC and SDN to solve LB issues in IoV	MPSO-CO algorithm	Less security and scalability
[3]	Energy aware load balancing for smart factories	Using improved PSO for energy aware load-balancing in manufacturing clusters	ELBS algorithm	Uncertain processing time, random scheduling, fuzzy data delivery
[4]	Load-balancing for connected car system	Load-balancing mechanism for minimizing deadline misses and total runtime	Load balancing optimization algorithm	Complexity in mobility pattern detection
[5]	Dynamic load-balancing	Dynamic load-balancing technique using graph partitioning	Graph partitioning and clustering	Less adaptive to dynamic load
[6]	Load-balancing for Mobile Edge Computing	Scalable and dynamic load-balancing for mobile edge computing	SDLB algorithm	Finding working load of MEC's is expensive
[7]	Load-balancing and authentication of EDC's	Authentication using shared key and load-balancing using BFS.	Key-based authentication and BFS based load balancing	Key management increases complexity
[8]	Real time efficient load-balancing	Real time load-balancing between Fog and EU	RTES algorithm	Less secure
[9]	Load-balancing large scale FC	Self similarity-based load-balancing and scheduling	SSLB algorithm	Less efficiency with fewer nodes

4.3.1 Authentication

The first step of any security system is to authenticate all the devices that will be connected to the network. This is to verify whether the connecting devices are authentic or not. For this, a mechanism must be employed for authentication and authorization. In a Fog network, a huge amount of Fog nodes and IoT devices are connected so it becomes important to have an identification of each individual device which is achieved by authentication [24]. The devices are connected in order to access the services provided by the Fog network. So, every individual device needs to be authenticated to the Fog network so that rogue or unauthorized devices do not get connected to the network. Authentication is the process of verifying whether a device has access to a particular resource or not.

4.3.2 Trust

Trust is another important factor that plays an important role in providing secure and reliable services. Trust means reliability, faith, and firm belief in something that is relied upon to act as guaranteed [25]. We will trust a system less if it does not deliver to its promises. IoT networks are supposed to provide security and reliability to the end users. To make such a thing possible, there is a requirement of a certain level of trust between the users and the Fog service provider. The Fog nodes that are providing services to the end users should be able to differentiate between genuine users and malicious users and the devices should also be able to validate whether the Fog nodes they are connecting to are secure. For this to happen, we need to make sure the trust model in place is reliable and secure. Some issues present in Trust are:

- Control: Control is one important aspect of trust. An end user will trust the system less if it gives less control to the user.
- Ownership: Ownership can be seen as a variation of trust, better ownership will provide a higher level of trust.
- Prevention: Cloud service providers use Service Level Agreements (SLA's) to improve the trust among end users; although cloud computing tries to prevent the breach of SLA rather than provide compensation when an SLA breach occurs.
- Security: Security plays a crucial role in developing trust among users. End users will trust a cloud service provider more if it provides a sophisticated level of security.

4.3.3 Network Security

In the Fog computing architecture, one thing that connects the end devices with Fog layer and Fog layer with the cloud layer is the network. So it is important to secure the network connecting different devices. One way of doing so is employing network isolation. By this, we can ensure the safety of the network and thwart any malicious attacks carried out by malicious users. An insecure network that is prone to security attacks may lead to loss of data, privacy, unwanted usage of resources and a lot more. So a secure network is a key to a secure and reliable system.

4.3.4 Users' Privacy

Security techniques must provide privacy of user's data, identity, usage of utilities and location. Preserving the privacy of end users in Fog is difficult as the Fog nodes are closer to the end nodes and they constantly collect sensitive data and send it to the cloud [24]. If an attacker finds a way into the network, he/she may steal confidential data such as identity, usage habits, location, etc. Since the Fog nodes are scattered, they cannot be controlled in a centralized way. Location information of end nodes is one of the most important data of a user. An intruder may steal location data and moving habits of an end user as they offload their location to the nearest Fog node. These privacy issues demand a requirement for more complex countermeasures.

4.3.5 Malicious Attacks

The fog computing environment is susceptible to a number of malicious attacks that can seriously undermine the working of the network and pose a great threat to the resources and data stored [24]. One such attack that comes into mind is the Denial of Service (DoS) attack. The attacking node requests for computation/storage services and continues to hog the resources by requesting an infinite number of resources. The other genuine nodes that require computation/storage services will not get the afore-mentioned services as the resources are hogged by the malicious node. The effect of this attack is increased when multiple compromised or malicious nodes launch the DoS attack. Such an attack is called the Distributed Denial of Service (DDoS).

One more such attack is called the Man in the Middle attack (MITM). In this attack, the attacker introduces himself/herself in between the communicating parties (the end nodes and the Fog layer in our case) and steals the data in the form of communication that happens between the two par-ties. Existing security techniques are not applicable to the Fog computing environment in light of the transparency of the framework. Such attacks occur because the rogue node becomes part of the network. So a robust authentication model needs to be placed in order to deny access to such users from accessing the network resources.

4.3.6 Access Control

Access control is required in a secure system which ensures that only authorized nodes are given access to the resources. There is a thin line between access control and authentication. Access control makes sure that the connecting node has the right to get authorization. We need access control in Fog computing to make sure that only authorized devices perform actions such as reading device data, updating device software or issuing a specific command [26]. Access control in IoT poses a great challenge due to an enormous amount of devices, each with different privileges and a limited amount of resources. A certain amount of work needs to be done to employ a robust access control mechanism as it introduces new challenges because we are dealing with a huge number of end devices with limited resources. Therefore, Fog computing infrastructure must have security measures capable of implementing access control.

4.3.7 *Intrusion Detection*

Intrusion detection techniques (IDT) alert the administrator when a breach of security is detected so that the administrator can take proper actions to thwart any malicious activities [26]. Such techniques must be present in a security system so that early detection of such malicious activities is possible. Most of the security techniques currently present tackle fewer attacks with low precision. The nature of the Fog environment makes it tough to detect such attacks and take appropriate actions. If such attacks go undetected, they may seriously undermine the system at a greater scale.

Implementing intrusion detection schemes in the IoT environment is itself a testing errand because of the way that the IoT environment works on a large scale, is highly mobile and is widely distributed. Also, the fact that the IoT devices possess limited resources makes the whole intrusion detection complicated. The security system should be such that it implements the intrusion detection schemes at both the Fog layer and the cloud layer. IDT at Fog layer ensures the safety of local infrastructure, whereas IDT at cloud layer ensures the safety of global infrastructure.

4.3.8 *Data Protection*

The Fog environment has to deal with huge amounts of information produced by the IoT devices. The data must be preserved at the communication level as well as the processing level. Data must be encrypted before transfer and also after processing. IoT devices are compelled because of the limited amount of resources they possess, which makes encrypting the data difficult. This is the reason they send the information over to the cloud for processing and analyzing. The integrity of the data must be preserved before and after the processing is done. Limited resources of the IoT devices and their lack of power to encrypt and decrypt the data poses a great challenge towards the security measures to provide data protection.

4.3.9 Other Challenges

There are other security challenges aside from the ones discussed above, such as malicious node identification, key management, virtualization, data aggregation, location privacy preservation. In rogue node detection, a malicious IoT node can pretend to be an authorized node and can steal the data generated by other IoT devices. Key management deals with the generation, exchange, storage and use of cryptographic keys in a cryptosystem. Successful key management is critical in Fog environment. There are several security issues in virtualization, like sensitive data in VM, hypervisor security, risks due to cloud service provider API's, re-source exhaustion, etc. Data aggregation also poses a risk in the form of data integrity and security. Data must be properly encrypted and decrypted in order to provide data security. Preserving location information in fog nodes remains a serious issue that requires attention [27].

Some of the distinguished characteristics help Fog computing contribute toward providing secure and reliable IoT environments. Fog computing could be a part of the security solution to ensure that the IoT devices are not vulnerable to security attacks.

4.4 Existing Security and Privacy Solutions

This subsection summarizes the work that has been done to enhance the security features in the Fog computing domain.

4.4.1 Access Control

Huang et al. [10] formulated a data access control plan for IoT devices in Fog computing. In this scheme, access policy and update policy are used to encrypt sensitive user data, and then the encrypted data is forwarded to the cloud servers. Using this, the scheme provides access control and authentication mechanism to the end users. The users, whose attributes abide by the access policy, can decode the cipher text. If a user needs to modify the data, the CSP will check the signature of the user, whether the user has attributes that satisfy the update policy, and hence can update the cipher text.

4.4.2 Data Protection

Stolfo et al. [11] proposed an approach to safeguard the user data in the cloud. The technique used by the author is called offensive decoy technology. In this technique, the author monitors data access in the cloud and detects abnormal data access patterns. When a malicious user tries to access the Fog network, huge amounts of fake information is provided to the malicious user using a data misinformation attack. The methodology combines two techniques, namely, User Behaviour Profiling (UBP) and Decoys. UBP involves tracking user behaviour, such as how frequently the user accesses his/her information from the cloud. The attacker who illegitimately gets access to the users' system might not know the inner details of the system and their search will be covering the entire system. This abnormal user access is detected and fake information is provided to the malicious user safeguarding the user data. The scheme focuses on intrusion detection and data protection.

4.4.3 Intrusion Detection

Gai et al. [12] discusses the various Intrusion Detection Schemes (IDS) that have been proposed for the FC. An Intrusion Detection Scheme is a tracking infrastructure or application that surveys all the communication that is occurring in the computing framework. The author discusses different IDS schemes. Anomaly-based detection works on the principle of detecting the malware signature. Signature-based detection monitors the traffic and senses inconsistencies and divergences in the traffic. Specification-based detection is similar to Anomaly-based detection but it needs clients to build up a conduct assessment. Stateful protocol analysis detection distinguishes asymmetrical occasions from routine streams in a session by utilizing a pre-decided pervasive profile. Hybrid intrusion detection schemes involve multiple intrusion detections working together based on the security demand.

4.4.4 Malicious Attacks

Alharbi et al. [13] proposed a Fog-based security framework called FOCUS. The suggested methodology, along with the help of VPN, provides double protection in the FC to ensure the security of the VPN server against malicious attacks like MITM attacks and DDoS attacks. The proposed system provides security in two phases. First, the communication channels are secured using a VPN server. To filter out malicious users and protect the VPN server, a challenge-response authentication scheme is used. The system is then implemented in the FC rather than in the CC as FC is closer to the end users compared to CC and provides fast and responsive security measures. The proposed infrastructure is used to protect the FC against malicious attacks, such as MITM and DDoS.

Deepali et al. [14] proposed a solution for resource provisioning and DDoS attack mitigation in the cloud using FC. The author proposes a model which defends cloud against DDoS attack and performs resource allocation using the Fog layer. The model includes two modules: Fog Defender and resource allocator. The Fog defender sits in between the IoT devices and the cloud. The traffic intended for the cloud passes through the intermediate Fog defender which detects and mitigates DDoS attacks using the defence scheme used by [21]. After that, the requests that are forwarded by the Fog defender are processed by the Fog servers and the response is sent back directly to the client according to the optimal response policy. The requests are forwarded to the cloud just when all the Fog servers are occupied and cannot serve the request in optimal time. This approach works only for the TCP SYN flood attack, which is a variant of the DDoS attack.

4.4.5 *Trust*

Khan et al. [15] discusses establishing trust in the cloud. Various challenges that are faced while establishing trust in the cloud environment are discussed. Some of them are:

- Diminishing Control: When a cloud service provider doesn't provide an appropriate amount of control to the end users.
- Lack of Transparency: The ability to easily access the data no matter where the data is present is not provided by the cloud service provider.

These issues are resolved using emerging technologies like:

- Remote Access Control: Remote access control is provided to cloud clients to give them more jurisdiction over their data.
- Reflection: Reflection mechanisms inform the end users about the strengths and weaknesses of the service provider.
- Certification: An independent security certification authority could certify the cloud services in terms of their security properties and capabilities.
- Private Enclaves: A set of a computing environment that a single authority controls which is connected by one or more networks. These enclaves provide certain capabilities that increase the trust factor of an organization.

Rahman et al. [16] proposed a fuzzy approach for evaluating the trustworthiness in Fog servers. The author takes into account three metrics: distance, reliability, and latency. To reflect the metrics in the Fog environment, a campus scenario is taken where 6 Fog servers and 500 end users are present. The study focuses on trust evaluation, where the metrics of these six Fog servers are quantified in order to obtain the values. To evaluate the Fog trust values, the study adopts a fuzzy approach where AND operator is used instead of the OR operator and the minimum value is taken for implication. Thus, each rule has its own trust value which is then aggregated to finally produce a graph on which the maximum operator is applied. This is followed by the de-fuzzification process using the centroid method. The trust value is the value corresponding to the center of gravity of the graph. Employing fuzzy approaches enables greater user control over the desired output degree.

4.4.6 Users' Privacy

Hur et al. [17] proposed a secure mechanism to remove redundant data with dynamic possession administration in cloud servers. Eliminating duplicate data is useful to minimize the storage and bandwidth requirements by removing the redundant data and storing just a single copy. However, it sometimes poses a problem when encrypted data is stored in the cloud storage and the proprietorship changes progressively. To counter this problem, the author proposes an architecture to remove redundant data from the system. The scheme follows some steps like key generation, data encryption, data decryption, data re-encryption, and key update. Using this scheme, the author manages to reduce the data redundancy in the cloud to enhance fine-grained ownership management.

4.4.7 Other Security Measures

Kahvazadeh et al. [18] proposed an SDN-based (master/slave) architecture exploiting a centralized controller at the cloud and distributed controllers at the edge of the system. By reducing the distance between the cloud and the end users, the suggested architecture yields a greater level of security and reduces the risk of attacks such as MITM. To overcome the security challenges, the author uses an SDN-based security architecture exploiting the control/data decoupling idea given by SDN [22] to build up a master-slave-based system.

Razouk et al. [19] proposed a middleware architecture to solve the security issues and unnecessary communications in the Fog network. Data is pre-processed at the edge of the network by the security middleware. Based on the received information, the middleware takes the decision of processing and storing the data at the Fog or sending it to the cloud for further processing. The proposed middleware offers various security properties such as access control, authentication and privacy.

The proposed middleware mediates between the IoT applications and the cloud to cope with various security issues present in the Fog computing paradigm. Rahbari et al. [20] proposed a hyper-heuristic (HH) algorithm for secure scheduling in Fog computing. The HH algorithm uses data mining techniques. The proposed technique comprises of two stages: training stage and testing stage. In the training stage, diverse work processes enter the framework. The algorithms of choice, including Genetic algorithm (GA), Particle Swarm Optimization (PSO), Ant Colony Optimization (ACO) and simulated annealing [23], are implemented and re-sources are allocated to modules in all work flows. The amount of energy consumed, network usage and running cost for each algorithm is achieved and the results are stored. The output is evaluated based on parameters such as network usage, energy consumption and execution time. The various research works focussed on load-balancing in Fog environments have been summarised in Table 4.3.

Table 4.3: Summarization of security approaches.

Paper	Problem Addressed	Description	Solution Proposed	Limitations
[10]	Secure data access control	Safeguarding data with Fine grained information access control	Data encryption scheme based on attribute based encryption/signature	Encryption overhead in FC
[11]	Mitigating insider theft attacks	Securing data in cloud using of defensive decoy technology	Data misinformation attack	Excessive storage requirement
[12]	Intrusion Detection	Analysis of different IDS Schemes like SBD, ABD, SPBD, SPAD and HID	IDS schemes like SBD, ABD, SPBD, SPAD, HID	Hard to implement, inability to deal with new threats
[13]	Security against malicious attacks (DDoS, MITM)	Fog Based security system named FOCUS	Use of VPN server along with challenge response authentication	Accuracy of Network traffic Classification
[14]	Resource provisioning and DDoS alleviation	Mitigating DDoS attack using Fog defender and resource provisioning	Using intermediate Fog defender between Fog and EU	Works only for TCP SYN attack, high processing time
[15]	Establish trust in cloud Computing	Techniques that can be used by Fog service provider to increase trust value	Remote access control, reflection, certification, private enclaves	Diminishing control, lack of transparency
[16]	Evaluating trustworthiness	Fuzzy approach to find the trustworthiness in FC	Fuzzy approach	Deciding what rule to use and implement
[17]	Secure de-duplication mechanism	Securing regular data de-duplication using data encryption and key generation	Encryption, key management	Encryption and key management overhead
[18]	SDN-based security for F2C	Securing F2C using SDN-based master/slave architecture	SDN-based master/slave architecture	Management issues of F2C controllers
[19]	Securing Fog and IoT devices	Using middleware architecture to solve security issues and unnecessary communications	Middleware architecture	Increased complexity and cost
[20]	Security aware scheduling	Comparing the proposed HH algorithm with GA, PSO, ACO, SA algorithms	Hyper-Heuristic algorithm	Increased execution cost

4.5 Discussion and Open Challenges

As discussed in the above sections, there are some open challenges that should be tended to in security and load-balancing techniques.

- In the load-balancing algorithms, the load should be balanced in a cost-effective manner with minimal execution cost.
- Some heuristic load-balancing techniques require a high amount of execution cost that increases the overall latency of the system.
- Some algorithms are less adaptive to the dynamic load balancing.
- To make the load-balancing more secure is another issue that needs to be addressed.
- Using key management in load-balancing algorithms increases the workload as the IoT devices possess less computational power.

Providing load balancing to billions of IoT devices requires a robust and secure architecture that can handle the dynamic incoming load requests.

Similarly, new security and privacy issues that require attention are found in Fog computing paradigm.

- Using key management in load-balancing algorithms increases the workload as the IoT devices possess less computational power.
- There is a need to outline a low multifaceted nature-based key management and authentication mechanism between Fog nodes and end users in the Fog network.
- Trust attributes of a Fog service need to be verified before the EU can trust a Fog service. An entity that verifies the trust attributes of a Fog network needs to be in place.
- The Fog-to-Fog communication in the Fog layer should have a low message overhead.
- Intrusion detection schemes need to be more accurate in order to detect abnormal behaviour.

IDS techniques should be applied in all the three tiers of the Fog architecture, because securing only one tier of the architecture does not guarantee the security of the system as a whole. Various other security and load-balancing challenges need to be addressed. Some of the works discussed in the paper can be extended to address more challenges in the future.

4.6 Conclusion

In this paper, we have examined various security and privacy issues in Fog computing. We also discussed different load balancing techniques which are required in order to efficiently utilize the resources. In addition to providing new features, like geo-distribution, low latency and location awareness, Fog computing also introduces new challenges, like security and load-balancing. To address these problems, multiple algorithms that promise to solve them have been proposed. The paper summarizes some of the issues present in the Fog computing paradigm and their solutions. The paper also points out the open challenges that are present in the existing state of the art load-balancing and security techniques. There are still some improvements that can be made in the proposed solutions which can be worked upon in the future.

References

[1] Mukherjee, M. et al. 2017. Security and privacy in fog computing: challenges. In IEEE Access, 5: 19293–19304.

[2] He, X., Ren, Z., Shi, C. and Fang, J. 2016. A novel load balancing strategy of software-defined cloud/Fog networking in the internet of vehicles. In China Communications, 13(Supplement 2): 140–149.

[3] Wan, J., Chen, B., Wang, S., Xia, M., Li, D. and Liu, C. 2018. Fog computing for energy-aware load balancing and scheduling in smart factory. In IEEE Transactions on Industrial Informatics.

[4] Chen, Y. A., Walters, J. P. and Crago, S. P. 2017. Load balancing for minimizing dead-line misses and total runtime for connected car systems in fog computing. 2017 IEEE International Symposium on Parallel and Distributed Processing with Applications and 2017 IEEE International Conference on Ubiquitous Computing and Communications (ISPA/IUCC), Guangzhou, pp. 683–690.

[5] Ningning, S., Chao, G., Xingshuo, A. and Qiang, Z. 2016. Fog computing dynamic load balancing mechanism based on graph repartitioning. In China Communications, 13(3): 156–164, March 2016.

[6] Ye Yu, Xin Li and Chen Qian. 2017. SDLB: A scalable and dynamic software load balancer for fog and mobile edge computing. pp. 55–60. In Proceedings of the Workshop on Mobile Edge Communications (MECOMM '17). ACM, New York, NY, USA.

[7] Puthal, D., Obaidat, M. S., Nanda, P., Prasad, M., Mohanty, S. P. and Zomaya, A. Y. 2018. Secure and sustainable load balancing of edge data centers in fog computing. In IEEE Communications Magazine, 56(5): 60–65, May 2018.

[8] Verma, Manisha, Bhardwaj, Neelam and Yadav, Arun. 2016. Real time efficient scheduling algorithm for load balancing in fog computing environment. International Journal of Information Technology and Computer Science, 8: 1–10. 10.5815/ijitcs.2016.04.01.

[9] Li, Changlong, Zhuang, Hang, Wang, Qingfeng and Zhou, Xuehai. 2018. SSLB: Self-similarity-based load balancing for large-scale fog computing. Arabian Journal for Science and Engineering. 10.1007/s13369-018-3169-3.

[10] Huang, Q., Yang, Y. and Wang, L. 2017. Secure data access control with ciphertext update and computation outsourcing in fog computing for internet of things. In IEEE Access, 5: 12941–12950.

[11] Stolfo, S. J., Salem, M. B. and Keromytis, A. D. 2012. Fog computing: mitigating insider data theft attacks in the cloud. 2012 IEEE Symposium on Security and Privacy Workshops, San Francisco, CA, pp. 125–128.

[12] Keke Gai, Meikang Qiu, Lixin Tao and Yongxin Zhu. 2016. Intrusion detection techniques for mobile cloud computing in heterogeneous 5G. Sec. and Commun. Netw. 9, 16 (November 2016): 3049–3058.

[13] Alharbi, S., Rodriguez, P., Maharaja, R., Iyer, P., Bose, N. and Ye, Z. 2018. FOCUS: A Fog computing-based security system for the Internet of Things. 2018 15th IEEE Annual Consumer Communications & Networking Conference (CCNC), Las Vegas, NV, pp. 1–5.

[14] Deepali and Bhushan, K. 2017. DDoS attack mitigation and resource provisioning in cloud using Fog computing. 2017 International Conference On Smart Technologies For Smart Nation (SmartTechCon), Bangalore, pp. 308–313.

[15] Khan, K. M. and Malluhi, Q. 2010. Establishing trust in cloud computing. In IT Professional, 12(5): 20–27, Sept.–Oct. 2010.

[16] Fatin Hamadah Rahman, Thien Wan Au, Shah Newaz, S. H. and Wida Susanty Suhaili. 2017. Trustworthiness in fog: A fuzzy approach. pp. 207–211. In Proceedings of the 2017 VI International Conference on Network, Communication and Computing (ICNCC 2017). ACM, New York, NY, USA.

[17] Hur, J., Koo, D., Shin, Y. and Kang, K. 2017. Secure data de-duplication with dynamic ownership management in cloud storage. 2017 IEEE 33rd International Conference on Data Engineering (ICDE), San Diego, CA, pp. 69–70.

[18] Sarang Kahvazadeh, Vitor B. Souza, Xavi Masip-Bruin, Eva Marn-Tordera, Jordi Garcia and Rodrigo Diaz. 2017. Securing combined fog-to-cloud system through SDN approach. In Proceedings of the 4th Workshop on Cross Cloud Infrastructures & Platforms (Crosscloud'17). ACM, New York, NY, USA, Article 2, 6 pages.

[19] Wissam Razouk, Daniele Sgandurra and Kouichi Sakurai. 2017. A new security middleware architecture based on Fog computing and cloud to support IoT con-strained devices. In Proceedings of the 1st International Conference on Internet of Things and Machine Learning (IML '17). ACM, New York, NY, USA, Article 35, 8 pages.

[20] Rahbari, D., Kabirzadeh, S. and Nickray, M. 2017. A security aware scheduling in Fog computing by hyper heuristic algorithm. 2017 3rd Iranian Conference on Intelligent Systems and Signal Processing (ICSPIS), Shahrood, pp. 87–92.

[21] Deepali and Bhushan, K. 2017. DDoS attack defence framework for cloud using Fog computing. 2017 2nd IEEE International Conference on Recent Trends in Electronics, Information & Communication Technology (RTEICT), Bangalore, pp. 534–538.

[22] Hu, F., Hao, Q. and Bao, K. 2014. A survey on software-defined network and openflow: from concept to implementation. IEEE Communications.

[23] Liu, X. and Liu, J. 2016. A task scheduling based on simulated annealing algorithm in cloud computing. International Journal of Hybrid Information Technology, 9(6): 403412.

[24] Mukherjee, M. et al. 2017. Security and privacy in fog computing: challenges. In IEEE Access, 5: 19293–19304. doi: 10.1109/ACCESS.2017.2749422.

[25] Alrawais, Arwa, Alhothaily, Abdulrahman, Hu, Chunqiang and Cheng, Xiuzhen. 2017. Fog computing for the internet of things: security and privacy issues. IEEE Internet Computing, 21: 34–42. 10.1109/MIC.2017.37.

[26] Abbasi, B. Z. and Shah, M. A. 2017. Fog computing: Security issues, solutions and robust practices. 2017 23rd International Conference on Automation and Computing (ICAC), Huddersfield, pp. 1–6.

[27] PeiYun Zhang, MengChu Zhou and Giancarlo Fortino. 2018. Security and trust issues in Fog computing: A survey. Future Generation Computer Systems, 88: 16–27.

5

Comparison of Various Techniques for Emergency Vehicle Detection using Audio Processing

Eshwar Prithvi Jonnadula and *Pabitra Mohan Khilar**

5.1 Introduction

The Vehicular Ad-Hoc Networks (VANETS) is a rising region of networking. It is a type of Mobile Ad-Hoc Network. The VANETS consists of three major modes of communication, namely, Vehicle to Vehicle (V2V), Infrastructure to Infrastructure (I2T) and Vehicle to Infrastructure (V2I) [6]. As of late, more mishap scenarios have come into existence. Because of this, roads are observed to be highly congested and occupied. With the assistance of committed short-extend correspondence (DSRC), Vehicular Ad-Hoc Networks sets up correspondence among different vehicles that are altering their course much of the time. Vehicles directly interact with other vehicles irrespective of their overloading, resulting in loss of information [5].

As of now, transportation has become an irreplaceable part of human life. Normally, 40% of the human population spends one hour on the road on average every day. Over time, the human race has become significantly dependent on transportation, due to this, transportation modes have opened the doors to new possibilities, but not without some drawbacks. To start with, the blockage has turned into an undeniable problem across the globe as the count of vehicles on the streets continues to increase. For instance, Beijing,

Department of Computer Science and Engineering National Institute of Technology, Rourkela.
Email: 714cs1038@nitrkl.ac.in
* Corresponding author: pmkhilar@nitrkl.ac.in

China, had an aggregate of four hundred thousand vehicles toward the start of this decade and added another eight hundred thousand that year. Blockages can cause an increase in gas utilization and air contamination, and also make it difficult to actualize plans for open transportation [12].

The spectrum of natural sounds is large and it incorporates the range of sounds generated in various real-world conditions. These sounds give us useful information about human activities. Such data is vital for applications that process sound and video streams. Cautioning sounds, for example, emergency vehicles, smoke alerts and medicinal checking alerts, are of an extraordinary significance, as they are generally intended to warn individuals of perilous circumstances. Programmed recognition of such sounds may have numerous applications for clever frameworks that need to react to their acoustic surroundings.

Over the most recent couple of decades, programmed processing of sound signs attracted extraordinary intrigue in both academia and industry. In any case, most efforts and resources have been directed toward discourse and music handling and less toward emergency sounds. The greater parts of works managing natural sounds are focused on the sound arrangement, e.g., blasts versus entryway pummel versus canine barks or location of unusual sound occasions. The fundamental research issue these works manage is picking an arrangement of reasonable sound highlights. Basic highlights being used for these undertakings are the Mel-frequency cepstral coefficients (MFCC), wavelet-based highlights and individual fleeting and recurrence highlights. The arrangement of sound categories is constrained significantly in these works, therefore, these are generally difficult to sum up. Along these lines, to make a dependable caution sound identifier, a more particular procedure ought to be planned.

This paper is divided into five sections as follows: In the first section, we briefly discussed VANETs and the importance of identification of emergency vehicles. In the second section, the previous works and the different techniques used by the authors are explained. The third section explains the different methods used in the identification of emergency vehicles. The fourth section gives comparative results of various methods explained in section three. The fifth section discusses the conclusion and the future work involved.

5.2 Related Works

The National Highway Traffic Safety Organization (NHTSA) has gathered rescue vehicle crash information for the United States of America between 1992 and 2011. There was an expected yearly average of 4500 car accidents and lot more damage crashes involving emergency vehicles. In the last two decades, 662 people were killed and 52,000 people were evaluated to be harmed in such crashes, including emergency vehicle drivers, travelers, non-inhabitants and tenants of different vehicles. According to the insights of crisis vehicle mischances in the United States of America, there were about 31,600 mishaps involving fire fighting vehicles that brought about 645 fatalities over a multi-year time frame (2000–2009) and 300 fatalities that happen each year amid police interests [11]. From the present issue area, it tends to be understood that there is a genuine requirement for an insightful movement administration framework for the compelling administration of both typical and emergency vehicles.

In view of this understanding, a few past works have attempted to bargain particularly with the errand of caution sound discovery. A general model of alert sound cannot be built easily, therefore, most research is focused on identifying specific cautions, ordinarily alarms of emergency vehicles of a particular nation. As expected, a vast number of research works do not show any performance gains since they don't show accurate results and for the most part don't consider moves in frequency because of the Doppler Effect. For instance, in the idea introduced in [4], the researchers attempt to identify a little arrangement of pre-chosen cautioning audio in a reenacted domain by cross connection.

In [3], a Machine Learning technique (ANN) was utilized to recognize law enforcement vehicles in Italy.

A different approach for distinguishing alarms of emergency vehicles in Italy is introduced in [9]. The framework keeps running progressively by evaluating the pitch frequency and contrasting it with pre-characterized alarm frequencies. Another straightforward framework for alarm identification that runs continuously is portrayed in [10]. In view of the periodicity of caution sounds, the aftereffects of autocorrelation are dissected by an ML-based classifier customized to acoustic crisis signals in Germany.

In [8], a strategy for distinguishing an emergency vehicle alarm sound in Taiwan is displayed. It utilizes frequency matching to find the longest basic subsequence.

5.3 Siren Detection

Sire detection is the process of identifying the presence of an emergency vehicle on the roads by the siren sound it produces using audio processing.

This section is divided into two parts. Part A discusses the basic siren detection using the pitch detection method. In Part B, we discuss the various machine learning-based methods.

5.3.1 Basic Pitch Based Detection

The issue of the siren detection has been assaulted with a procedure chipping away at two levels. First MDF (Module Difference Function), a period space strategy, intends to group each bit of the sound motion as pitched or unhitched. This initial step can be isolated in MDF count and Peak Looking. The Peak looking gives us the estimation of the pitch frequency. Toward the end of the main stage, we get a flag speaking to the pitch developing after some time, we call this Pitch (t).

Also, Pitch (t) is investigated with the end goal to perceive a period design of the coveted siren appearance or nonappearance of the siren.

$$MDF(w,l) = \sum_{n=0}^{ws-1} |y(n+l)\%ws - y(n)| \tag{5.1}$$

where

y(n) is the audio signal at nth sample
l is the lag
N is the length of audio signal w is the window number
ws is the window size

Using the MDF vs the lag plot, the pitch of the signal is detected.

$$pitch(w) = \frac{sr}{l} \tag{5.2}$$

where

sr is the Sample Rate
l is the lag at which MDF is minimum
w is the window number

Here, Pitch is the basic fundamental frequency of the sound or audio signal. The window is the small part of the audio signal. The audio signal is divided into a number of windows for the purpose of easy processing of the audio signal. The sample rate is the rate at which the analogue signal is converted to a digital audio signal. Lag is nothing but a particular instance of the sample.

Emergency signals all in all have an occasional example which rehashes over a brief length of time. Moreover, they additionally have a place with particular frequency groups which loans them the high pitch sound that they are typically connected with.

Algorithm 1: Algorithm to find Module Difference Function

---

procedure MDF(*y, l, ws*)
$r \leftarrow 0$ ▷ r stores the result
$i \leftarrow 0$
while *i f* = *ws* **do**
$temp \leftarrow |y(i+l)\%ws - y(i)|$ ▷ l is the lag; ws is the window size
$r \leftarrow r + temp$ $i \leftarrow i + 1$
return *r*

We use these qualities relating to emergency signals by utilizing a pitch identification calculation.

An Altered Pitch Discovery (MDF) calculation, which is a less computationally costly form of the autocorrelation work, is utilized to discover the pitch. Utilizing the MDF versus the lag plot, the pitch is distinguished. An emergency signal estimator that ascertains the division of time for which the pitch stays inside the frequency band for emergency signals predicts the nearness of emergency signals in the sound example.

Algorithm 2: Algorithm to find Pitch

---

procedure PITCH(*ws*)
pitch list[ ]

$nw \leftarrow \int \dfrac{len(y)}{ws}$ ▷ nw is the number of windows; ws is the window size

$i \leftarrow 0$
while $i\ f = nw$ **do**
mdf list[ ]
$y\ clip = y[i * ws : i * ws + ws]$
$j \leftarrow 0$
while $j\ f = ws$ **do**
$temp \leftarrow (MDF\ (y\ clip,\ j,\ ws)\ mdf\ list.add(temp)$
min value $= min(mdf\ list)$
min index $= mdf\ list.index(min\ value)$ *pitch detected* $= \dfrac{sr}{min\ index}$
pitch list.add(pitch detected)
return *pitch list*

From the two algorithms above, we get the pitch of each window. The window domain is converted to time domain as follows

$$time = \frac{w * ws}{sr} \tag{5.3}$$

where

w is the window number
ws is the window size
sr is the sample rate

Now that we have time domain and pitch at every instance of time, we draw a Pitch VS Time graph as shown in Figure 5.4.

The probability of presence of emergency vehicle is obtained by simply dividing the pitch obtained by the standard pitch frequency of emergency vehicle as per the standard.

5.3.2 Machine Learning Techniques

Machine learning (ML) is a field of AI that utilizes statistical techniques to enable digital computers to "learn" (e.g., process information without being given explicit instructions).

In this part of subsection, we briefly discuss the Artificial Neural Network which is used in our comparative study of identification of emergency vehicles.

Artificial Neural Networks The idea of ANN is formulated upon the fact that the human mind works by making the correct networks which can be reproduced using silicon and wires in place of neurons and dendrites. The human brain is comprised of around 8600 crore nerve cells called neurons. These are inter connected to other cells with the help of structures called axons. Stimuli from various sources such as inputs from sensory organs and other external sources are processed by dendrites. These inputs transform into electrical signals which travel through the neural network quickly. A nerve cell in a network decides whether it should forward the signal to other nerve cell or not. The basic structure of ANN is shown in Figure 5.1.

In a similar fashion, an ANN is comprised of multiple nodes which imitate the biological nervous system, specifically the neural connections of the human brain. The neurons are interconnected and interact among themselves. The nodes in the network take data as input and perform a basic operation on it. This result is then forwarded to other neurons. The output generated at each node is termed as its activation If the output generated by the neural network is 'good or desired' then adjustment of weights is not required. On the contrary, if the neural network produces 'poor or undesired' output then the network modifies the weights such that further computations result in improved output.

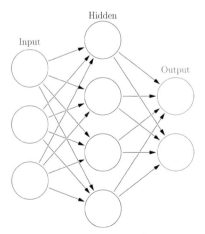

Figure 5.1: Basic structure of ANN [1].

In this method of machine learning, we use the feature as the input layer and based on the requirement we add hidden layers. The final output layer consists of only one node which gives the output as either 1 (Emergency) or 0 (Non-Emergency).

Feature Extraction We used 34 features extracted from each audio sample. It segregates the input signal into short window frames and then computes the features for individual frame. This method produces a series of feature vectors for the entire signal.

- **Zero Crossing Rate (0):** The number of times the sign of a time series change within a frame. It approximates the frequency which is significant in a time frame.

$$ZCR = \frac{1}{2} \sum_{m=-\infty}^{+\infty} \left| sig(x(m)) - sig(x(m-1)) \right|$$

$$sig(x(n)) = \begin{cases} 1 & x(n) \geq 0 \\ -1 & x(n) \leq 0 \end{cases}$$

- **Energy (1):** The sum of squares of the signal values.

$$Energy = \sum_{-\infty}^{+\infty} |x(n)|^2$$

$x(n)$ is the discrete time signal

- **Entropy of Energy (2):** The entropy of a signal is a measure of the amount of information a signal carries. It can be understood as a measure of sudden changes.

$$Entropy = -\sum_{i} p(x_i) ln(p(x_i))$$

$p(x_i)$ is the probability for the signal to take values x_i

- **Spectral Centroid (3):** The spectral centroid is a measure which indicates where the "centre of mass" lies in the spectrum.

$$Spectral\ Centroid = \frac{\sum_{k=1}^{N} kF[k]}{\sum_{k=1}^{N} F[k]}$$

$F[k]$ is the amplitude corresponding to bin k in DFT spectrum

- **Spectral Spread (4):** The second central moment of the spectrum.

$$Spectral\ Spread = \sum_{k=1}^{N} (k - SC)^2 F[k]$$

- **Spectral Entropy (5):** The entropy of the normalized spectral energies for a set of sub-frames.

$$Spectral\ Entropy = -\sum_i p(F[k])ln(p(F[k]))$$

$p(F[k])$ is the probability for the signal to take values $F[k]$

- **Spectral Flux (6):** Spectral flux is a proportion of how quick the power spectrum of a signal is fluctuating which is determined by comparing the previous frame of the power spectrum to the other frame.

$$Spectral\ Flux = \sum_{-\infty}^{+\infty}(F[k] - F[k+1])^2$$

- **Spectral Rolloff (7):** Spectral roll-off is defined as the Nth percentile of the power spectral distribution, where N is usually 85% or 95%. The roll-off point is the frequency below which the N% of the magnitude distribution is concentrated.

- **MFCCs (8–20):** Mel Frequency Cepstral Coefficients form a cepstral depiction where the frequency bands are distributed according to the Mel-scale and not linear. We use 13 Mel-frequency cepstral coefficients to describe the spectral shape of the signal. The log-energy outputs of the nonlinear Mel-scale filter-bank is taken as input and discrete cosine transform (DCT) is applied to produce the output as the coefficients.

- **Chroma Vector (21–32):** The spectral energy is represented by the twelve element buckets where each bucket represents twelve equal pitch-tempered pitch classes of western music.

- **Chroma Deviation (33):** The standard deviation of the 12 chroma coefficients.

5.4 Results

In this part, comparison of the various machine learning techniques for the classification of emergency vehicle detection is explained. These are implemented in python. We have taken an audio dataset provided by Google [2].

Using Algorithm 1 we find the MDF. This is used for a particular window to get the MDF VS Lag plot as shown in Figure 5.2.

This plot of MDF VS Lag is used to find out the pitch of a particular window. Then we easily plot the Pitch VS Time plot as shown in Figure 5.3.

The probability of the presence of an emergency vehicle is obtained dividing the pitch by the standard pitch frequency of emergency vehicle siren.

Then we obtain the Probability VS Time plot as shown in Figure 5.4.

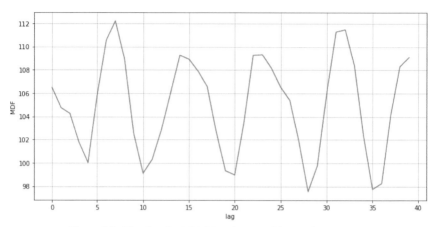

Figure 5.2: The plot of MDF VS Lag for a small interval in a window.

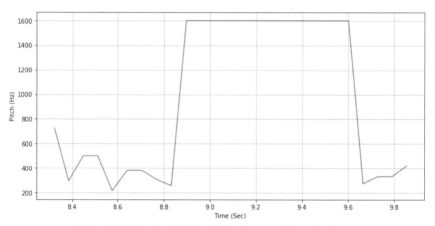

Figure 5.3: The plot of Pitch VS time for a small interval of time.

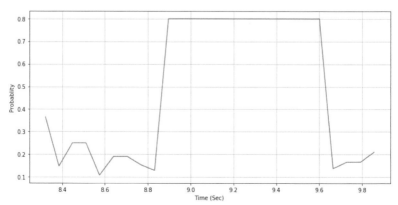

Figure 5.4: The plot of Probability VS time for a small interval in time.

The parameters [7] used for the comparisons are

1. **True Positive Rate (TPR)** $= \dfrac{TP}{TP + FN}$

2. **True Negative Rate (TNR)** $= \dfrac{TN}{FP + TN}$

3. **Positive Predictive Value (PPV)** $= \dfrac{TP}{TP + FP}$

4. **Negative Predictive Value (NPV)** $= \dfrac{TN}{TN + FN}$

5. **False Positive Rate (FPR)** $= \dfrac{FP}{FP + TN}$

6. **False Discovery Rate (FDR)** $= \dfrac{FP}{FP + TP}$

7. **False Negative Rate (FNR)** $= \dfrac{FN}{FN + TP}$

8. **Accuracy (ACC)** $= \dfrac{TP + FP}{TP + FP + TN + FN}$

9. **F1 Score (F1)** $= \dfrac{2TP}{2TP + FP + FN}$

We have made a comparison for Artificial Neural Networks by incrementing the number of hidden layers and increasing the features used, thereby increasing the accuracy of perdition.

The following are the architecture of the ANN's used, as shown below in Figure 5.5 and Figure 5.6.

Using these two architectures, we calculate the different parameters and compare them to find which gives the better performance in the identification of emergency vehicles. We see that the ANN with three hidden layers gives 3%

Figure 5.5: Architecture of one hidden layer ANN.

Figure 5.6: Architecture of three hidden layer ANN.

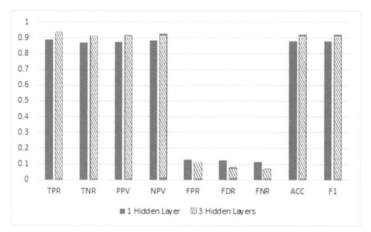

Figure 5.7: Comparison of ANNs.

more accuracy than one hidden layer ANN in the identification of emergency vehicles, as shown in Figure 5.7.

5.5 Conclusion

An increased number of vehicles does not just build the reaction delay of emergency vehicles, yet it increments the odds for them being engaged with mischances. The emergency vehicle entering a crossing point at speed on a red light poses a danger to activity on various streets and can cause mischances.

This paper demonstrates a comparison of several techniques for the detection of emergency vehicles using machine learning. We have also found out that the artificial neural network with three hidden layers has the best accuracy rate, i.e., 3% more than the one hidden layer ANN. So, this ANN can be deployed in real time to determine the existence of emergency vehicles.

Audio analysis may always not be correct, as we can see in the results mentioned above in Figure 5.7. This can be overcome by improving the ability to detect emergency vehicles, using traffic cameras to get actionable real-time data or information. Both audio and video detection can together indicate the presence of an emergency vehicle on the road.

References

[1] ANN Wikipedia. 2018. https://en.wikipedia.org/wiki/Artificial_neural_network, [Online; accessed Nov-2018].
[2] AudioSet by Google. 2018. https://research.google.com/audioset/dataset/ emergency_vehicle. html, [Online; accessed Nov-2018].
[3] Beritelli, F., Casale, S., Russo, A. and Serrano, S. 2006. An automatic emergency signal recognition system for the hearing impaired. pp. 179–182. *In*: Digital Signal Processing Workshop, 12th-Signal Processing Education Workshop, 4th IEEE.

[4] Bernstein, E. R., Brammer, A. J. and Yu, G. 2014. Augmented warning sound detection for hearing protectors. The Journal of the Acoustical Society of America, 135(1): EL29–EL34.

[5] Bhoi, S. K. and Khilar, P. M. 2013. Vehicular communication: a survey. IET Networks, 3(3): 204–217.

[6] Bhoi, S. K. and Khilar, P. M. 2014. Sir: a secure and intelligent routing protocol for vehicular ad hoc network. IET Networks, 4(3): 185–194.

[7] Grover, J., Prajapati, N. K., Laxmi, V. and Gaur, M. S. 2011. Machine learning approach for multiple misbehavior detection in vanet. pp. 644–653. *In*: International Conference on Advances in Computing and Communications. Springer.

[8] Liaw, J. J., Wang, W. S., Chu, H. C., Huang, M. S. and Lu, C. P. 2013. Recognition of the ambulance siren sound in Taiwan by the longest common subsequence. pp. 3825–3828. *In*: Systems, Man, and Cybernetics (SMC), 2013 IEEE International Conference on IEEE.

[9] Meucci, F., Pierucci, L., Del Re, E., Lastrucci, L. and Desii, P. 2008. A real-time siren detector to improve safety of guide in traffic environment. pp. 1–5. *In*: Signal Processing Conference, 2008 16th European IEEE.

[10] M., Schafer, A., R. 2010. Integrated circuit for detection of acoustic emergency signals in road traffic. pp. 562–565. *In*: Mixed Design of Integrated Circuits and Systems (MIXDES), 2010 Proceedings of the 17th International Conference IEEE.

[11] Nellore, K. and Hancke, G. P. 2016. Traffic management for emergency vehicle priority based on visual sensing. Sensors, 16(11): 1892.

[12] Zhang, J., Wang, F. Y., Wang, K., Lin, W. H., Xu, X., Chen, C. et al. 2011. Data-driven intelligent transportation systems: A survey. IEEE Transactions on Intelligent Transportation Systems, 12(4): 1624–1639.

6

Cryptanalysis of a Robust ECC-Based Provable Secure Authentication Protocol with Privacy Preserving for Industrial Internet of Things

Diksha Rangwani, Dipanwita Sadhukhan* and Sangram Ray

6.1 Introduction

Wireless sensor network (WSN) is an emerging Internet-based global autonomous architecture facilitating information exchange among different communicating entities [1]. This technology has become popular in recent days due to its user-centric services, scalability, minimal overhead and efficiency. Moreover, it consists of tens to thousands of spatially distributed low-cost, low power-consuming sensor nodes which communicate through a wireless channel to share information and monitor any physical or environmental change in the system [2]. The general architecture of WSN consists of a gateway and many sensor nodes. Since sensor nodes have limited resources and low computation capabilities, gateway provides connectivity and performs data aggregation and forwarding between sensor nodes and other components in the network [3]. WSN can be applied in various areas,

Department of Computer Science and Engineering National Institute of Technology Sikkim, Ravangla, Sikkim-737139, India.
Emails: diksharangwani@gmail.com; sangram.ism@gmail.com
* Corresponding author: dipanwitasadhukhan2012@gmail.com

such as coal mine monitoring, agricultural field monitoring, patient health monitoring, battle field monitoring and other real life scenarios which are difficult for humans to reach. Recently, an application of WSN, Industrial Internet of Things (IIoT), has emerged as the most important infrastructure. In the present scenario, Industrial Internet of Things has become more important in the perspective of industry as digitization has become a business priority. By combining machine-learning approach and cloud technology, IIoT has achieved exceptional heights of productivity, efficiency, and performance [1].

Along with the various advantages of WSN/IIoT come several challenges, such as key management, data confidentiality and user authentication for validation of user legitimacy. As the wireless channels are more prone to security threats, verifying the legitimacy of user is one of the key challenges for making WSN/IIoT secure. Therefore, many different remote user authentication and key management schemes were proposed for making communication in WSN secure. Generally, in WSN, the communicating parties authenticate themselves mutually, i.e., the user needs to log in to the gateway whenever it needs any of the environmental data being collected by the sensor nodes. As the sensor nodes have limited resources and capabilities, traditional Public Key Infrastructure (PKI) with high computational overhead becomes incompatible for use, although the system must maintain high security-performance trade-off. Hence, the above discussion identifies that the greatest challenge for WSN/IIoT is making it secure, efficient, cost effective and lightweight.

6.1.1 Literature Review

The work which became the foundational stone for the authentication protocols was carried out by Das [4] in 2009. Das [4] proposed a user authentication scheme for WSN using two factors, i.e., password and smart-card. However, in 2010, Khan et al. [5] identified that Das's scheme [4] did not provide proper mutual authentication, user anonymity, key agreement, and was not resilient to masquerade attacks, gateway bypassing attack and offline password guessing attack. Simultaneously, He et al. [6] enhanced Das's [4] protocol by improving mutual authentication phase. Yet, in 2011, Lee et al. [7] depicted that the scheme did not preserve user anonymity and suffered from secret information leakage.

In the same year, Yeh et al. [8] proposed an Elliptic Curve Cryptography (ECC)-based two-factor user authentication scheme for WSN. Unfortunately, the scheme was not able to provide suitable mutual authentication and user anonymity nor prevent stolen smart card attack. In 2013, Shi and Gong [9] designed an ECC-based improved user authentication scheme covering almost all of the loopholes of Yeh et al.'s [8] scheme. Later, Choi et al. [10] illustrated that the scheme in [9] was vulnerable to stolen smart-card attack and unknown key-share attack. They also proposed an efficient scheme for WSN using ECC. In 2014, Nam et al. [11] proposed a novel authentication scheme for WSN, although it lacked some basic functionality [1].

In 2016, Das et al. [12] and Xue et al. [13] proposed remote user authentication scheme for WSN that was provably efficient and lightweight using irreversible one-way cryptographic hash function and symmetric-key cryptography. Although Das et al.'s protocol included several new features, like password protection, secure key agreement, dynamic node addition, etc., Wu et al. [14] showed that the scheme proposed by Das [12] was not resilient to offline password guessing attack and desynchronization attack. Later that same year, Amin and Biswas [15] pointed out that Wu et al.'s scheme [14] suffered from lack of user anonymity and lacked the ability to counter offline password guessing attack, privileged insider attack, stolen smart card attack and user impersonation attack.

Furthermore, Jiang et al. [16] depicted that the scheme proposed by Amin et al. [17] for WSNs is prone to offline password guessing attack and tracking attack. Then, an improved version of the scheme was proposed by Jiang et al. [16] using Rabin cryptosystem. As the scheme used Rabin cryptosystem, it had higher commutation overhead [18]. Hence, Gope and Hwang [18] proposed a user authentication scheme for WSN which was efficient, secure, lightweight and also preserved user anonymity. In 2016, Li et al. [19] proved that the scheme proposed by Gope and Hwang [18] was vulnerable to security attacks, such as stolen smart-card attack and de-synchronization attack.

Recently, in 2018, Li et al. [1] has proposed a secure user authentication ECC-based three factor privacy preservation scheme for IIoT. Li et al. [1] has used various formal and informal security analyses for proving the robustness of the scheme and demonstrates that the scheme is secure against various security attacks. However, in this paper we have found that the scheme is not resilient to User Impersonation Attack, Sensor Node Impersonation Attack, Session Specific Temporary Information Attack, Denial of Service Attack, Replay Attack and Privileged Insider Attack.

6.1.2 Our Contribution

In this paper, we have considered some practical assumptions to mathematically prove that Li et al.'s scheme [1] is not resilient to User Impersonation Attack, Sensor Node Impersonation Attack, Session Specific Temporary Information Attack, Denial of Service Attack, Replay Attack and Privileged Insider Attack.

6.1.3 Organization of the Paper

The rest of the paper is organized as follows: Section 6.2 illustrates Li et al.'s scheme [1] in brief. The cryptanalysis of the Li et al.'s scheme [1] that shows the aforementioned attacks persist in the scheme is given in section 6.3, and finally, a conclusion to the paper is given in section 6.4.

6.2 Review of Li et al.'s Scheme

This section contains the review of Park et al. [1] scheme for mobile commerce environment. The scheme can be divided into four phases, namely, (i) System initialization phase, (ii) User registration phase, (iii) Mutual authentication and key exchange phase and (iv) Password change phase. A brief description of each phase is illustrated in the subsections below, with notations described in Table 6.1.

Table 6.1: Notations used in Li et al.'s [1] scheme.

Notation	Description
U	A mobile user
GW	A gateway node
SN	A sensor node
ID_U, PW_U	U's identity and password
ω	GW's secret identity and master secret key
SN_{id}	SN's identity
SK	A session key shared between U and SN
$h(\cdot)$	One-way hash function
$\boxed{?}$	XOR operation
$\|$	Concatenation operation
$Gen(.)$	Generative function of fuzzy extractor
$Rep(.)$	Reproductive function of fuzzy extractor
x, X	Secret/public key pair of GW

6.2.1 Registration Phase

Here, registration phase depicts individual registration for both sensor node and user into the gateway of the IIoT network. The detail registration procedures are given in the following subsections.

6.2.1.1 Sensor Node Registration

Gateway GW selects a unique identity SN_{id} for each sensor node and computes the secret key $K_{gs} = h(SN_{id}\|\omega)$. GW stores SN_{id} in its memory and (SN_{id}, K_{gs}) is stored in sensor node. After successful registration, sensor nodes are deployed in the target region of the network.

6.2.1.2 User Registration

Step 1: User U randomly selects an identity ID_U, password PW_U, and imprints his/her own biometric BIO_U. Then, through fuzzy extractor smart-device, extracts the biometric information in smart device as $Gen\,(BIO_U) = (R_U, P_U)$, where (R_U, P_U) are the secret and public strings of the user. Next, user selects a random number r_U to compute $HPW_U = h(PW_U||r_U)$ and, finally, sends the registration request message containing (i) ID_U (ii) HPW_U (iii) R_U to GW.

Step 2: After receiving the registration request from U, GW checks if ID_U is already used by another user or not. If it is used, then GW asks him/her to choose a new identity. After receiving the valid identity ID_U, GW computes $B_1 = h(ID_U||HPW_U||R_U)$, $B_2 = h(ID_U||\omega)$ and $B_3 = h(HPW_U||R_U) \oplus B_2$. Lastly, GW forwards a reply message composed of (i) B_1 (ii) B_3 (iii) public key of gateway X to user.

Step 3: After receiving the message from GW, U stores $(P_U, r_U, B_1, B_3, X, Gen(\cdot), Rep(\cdot))$ into his/her smart device.

6.2.2 Authentication and Key Agreement (AKA) Phase

To access the sensed data, the user first needs to authenticate himself/herself as legitimate user to the gateway GW. Similarly, each sensor node SN must authenticate itself to the gateway in order to communicate with the users. The procedure of authentication among all the communicating parties of the network as well as the final session key agreement between U and SN for further data exchange is given below in a step-wise manner, where $A \rightarrow B$: M means message M is sent to communicating party B from another communicating party A.

Step 1: $U \rightarrow GW$: M_1

U feeds identity ID_U, password PW_U and imprints biometric information BIO_U on the smart device. The smart device computes (i) $R_U = Rep(BIO_U, P_U)$, where $Rep(.)$ is the reproductive function of fuzzy extractor and (R_U, P_U) are the secret and public strings of the user. Then, it calculates $B_1' = h(ID_U||h(PW_U||r_U)||R_U)$, where r_U is the random number generated by user during registration, and checks B_1' is same as B_1 or not. If both are not same, then the session is terminated. Otherwise, U produces a random number $a \in Z_n^*$, and calculates (i) $B_2 = B_3 \oplus h(h(PW_U||r_U)||R_U)$, (ii) $D_1 = aP$, (iii) $D_2 = aX$, where X is the public key of the gateway, (iv) $DID_U = ID_U \oplus h(D_2)$, (v) $D_3 = SN_{id} \oplus B_2 \oplus h(D_2)$, and (vi) $D_4 = h(B_2||D_2||SN_{id})$. Finally, the login request message M_1 is generated as concatenating the calculated values of DID_U, D_1, D_3, D_4 as $M_1 = \{DID_U, D_1, D_3, D_4\}$ and it is forwarded to GW.

Step 2: $GW \rightarrow SN: M_2$

After receiving the login request message, GW calculates $D_2 = xD_1$, $ID_U = DID_U \oplus h(D_2)$, and checks if calculated ID_U is present in its memory or not? If it is there, then GW computes $B_2 = h(ID_U||\omega)$, where ω is the secret identity and master secret key of gateway, $SN_{id} = D_3 \oplus B_2 \oplus h(D_2)$ and $D_4' = h(B_2||D_2||SN_{id})$. Then, it checks whether D_4' is equal to D_4 or not. If $D_4' \neq D_4$, then the session is terminated. Else, GW computes $D_5 = h(SN_{id}||\omega)$. Next, GW generates a random number r_G, calculates $D_6 = D_5 \oplus r_G$ and $D_7 = h(D_1||r_G||D_5||SN_{id})$. Lastly, GW sends $M_2 = \{D_1, D_6, D_7\}$ to SN.

Step 3: $SN \rightarrow GW: M_3$

After receiving M_2 from GW, SN computes $r_G = K_{gs} \oplus D_6$, where K_{gs} is the secret key of sensor node, $D_7' = h(D_1||r_G||K_{gs}||SN_{id})$, and checks whether D_7' is the same as D_7 or not. If it is false, session is terminated. Otherwise, SN generates $b \in Z_n^*$, a random number to compute D_8, where $D_8 = bP$, and then computes session key as $SK = h(D_1||D_8||bD_1)$, $D_9 = h(K_{gs}||D_8||r_G||SN_{id})$ and $D_{10} = h(SN_{id}||SK)$. Finally, SN sends message $M_3 = \{D_8, D_9, D_{10}\}$ to GW.

Step 4: $GW \rightarrow U: M_4$

Upon receiving M_3, GW computes $D_9' = h(D_5||D_8||r_G||SN_{id})$, and checks whether $D_9' \neq D_9$. If the condition holds, the session is terminated. Else, GW computes $D_{11} = h(ID_U||D_1||D_8||B_2)$, and forwards $M_4 = \{D_8, D_{10}, D_{11}\}$ to U.

After receiving M_4, the smart device computes $D_{11}' = h(ID_U|D_1||D_8||B_2)$, and checks whether computed D_{11}' and received D_{11} are both the same or not. If they are not the same, communication is closed. Else, U authenticates GW as legitimate one. Then, the smart device computes $SK = h(D_1||D_8||aD_8)$, $D_{10}' = h(SN_{id}||SK)$, and checks if $D_{10}' = D_{10}$. If it is false, the session termination takes place. Otherwise, U authenticates SN as legitimate one and starts communication using negotiated session key.

6.3 Cryptanalysis of Li et al.'s Scheme

As mentioned in section 1.2, the remote user authentication scheme developed by Li et al. [1] suffers from some security flaws, which are conferred below. Our analysis is based on some simple practical assumptions [22, 23] which are very common in present scenario.

6.3.1 User Impersonation Attack

An adversary $\grave{A}$ pretending to be a legitimate user in order to retrieve secret information from the system is termed as user impersonation attack [23]. It can be easily proved that, by following simple steps, any adversary $\grave{A}$ can easily impersonate himself/herself as the legitimate user only by acquiring valid user's identity ID_U. Usually, user selects low entropy identity which can be easily obtained by the adversary $\dot{A}$. Now, the step-wise representation shows that the scheme is vulnerable to user impersonation attack after acquiring any valid user's identity.

Step 1: Adversary $\dot{A}$ has to morph the authentication request sent by the user. It needs to generate the login request message $\{DID_U, D_1, D_3, D_4\}$ which is being sent through an insecure channel. So, any adversary $\dot{A}$ can easily capture this message $\{DID_U, D_1, D_3, D_4\}$ of the current session.

Step 2: After obtaining the login request message of the user, the adversary $\dot{A}$ can calculate $h(D_2)$ = acquired $ID_U \oplus$ public DID_U, B_2 = public $D_3 \oplus$ public $SN_{id} \oplus$ calculated $h(D_2)$.

Step 3: To generate valid authentication request, adversary $\dot{A}$ generates random number $\bar{a}$ and then calculates $\overline{D_2} = \bar{a}X$ as X is the public key of the gateway, $h(\overline{D_2}) = h(\bar{a}X)$, $\overline{DID_U}$ = acquired $ID_U \oplus h(\overline{D_2})$, $\overline{D_1} = \bar{a}P$, $\overline{D_3}$ = public $SN_{id} \oplus B_2$ (calculated in step 2) $\oplus h(\overline{D_2})$, $\overline{D_4} = h$ (calculated $B_2||\overline{D_2}||$public SN_{id}). Finally, adversary $\dot{A}$ forwards the message $\{\overline{DID_U}, \overline{D_1}, \overline{D_3}, \overline{D_4}\}$ to gateway.

Step 4: After receiving the authentication request from adversary $\dot{A}$ with ID_U, the gateway computes $\overline{D_2}' = x\overline{D_1}$, $ID_U' = \overline{DID_U} \oplus h(\overline{D_2}')$ $B_2' = h(ID_U'||\omega)$, $SN_{id}' = \overline{D_3} \oplus B_2' \oplus h(\overline{D_2}')$, $\overline{D_4}' = h(B_2'||\overline{D_2}'||SN_{id}')$ and verifies if $\overline{D_4}' = \overline{D_4}$. Here, this verification would be successful as all the values are calculated on the basis of the message that has been sent by the adversary $\dot{A}$.

Step 5: All the further steps are carried out in a similar way as described in section 2.2, as in those steps only the gateway and sensor node are involved. Now, in the last phase of authentication, where the gateway sends the message $\{D_9, D_{10}, D_{11}\}$ to the user, the message is again captured by the adversary $\dot{A}$ as it is being sent through an insecure channel. Lastly, the adversary $\dot{A}$ calculates the session key $SK = h(\overline{D_1}||D_8||\bar{a}D_8)$. In the same way, the sensor node also calculates similar session key $SK = h(\overline{D_1}||D_8||b\overline{D_1})$. Since, $\overline{D_1}$ and D_8 both are available to the adversary $\dot{A}$ and the sensor node, the condition of calculating same session key SK depends on the similarity of $\bar{a}D_8$ and $b\overline{D_1}$, which is proved in the following theorem.

Theorem: The partial session key $\bar{a}.D_8$ is similar to $b\overline{D_1}$

Proof:

$\bar{a}D_8 = \bar{a}.b.P$ (Since $D_8 = b.P$ in section 2.2)

$\quad = b.\bar{a}.\ P = b.\overline{D_1}$ (Since $\overline{D_1} = \bar{a}.P$ in section 3.1).   ∎

Hence, Li et al.'s scheme [1] is vulnerable to user impersonation attack.

6.3.2 Sensor Node Impersonation Attack

It is presumed that adversary $\grave{A}$ acts as a valid sensor node and generates a valid session key. Here, the memory of the sensor node is preloaded with SN_{id} and K_{gs}, where SN_{id} is the identity of each sensor node and K_{gs} is the corresponding secret key. It is considered that the adversary $\grave{A}$ captures the sensor node and obtains secret K_{gs} by carrying out power analysis [24] over the captured sensor node. The sensor node capture attack is explained in detail in [24]. The occurrence of this attack is represented below using the following simple mathematical steps.

Step 1: During authentication phase, gateway sends $M_2 = \{D_1, D_6$ and $D_7\}$ through public channel to the sensor node. Hence, adversary $\grave{A}$ easily captures D_1, D_6 by eavesdropping the channel and calculates $r_G = D_6 \oplus$ captured K_{gs}. Similarly, D_8, D_9 and D_{10} are sent over insecure channel. Hence, adversary $\grave{A}$ gets D_8 by snooping.

Step 2: Then, the adversary $\grave{A}$ generates a random number $\overline{b} \in Z_n^*$ to compute (i) $\overline{D_8} = \overline{b}.P$, (ii) $\overline{SK} = h(\text{public } D_1||\overline{D_8}||\overline{b}.\text{public } D_1)$, (iii) $\overline{D_9} = h(\text{captured } K_{gs}||\overline{D_8}||\text{calculated } r_g||\text{public } SN_{id})$, and (iv) $\overline{D_{10}} = h(\text{public } SN_{id}||\overline{SK})$. Finally, adversary $\grave{A}$ sends $\overline{D_8}$, $\overline{D_9}$ and $\overline{D_{10}}$ to gateway.

Step 3: After receiving the message from adversary $\grave{A}$, gateway calculates $\overline{D_9}$' $= h(K_{gs}||\overline{D_8}||r_G||SN_{id})$ and then verifies if $\overline{D_9}$' $= \overline{D_9}$ holds or not. According to the scheme [1], if the condition is true then the gateway continues the further process, otherwise session is terminated. Here, the verification will be successful since the parameter $\overline{D_8}$ is obtained from the adversary $\grave{A}$ impersonated a sensor node and K_{gs}, r_G, SN_{id} are calculated by the gateway. Furthermore, gateway calculates $D_{11} = h(ID_U||D_1||\overline{D_8}||B_2)$ and sends $\overline{D_8}$, D_{10} and D_{11} to user.

Step 4: After getting the message from gateway, user calculates D_{11}' $= h(ID_U||D_1||\overline{D_8}||B_2)$ and verifies if D_{11}' $= D_{11}$ is true or not. However, verification will be successful as the parameters used to verify the message are either sent by the adversary $\grave{A}$ via gateway or are public. Finally, the user calculates $\overline{SK} = h(D_1||\overline{D_8}||\overline{a}.\overline{D_8})$ and $\overline{D_{10}} = h(SN_{id}||\overline{SK})$. The user verifies the legitimacy of the gateway by comparing received and calculated $\overline{D_{10}}$. As we have mentioned earlier, all the validation parameters are provided by adversary $\grave{A}$ or are public. Hence, like earlier, the verification will be successful. In this scenario, by infusing some wrong credentials to the gateway and user, the adversary $\grave{A}$ is now able to generate a valid session key between the adversary $\grave{A}$ and the user.

    Hence, Li et al.'s scheme [1] is vulnerable to sensor node impersonation attack.

6.3.3 Session Specific Temporary Information Attack

If any temporary information, particular for the current session, like any random number, is inadvertently disclosed to the adversary $\dot{A}$, he/she can easily compute the session key of the current session. This attack is termed as Session specific temporary information attack [25, 26]. In Li et al.'s scheme [1], the session key is calculated as:

$SK_U = h(D_1||D_8||aD_8)$ at user side

$SK_{SN} = h(D_1||D_8||bD_1)$ at sensor node side

Here, the parameters of the session key D_1, D_8 are sent through public channel which can easily be captured by any adversary $\dot{A}$ by eavesdropping. Hence, the secrecy of the session key of that particular session depends only upon the secrecy of random number a or b. If somehow any of the secret temporary information is accidentally disclosed to any adversary $\dot{A}$, it can easily compute $a.D_8$ or $b.D_1$. In this condition, adversary $\dot{A}$ calculates session key SK either as $SK = h(D_1||D_8||aD_8)$ or $SK = h(D_1||D_8||bD_1)$, which leads to session key leakage. Hence, Li et al.'s scheme [1] is not resilient to session specific temporary information attack.

6.3.4 Denial of Service Attack

Interruption in legitimate users' access to the services provided by the system due to bad allocations of system resources is termed as denial of service attack [27, 28]. Here, the sensor node sends D_{10} to the gateway and gateway forwards it to user without any verification of the integrity of the message containing D_{10}. Now, the adversary $\dot{A}$ intentionally changes D_{10} to D_{10}', as it is forwarded through insecure channel. In this scenario, the user calculates a valid session key $SK' = h(D_1||D_8||aD_8)$ and further D_{10}' as D_{10}' $= h(SN_{id}||SK')$ to check if calculated D_{10}' is the same as received D_{10} for verifying the legitimacy of the gateway. However, due to modifications done by the adversary $\dot{A}$ in D_{10}, it will not match. Thus, the legitimate parties will not be able to communicate with each other although both are legal communicating parties. Thus, the service will remain unreachable to the user due to the presence of adversary $\dot{A}$. Hence, Li et al.'s scheme [1] suffers from denial of service attack.

6.3.5 Replay Attack

The security attack where valid data transmitted in any previous session is fraudulently repeated in later session to generate authentic session key is called a replay attack [27, 28]. Adversary $\dot{A}$ eavesdrops any authentication request message, like $M_1 = \{DID_U, D_1, D_3, D_4\}$, and forwards it to gateway in later session. As message M_1 does not contain any fresh timestamp or random nonce generated by the user for that current session, the gateway will validate the message sent by the adversary $\grave{A}$ as fresh and authenticate the adversary $\grave{A}$ as legitimate user on the basis of the previous communicated parameters in that current session. Later, if somehow it can manage to get a random number generated in current session, then it can calculate the session key as well. Hence, Li et al.'s scheme [1] is vulnerable to replay attack.

6.3.6 Privileged Insider Attack

The PKI-based schemes that include trusted third party, for example, gateway or base-stations, usually suffer from insider attack [26, 28]. The insider receives some secret credentials of the communicating user during the conversation that could be used by the vulnerable insider to act as a legitimate user. In Li et al.'s scheme [1] the gateway receives the registration request message $M_1 = \{DID_U, D_1, D_3, D_4\}$. Now, when the insider needs to forward D_1 to the sensor node instead of sending the original D_1, it generates $\bar{a} \in Z_n^*$ and computes $\overline{D_1} = \bar{a}.P$, then follows the rest of steps as explained in section 2.2. After that, insider/adversary $\grave{A}$ calculates $D_5 = h(SN_{id}||\omega)$, generates a random number $\overline{r_G}$ and computes $\overline{D_6} = D_5 \oplus \overline{r_G}$. Then, insider changes D_7 as $\overline{D_7} = h(\overline{D_1}||\overline{r_G}||D_5||SN_{id}')$ and forwards $\{\overline{D_1}, \overline{D_6}, \overline{D_7}\}$ to sensor node. Furthermore, the verifications at sensor node are successful as the data provided to sensor node is through the gateway/insider. Finally, both the sensor and the insider have the same session key as $SK = h(\overline{D_1}||D_8||aD_8)$ or $h(\overline{D_1}||D_8||b\overline{D_1})$. Now, the insider can directly access the data communicated between user and the sensor node. Hence, Li et al.'s scheme [1] is not resilient to privileged insider attack.

6.4 Conclusion

To make a secure key exchange protocol for IIoT, Li et al. designed an improved and robust protocol. Furthermore Li et al. claimed that their protocol is provably secure against all possible cryptographic attacks. After analyzing the protocol in detail, some security attacks, like user impersonation attack, sensor node impersonation attack, session specific temporary information attack, denial of service attack, replay attack and privileged insider attack, were discovered. In this paper, the detailed description of the abovementioned attacks of Li et al.'s scheme [1] is given. In future we will eradicate these aforesaid security vulnerabilities and will propose a more efficient, robust and secure remote user authentication protocol for IIoT.

References

[1] Li, X., Niu, J., Bhuiyan, M. Z. A., Wu, F., Karuppiah, M. and Kumari, S. 2018. A robust ECC-based provable secure authentication protocol with privacy preserving for industrial internet of things. IEEE Transactions on Industrial Informatics, 14(8): 3599–3609.

[2] Ahmed, M. R., Huang, X., Sharma, D. and Cui, H. 2012. Wireless sensor network: characteristics and architectures. World Academy of Science, Engineering and Technology, International Journal of Electrical, Computer, Energetic, Electronic and Communication Engineering, 6(12): 1398–1401.

[3] Li, X., Ibrahim, M. H., Kumari, S., Sangaiah, A. K., Gupta, V. and Choo, K. K. R. 2017. Anonymous mutual authentication and key agreement scheme for wearable sensors in wireless body area networks. Computer Networks, 129: 429–443.

[4] Das, M. L. 2009. Two-factor user authentication in wireless sensor networks. IEEE Transactions on Wireless Communications, 8(3): 1086–1090.

[5] Khan, M. K. and Alghathbar, K. 2010. Cryptanalysis and security improvements of 'two-factor user authentication in wireless sensor networks'. Sensors, 10(3): 2450–2459.

[6] He, D., Gao, Y., Chan, S., Chen, C. and Bu, J. 2010. An enhanced two-factor user authentication scheme in wireless sensor networks. Ad Hoc and Sensor Wireless Networks, 10(4): 361–371.

[7] Lee, C. C., Li, C. T. and Chen, S. D. 2011. Two attacks on a two-factor user authentication in wireless sensor networks. Parallel Processing Letters, 21(01): 21–26.

[8] Yeh, H. L., Chen, T. H., Liu, P. C., Kim, T. H. and Wei, H. W. 2011. A secured authentication protocol for wireless sensor networks using elliptic curves cryptography. Sensors, 11(5): 4767–4779.

[9] Shi, W. and Gong, P. 2013. A new user authentication protocol for wireless sensor networks using elliptic curves cryptography. International Journal of Distributed Sensor Networks, 9(4): 730831.

[10] Choi, Y., Lee, D., Kim, J., Jung, J., Nam, J. and Won, D. 2014. Security enhanced user authentication protocol for wireless sensor networks using elliptic curves cryptography. Sensors, 14(6): 10081–10106.

[11] Nam, J., Kim, M., Paik, J., Lee, Y. and Won, D. 2014. A provably-secure ECC-based authentication scheme for wireless sensor networks. Sensors, 14(11): 21023–21044.

[12] Das, A. K. 2016. A secure and robust temporal credential-based three-factor user authentication scheme for wireless sensor networks. Peer-to-peer Networking and Applications, 9(1): 223–244.

[13] Xue, K., Ma, C., Hong, P. and Ding, R. 2013. A temporal-credential-based mutual authentication and key agreement scheme for wireless sensor networks. Journal of Network and Computer Applications, 36(1): 316–323.

[14] Wu, F., Xu, L., Kumari, S. and Li, X. 2018. An improved and provably secure three-factor user authentication scheme for wireless sensor networks. Peer-to-Peer Networking and Applications, 11(1): 1–20.

[15] Amin, R. and Biswas, G. P. 2016. A secure light weight scheme for user authentication and key agreement in multi-gateway based wireless sensor networks. Ad Hoc Networks, 36: 58–80.

[16] Jiang, Q., Zeadally, S., Ma, J. and He, D. 2017. Lightweight three-factor authentication and key agreement protocol for internet-integrated wireless sensor networks. IEEE Access, 5: 3376–3392.

[17] Amin, R., Islam, S. H., Biswas, G. P., Khan, M. K., Leng, L. and Kumar, N. 2016. Design of an anonymity-preserving three-factor authenticated key exchange protocol for wireless sensor networks. Computer Networks, 101: 42–62.

[18] Gope, P. and Hwang, T. 2016. A realistic lightweight anonymous authentication protocol for securing real-time application data access in wireless sensor networks. IEEE Trans. Industrial Electronics, 63(11): 7124–7132.

[19] Li, X., Niu, J., Bhuiyan, M. Z. A., Wu, F., Karuppiah, M. and Kumari, S. 2018. A robust ECC-based provable secure authentication protocol with privacy preserving for industrial internet of things. IEEE Transactions on Industrial Informatics, 14(8): 3599–3609.

[20] Hossain, M. S. and Muhammad, G. 2016. Cloud-assisted industrial internet of things (IIoT)–enabled framework for health monitoring. Computer Networks, 101: 192–202.

[21] Dodis, Y., Reyzin, L. and Smith, A. 2004. Fuzzy extractors: How to generate strong keys from biometrics and other noisy data. International Conference on the Theory and Applications of Cryptographic Techniques. Springer, Berlin, Heidelberg, 523–540.

[22] Kumari, S., Khan, M. K., Muhaya, F. B. and Kumar, R. 2013. Cryptanalysis of a robust smart-card-based remote user password authentication scheme. 2013 International Symposium on Biometrics and Security Technologies (ISBAST), IEEE, 247–250.

[23] Limbasiya, T. and Karati, A. 2018. Cryptanalysis and improvement of a mutual user authentication scheme for the Internet of Things. 2018 International Conference on Information Networking (ICOIN), IEEE, 168–173.

[24] Wu, F., Xu, L., Kumari, S., Li, X., Shen, J., Choo, K. K. R., Wazid, M. and Das, A. K. 2017. An efficient authentication and key agreement scheme for multi-gateway wireless sensor networks in IoT deployment. Journal of Network and Computer Applications, 89: 72–85.

[25] Sadhukhan, D. and Ray, S. 2018. Cryptanalysis of an elliptic curve cryptography based lightweight authentication scheme for smart grid communication. 2018 4th International Conference on Recent Advances in Information Technology (RAIT), IEEE, 1–6.

[26] Islam, S. H. and Biswas, G. P. 2011. Comments on ID-based client authentication with key agreement protocol on ECC for mobile client-server environment. International Conference on Advances in Computing and Communications Springer, Berlin, Heidelberg, 628–635.

[27] Stallings, W. 2006. Cryptography and Network Security, 4/E. Pearson Education India.

[28] Ray, S., Biswas, G.P. and Dasgupta, M. 2016. Secure multi-purpose mobile-banking using elliptic curve cryptography. Wireless Personal Communications, 90(3): 1331–1354.

7

Cryptanalysis of 2PAKEP

Provably Secure and Efficient Two-Party Authenticated Key Exchange Protocol for Mobile Environment

*Dipanwita Sadhukhan** and *Sangram Ray*

7.1 Introduction

Mobility is a tendency that involves mobile internet connectivity on an anywhere-anytime basis in the heterogeneous wireless network of multiple technologies. Modern information and communication technology (ICT) based on mobile internet devices brings a rapid advancement in the common life of the mobile users by providing various anytime–anywhere services, such as mobile banking, smart healthcare, file transferring, online shopping, e-payment, etc. Mobile commerce has several other utilizations in daily life, like mobile banking, online shopping, e-mailing and much more. To facilitate clients with all these advantages, they have to share their secret information/credentials, i.e., bank details, password, etc., via public channel [1]. Maintaining the security, confidentiality and anonymity of a client's data are the main concern for establishing a secure communication, so that the user can share their data confidently. These features and services expedite the overall development of communication technology [2]. However, the flourishing internet technology has fetched several accompanying challenges

Department of Computer Science and Engineering National Institute of Technology Sikkim Ravangla, Sikkim-737139.
Email: sangram.ism@gmail.com
* Corresponding author: dipanwitasadhukhan2012@gmail.com

to the security of the internet communication and severe issues to the privacy preservation of the user credentials [3]. Due to the openness of the network transmission, any adversary can eavesdrop or simply monitor the channel to obtain sensitive user information or may modify, replay or just delete the sensed data for his own gain. Thus, various attacks like impersonation, replay, man-in-the-middle, stolen verifier, masquerading, bypassing, and insider attacks may occur to the user. In this scenario, two-party authentication and a shared session key negotiation mechanism using public key infrastructure (PKI) has become a crucial solution, providing secure communication between the user and the server over an insecure public channel [4]. The primary objective of two party authentication and key exchange protocol (2PAKE) is to preserve the confidentiality of the communicated messages over the network and preserve the network security.

7.1.1 Literature Review

The fundamental goal of the proposing a 2PAKE protocol is to provide a virtually independent and secure communication among the concerning parties over an insecure channel. In the last decade, several low entropy password-based authenticity protocols have been proposed. Bellovin and Merritt [5] first introduced two party password-based authentication and key exchange protocol. Along with the increment of the number of security threats, communication and computation efficiency have become crucial factors for practical effectiveness of those schemes [6]. A large number of related studies have been published in this field [7–9] of authentication and key exchange using smart card. Yang and Chang [10] developed an identity-based 2PAKE scheme using ECC in 2009. Yet, it was identified by Yoon and Yoo [11] that the scheme did not support perfect forward secrecy and the scheme was unable to resist impersonation attack; a modified version of the scheme that could overcome the identified security breaches was also proposed by them. Later, in 2012, He et al. [12] exhibited that Yoon and Yoo's protocol still lacked perfect forward secrecy and they proposed an enhanced research on identity-based authentication and key exchange. However, Chou et al. [13] detected that there was an imperfection in the private key corroboration process in He et al.'s scheme. Additionally, in 2015, Yang et al. [14] also claimed that He et al.'s scheme was vulnerable to key share attack and impersonation attack. On the basis of the authentication and key exchange scheme proposed by Yang et al. [14], Chen et al. [15] have also proposed another scheme which suffered from offline password guessing attack. Later, in 2017, Qi and Chen [4] proposed two party authentication scheme and key agreement provision for mobile environments by using ECC. However, in 2018, Park et al. [1] claimed that Qi and Chen's protocol cannot resist privileged-insider attack, impersonation attack, and offline password guessing attack. They also demonstrated that the scheme of Qi and Chen [4] was unable to support user anonymity and proficient password change phase. Later, Park et al. [1] proposed a protocol named 2PAKEP: provably secure and efficient two party authentications and key exchange protocol for mobile environment [3]. The scheme [1] introduced a secure mutual authentication that provides perfect forward secrecy, user anonymity and session key protection. The researchers claimed that the scheme is well protected against nearly all acclaimed security flaws. To make the scheme user-friendly, there has a provision for password change.

7.1.2 Motivation and Contribution

It has been detected that researchers claims regarding 2PAKEP [1] are not fully satisfactory in terms of security analysis. In this research, we have demonstrated that Park et al.'s [1] scheme suffers from impersonation attack, privileged insider attack, known session specific temporary information attack, many user logged-in problem and clock synchronization problem. Using some valid practical assumptions, we have proved mathematically that the scheme is simply vulnerable to the aforementioned security threats.

7.1.3 Paper Outline

The rest of the paper is arranged as follows: review of the Park et al.'s scheme is briefly described in section 7.2. Section 7.3 analyzes the security weakness of the scheme of Park et al. and, finally, section 7.4 concludes the paper.

7.2 Review of Park et al.'s [1] Scheme

This section contains the review of Park et al. [1] scheme for mobile commerce environment. The scheme can be elucidated into four phases, namely, (i) System initialization phase, (ii) User registration phase, (iii) Mutual authentication and key exchange phase and (iv) Password change phase. The brief description of each phase is illustrated below and the notations are described in Table 7.1.

7.2.1 System Initialization Phase

Initially, in this phase, server S considers an elliptic curve $E/F_p(a,b)$ with a base point P of order n where n is a large prime number. Then, it computes its public key $Q_S = d_S.P$, where d_S is the long term private key of the server. Finally, the server S selects two collision-free one way hash functions $H_1(.)$ and $H_2(.)$. The parameters $\{E/F_P, P, Q_S, n, H_1()$ and $H_2()\}$ are publically published.

Table 7.1: Notations used in Park et al.'s [1] scheme.

Notation	Description
U	Mobile user
S	The Server
$\breve{A}$	An adversary
ID_u	Identity of user
PW_u	Password of user
d_S	Private key of server
Q_S	Public key of server
SK	Session key
SK_{FA}	Secret key of A
kdf	One way key derivation function
$H_1(), H_2()$	Collision-resistant One way hash function
$\oplus$	Exclusive OR operation
$\|$	Concatenation operation
P	Base point in Elliptic curve
E/F_p	Elliptic curve E over prime field F_p where p is large prime

7.2.2 User Registration Phase

The user U must register to server S to get access to different available services. The detailed description of the registration phase is given in the following steps.

Step 1: Initially, the user U selects its user identity ID_u and password PW_u and generates two random number a_u and b_u. Then, it calculates $RPW = H_2(ID_u\|PW_u)$, $v = RPW \oplus a_u$ and $C = H_2(ID_u\|PW_u\|a_u)$. Finally, user U transmits $\{ID_u,(RPW \oplus b_u)\}$ to server S.

Step 2: After receiving the sent message from the user, it calculates $H_2(ID_u)$ and compares it with the database to verify the freshness of the newly arrived registration request. If ID_u already exists in the database, then the server requests the user to send new identity for a fresh registration.

Step 3: The server S calculates $l = H_1(d_S) \oplus (RPW \oplus b_u) \oplus H_2(d_S\|ID_u)$ and stores $H_2(d_S\|ID_u)$ along with ID_u. Finally, server S sends l to user U.

Step 4: After receiving from the server, the user U calculates $l' = l \oplus b_u = H_1(d_S) \oplus RPW \oplus H_2(d_S\|ID_u)$. Finally, the user U stores l', v and C in the smart card or mobile.

7.2.3 *Mutual Authentication and Key Exchange Phase*

The following steps are given to illustrate this phase.

Step 1: User takes ID_u and PW_u as an input using the smart card or mobile device, then calculates $RPW = H_2(ID_u||PW_u)$, $a_u = v \oplus RPW$ and $C_u' = H_2(ID_u||PW_u||a_u)$. Then, the U compares calculated C_u' with stored C. If the condition satisfies, then the user selects a random number r_u from Z_p^* and computes $R_u = r_u.P$, $R = r_u.Q_S$, $CID_u = l' \oplus RPW = H_1(d_S) \oplus H_2(d_S||ID_u)$. After that, the user computes $Auth_u = H_2(ID_u||R||CID_u||T_u)$, where T_u is the current time stamp generated by the user U. Finally, the user sends $Msg_1 = \{Auth_u, CID_u, R_u, T_u\}$ to the server.

Step 2: Receiving Msg_1 from the user, the server first checks $|T_u^* - T_u| < \Delta T$, where ΔT stands for maximum transmission delay and T_u^* stands for the arrival time of the message. If the condition satisfies, then the server calculates $H_2(d_S||ID_u) = CID_u H_1(d_S)$. Also, the server retrieves the identity of the user ID_u from the database and calculates $R^* = d_S.R_u$ and $Auth_u^* = H_2(ID_u||R^*||CID_u||T_u)$ to compare calculated $Auth_u^*$ with received $Auth_u$. If both are the same, then the server selects a random number $r_S \in Z_p^*$ and computes $R_S = r_S.P$, $Auth_S = H_2(ID_u||R^*||SK_S||T_S)$, where $SK_S = r_S.R_u$ and T_S is the current time stamp generated by the server S. Finally, the server sends $Msg_2 = \{Auth_S, R_S, T_S\}$ to the user.

Step 3: After receiving Msg_2 from server, the client checks $|T_S^* - T_S| < \Delta T$, where ΔT stands for maximum transmission delay and T_S^* stands for the arrival time of the message. If it holds, then the user computes $SK_u = r_u.R_S$, $Auth_S^* = H_2(ID_u||R||SK_u||T_S)$. After that, the user compares calculated $Auth_S^*$ with received $Auth_S$ and, if it satisfies, then the user calculates the session key $SK = kdf(ID_u||SK_u||T_u||T_S)$. The user also the user calculates $Auth_{us} = H_2(R||SK||T_u')$. T_u' is the timestamp generated by user U. Finally, the user sends $Msg_3 = \{Auth_{us}, T_u'\}$ to the server.

Step 4: After receiving Msg_3, the server first validates the timestamp $|T_u'' - T_u'| < \Delta T$, where ΔT stands for maximum transmission delay and T_u'' stands for the arrival time of the message. If this condition is fulfilled successfully, then the server computes $SK' = kdf(ID_u||SK_u||T_u||T_S)$ and $Auth_{us}^* = H_2(R^*||SK'||T_u')$. After that, the server compares computed $Auth_{us}^*$ with received $Auth_{us}$. If it is true, the server stores the session key SK and the session key is generated between the server S and user U.

7.2.4 *Password Change Activity*

User sometimes needs to change the password and, for this operation, involvement of the server is unnecessary. The following steps describe the whole password change activity.

Step 1: Firstly, the server takes ID_u, old PW_u as an input from the mobile device or smart card.

Step 2: After taking the input, the smart card calculates $RPW = H_2(ID_u||PW_u)$, $a_u = v \oplus RPW$ and $C' = H_2(ID_u||PW_u||a_u)$. After that, it compares calculated C' with previously stored C. If both of them are equal, then it asks the user for a new password.

Step 3: User picks a new password PW_{new} and stores it into the device.

Step 4: After getting PW_{new}, the device calculates $RPW_{new} = H_2(ID_u||PW_{new})$, $v_{new} = RPW_{new} \oplus a_u$ and $C_{new} = H_2(ID_u||PW_{new}||a_u)$. The user also calculates $l_{new} = l' \oplus RPW \oplus RPW_{new} = H_1(d_S) \oplus RPW_{new} \oplus H_2(d_S||ID_u)$. Finally, it exchanges l', v, C with l_{new}, v_{new} and C_{new} in the smart card, respectively.

7.3 Cryptanalysis of PARK et al.'s Scheme

As demonstrated in section II, Park et al.'s scheme [1] provides an efficient Two Party Authentication and Key Exchange protocol (2PAKE) for mobile commerce environment that accomplishes a secure mutual authentication and session agreement between user and server using one way lightweight cryptographic hash function and XOR function. Although there exists several identity and password-based mutual authentication and key exchange schemes [16–19] using hash and XOR function, this scheme also incorporates ECC-based point multiplication function for granting better security strength to the session key in compared to RSA-based cryptography. However, in contrast to the claim of the researchers of the paper [1], this scheme encompasses some security breaches that are discussed below.

7.3.1 User Impersonation Attack

Whenever an adversary attempts to impersonate himself as a legitimate user to the server by stealing some of the personal credentials of the user, the adversary successfully executes this attack [18, 20, 21]. Generally, the corresponding server initially verifies the legitimacy of the requesting user for registration from any trusted third party or certificate authority, but Park et al.'s scheme does not provide any initial verification of identity of the user. Suppose that an adversary $\tilde{A}$ pilfers the identity ID_u Dolev-Yao (DY) the art model [21] of a valid user U and then registers himself. Moreover, the identity ID_u is sent to the server S by the user U through a communication channel without encrypting it. This indicates that the user identity is susceptible to the attacker as it is transmitting through a communication channel. Let us assume that there exists a malicious client in between the user and the server who can intercept all the communication messages between the two parities. The attacker just intercepts the communication channel to get the communicated messages during the previous session that contains ID_u, $(RPW \oplus b_u)$ and l. Based on these valid assumptions, it has been shown that Park et al.'s scheme is vulnerable to user impersonation attack. The procedure is demonstrated below.

Step 1: The adversary acquires the knowledge of ID_u, $(RPW \oplus b_u)$ and l. The server calculates l as $l = H_1(d_S) \oplus (RPW \oplus b_u) \oplus H_2(d_S||ID_u)$. As the adversary has the knowledge of $(RPW \oplus b_u)$ he can compute $l \oplus (RPW \oplus b_u)$ $= H_1(d_S) \oplus H_2(d_S||ID_u)$ which is the same CID_u calculated by the user during authentication phase. CID_u is one of the components of the authentication request sent by the user U.

The adversary selects a random number r_a, such that $r_a \in Z_p^*$, and calculates $R_a = r_a.P$ and $R' = r_a.Qs$, where both P and Q_s are publically disclosed.

Next, the adversary generates $Auth_a = H_2(ID_u||R||CID_u||T_a)$, where T_a is the current timestamp recorded by the adversary.

Finally, the adversary transmits an authentication request of Msg_1 composed of $\{Auth_u, CID_u, R_a, T_u\}$ to the server without any knowledge of the legitimate user.

Step 2: After receiving the authentication request, the server validates the timestamp and computes $H_2(d_s||ID_u) = CID_u \oplus H_1(d_s)$. Next, it computes $R^{**} = d_s$ received R_a and $Auth_a^* = H_2(ID_u||R'^*||CID_u||T_a)$ to compare with the received $Auth_a$.

Next, the server generates $r_s \in Z_p^*$ and calculates $R_s = r_s.P$ and $SK_s = r_s.R_a$. Finally, the authentication response is generated as $Msg_2 = \{Auth_s||R_s||T_s\}$, where T_s is the current timestamp and $Auth_s = H_2(ID_u||R^*||SK_s||T_s)$.

Step 3: Upon receiving the response from the server, the adversary easily calculates the final session key as $SK_a = kdf(ID_u||SK_a||T_a||T_s)$. Similarly, the same session key will be calculated by the server as $SK_a = kdf(ID_u||received$ $SK_a||T_a||T_s)$.

By intercepting some valid messages of the legitimate user, the adversary easily achieves mutual authentication and negotiates a valid session key with the server. Therefore, it can be said that Park et al.'s scheme does not endure user impersonation attack.

7.3.2 *Many Logged-In User's Problem*

Consider the circumstances where the smart card/device of the user is lost or the information/credentials stored into the smart card are accidentally revealed to more than one person who all came to know about the credentials (v, l' and C) and the identity ID_u of the user U and may endeavour to login to the server at the same time. In this situation, different login requests may be generated and more than one adversary who knows the credentials can log in to the server at the same time. They just need to select a random number $r_u \in Z_p^*$ and execute some required steps of mutual authentication of Prak et al.'s scheme. Different session keys would now be generated for each adversary. They all will be successfully logged in because they all employ the same authentication procedure using valid credentials. The server will not be able to detect the situation. This attack is displayed by Islam et al. [22] in 2011.

7.3.3 Privileged Insider Attack

Identity-based cryptosystem (IBC) with user identity and password as parameters of the authentication generally suffers from the key escrows problem [21]. These schemes are vulnerable to insider attack as the remote server knows the user identity and other valuable secret information of the user due to the access of the repository [22]. In the registration phase, the user delivers the registration request which contains the real identity of the user U, ID_u to the server. If any privileged insider from the server side gets the identity ID_u of the user U he may attempt to impersonate U in order to access the remote server. The insider can easily re-register himself as the valid user for the next session as described in section 3.1 without facing any problems. Moreover, the insider obtains the knowledge of l, where $l = H_1(d_s) \oplus (RPW \oplus b) H_2(d_s||ID_u)$ as l stays with the server. In this scenario, if the insider deliberately steals the smart card of the user U, he would be able to get l', v and C. Now, the following steps may be executed by the insider to authenticate himself as a valid user.

a. Insider computers $l' \oplus l = b_u$ and retrieves b_u, one of the secret parameters of the user.

b. Insider has the information of the user's $RPW \oplus b_u$. From the previous knowledge of b_u, he calculates $RPW \oplus b_u \oplus b_u = RPW$. Now, he acquires the knowledge of RPW.

c. Next, he computes a_u, other secret information about the user as $v \oplus RPW = a_u$.

d. After gaining the credentials of the user, the insider generates current timestamp T_i and selects a random number $r_i \in Z_p^*$ and calculates $R_i = r_i.P$ and $R = r_i.Q_S$, where P and Q_s are both publically disclosed parameters.

e. Then, he calculates $CID_u = l' \oplus RPW$ and computes the $Auth_u = H_2(ID_u||R||CID_u||T_i)$.

f. Finally, he can successfully transmit a valid authentication request Msg_1 containing $\{Auth_u, CID_u, R_u, T_i\}$.

g. After receiving the Msg_2 = {$Auth_s$, R_s, T_s}, the user computes $SK_u = r_u.R_s$ and $SK = Kdf(ID_u||SK_u||T_i||T_s)$. He also computes $Auth_{us} = H_2(R||SK||T_i')$, where T_i' is the current time stamp.

h. Finally, the server validates the $Auth_{us}$ and agrees with the session key SK between the privileged insider impersonating as the valid user and the server. Now, the insider can obtain all the information communicating between the user U and the server S.

Thus, it can be stated that the scheme suffers from privileged insider attack.

7.3.4 *Known Session Specific Temporary Information Attack*

If some of the session-related temporary information is accidentally unveiled, then the exposure of this sensitive information would not anyhow directly compromise the session key, i.e., the secrecy of the session key is preserved. Cheng et al. [23] and Islam et al. [22] have identified this attack in their researches. In Park et al.'s scheme, session key is calculated as $SK = kdf$ $(ID_u||SK_u||T_u||T_s)$, where the only secret parameter is SK_u, which is calculated as $SK_u = r_u.R_s$ where R_s is publically disclosed. In this scenario, if the secret information r_u is somehow revealed, then an adversary could easily calculate SK_u by carrying out a simple elliptic curve point multiplication operation. The other information of the session key SK that is T_u and T_s are openly transmitted through communication channel. That means by just eavesdropping the communication channel the calculation of session key is possible. So, the hardness of the session key lies on the confidentiality of r_u. According to the definition of the known session specific temporary information attack by Cheng et al. [23], somehow disclosure of any of the contributory part (here r_u) of the session key to any outsider causes the declaration of the session key. From the above discussion, it can be acknowledged that the session key is not very secure. Hence, it can be concluded that the scheme is vulnerable to known session specific temporary information attack.

7.3.5 *Clock Synchronization Problem*

To prevent replay attack and man-in-the-middle-attack, several schemes employ a timestamp mechanism. However, timestamp evokes clock synchronization problem in large networks like the mobile communication network. All the schemes utilizing the concept of timestamp must synchronize their clock with the global clock for proper functionality. In large networks, like mobile network or sensor network, transmission delay due to high traffic is very usual and random. To predict this delay is practically impossible [24]. Hence, it can be predicted that replay attack may exist in Park et al.'s scheme or the scheme may not execute properly.

7.4 Conclusion

To make a secure two party authenticated key exchange protocol, Park et al. designed a 2PAKE protocol [1] with some improvements over the Qi and Chang protocol [4]. Furthermore, Park et al. claimed that their 2PAKE protocol is provably secure against all possible cryptographic attacks. After analyzing the 2PAKE protocol in detail, it is shown that user impersonation attack, many logged in user's problem, privileged insider attack and known session specific temporary information attack and clock synchronization problem exist in the scheme. Moreover, the time stamp is used in Park et al.'s scheme, which may create clock synchronization problem while using the scheme in a large network like mobile commerce environment. In this paper, the detailed description of the abovementioned attacks are given. In the future, we will remove these security vulnerabilities and propose an efficient and secure 2PAKE protocol.

References

[1] Park, K., Park, Y., Park, Y. and Das, A. K. 2018. 2PAKEP: Provably secure and efficient two-party authenticated key exchange protocol for mobile environment. IEEE Access, 6: 30225–30241.

[2] Almuhaideb, A., Le, P. D. and Srinivasan, B. 2011. Two-party mobile authentication protocols for wireless roaming networks. Proc. IEEE NCA'II, pp. 285–288.

[3] Yang, H., Zhang, Y. and Zhou, Y. 2012. A two-party identity-based key agreement protocol with explicit authentication. Wireless Communications, Networking and Mobile Computing (WiCOM), 2012 8th International Conference. IEEE, pp. 1–4.

[4] Qi, M. and Chen, J. 2017. An efficient two-party authentication key exchange protocol for mobile environment. International Journal of Communication Systems, 30(16): p.e3341.

[5] Bellovin, Steven M. and Michael Merritt. 1992. Encrypted key exchange: Password-based protocols secure against dictionary attacks. Research in Security and Privacy, 1992. Proceedings, IEEE Computer Society Symposium on, pp. 72–84.

[6] Saeed, M., Shahhoseini, H. S., Mackvandi, A., Rezaeinezhad, M. R., Naddafiun, M. and Bidoki, M. Z. 2014 August. A secure two-party password-authenticated key exchange protocol. pp. 466–474. *In*: Information Reuse and Integration (IRI), 2014 IEEE 15th International Conference on IEEE.

[7] Boyko, V., MacKenzie, P. and Patel, S. 2000. Provably secure password-authenticated key exchange using Diffie-Hellman. pp. 156–171. *In*: International Conference on the Theory and Applications of Cryptographic Techniques. Springer, Berlin, Heidelberg.

[8] Bresson, E., Chevassut, O. and Pointcheval, D. 2004 March. New security results on encrypted key exchange. pp. 145–158. *In*: International Workshop on Public Key Cryptography. Springer, Berlin, Heidelberg.

[9] Chang, Y. F. 2007. Non-interactive t-out-of-n oblivious transfer based on the RSA cryptosystem. pp. 45–50. *In*: Intelligent Information Hiding and Multimedia Signal Processing, 2007. IIHMSP 2007. Third International Conference. Vol. 2, IEEE.

[10] Yang, J. H. and Chang, C. C. 2009. An ID-based remote mutual authentication with key agreement scheme for mobile devices on elliptic curve cryptosystem. Computers & Security, 28(3-4): 138–143.

[11] Yoon, E. J. and Yoo, K. Y. 2009 August. Robust ID-based remote mutual authentication with key agreement scheme for mobile devices on ECC. pp. 633–640. *In*: Computational Science and Engineering, 2009. CSE'09. International Conference on Vol. 2, IEEE.

[12] Debiao, H., Jianhua, C. and Jin, H. 2012. An ID-based client authentication with key agreement protocol for mobile client–server environment on ECC with provable security. Information Fusion, 13(3): 223–230.

[13] Chou, C. H., Tsai, K. Y. and Lu, C. F. 2013. Two ID-based authenticated schemes with key agreement for mobile environments. The Journal of Supercomputing, 66(2): 973–988.

[14] Yang, H., Chen, J. and Zhang, Y. 2015. An improved two-party authentication key exchange protocol for mobile environment. Wireless Personal Communications, 85(3): 1399–1409.

[15] Chen, B. L., Kuo, W. C. and Wuu, L. C. 2014. Robust smart-card-based remote user password authentication scheme. International Journal of Communication Systems, 27(2): 377–389.

[16] Tan, Z. 2010a. An enhanced three-party authentication key exchange protocol for mobile commerce environments. JCM, 5(5): 436–443.

[17] Tan, Z. 2010b. An improvement on a three-party authentication key exchange protocol using elliptic curve cryptography. Journal of Convergence Information Technology, 5(4): 120.

[18] Islam, S. H., Amin, R., Biswas, G. P., Farash, M. S., Li, X. and Kumari, S. 2017. An improved three party authenticated key exchange protocol using hash function and elliptic curve cryptography for mobile-commerce environments. Journal of King Saud University-Computer and Information Sciences, 29(3): 311–324.

[19] Ray, S., Biswas, G. P. and Dasgupta, M. 2016. Secure multi-purpose mobile-banking using elliptic curve cryptography. Wireless Personal Communications, 90(3): 1331–1354.

[20] Turkanović, M., Brumen, B. and Hölbl, M. 2014. A novel user authentication and key agreement scheme for heterogeneous ad hoc wireless sensor networks, based on the Internet of Things notion. Ad Hoc Networks, 20: 96–112.

8

Self-Stabilizing Attack Graph Model for Intrusion Detection in Cyber Physical Systems

M Sangeetha,* Mathan Kumar M, Rishi Vikram N and
Sakthi Kavin S S

8.1 Introduction

Cyber physical systems (CPSs) are large scale, geographically dispersed, federated, heterogeneous, life-critical systems that comprise sensors, actuators and control and networking components that interact extensively with each other under the monitoring of the computational intelligence [1]. Embedded systems form the basis of all devices that are currently growing. As the dimensions of the devices become smaller, the possibility of combining multiple devices becomes higher, thereby introducing the ability to solve #complex real-time problems [2].

CPS automates the physical systems and synchronizes the tasks to increase the profit of the organization implementing those schemes. However, the vulnerabilities in the CPS paves the way for intrusions to happen. An intrusion may even break down the entire system or sabotage the whole industry. Though modern technologies provide many advantages, it introduces few shortcomings where intrusions can happen.

Department of Computer Science and Engineering, Coimbatore Institute of Technology, Coimbatore, Tamil Nadu, India.
Emails: mathancse.cit@gmail.com; rishi.vikram.1@gmail.com; sakthikavincit@gmail.com
* Corresponding author: citcsesangi@gmail.com
# Complex Real time problems include Medical Instrument failure, Industrial equipment risks, Unauthorized unmanned vehicle control, etc.

Therefore, a mechanism is needed to safeguard the system from the intrusions [3]. Safety critical system is a system wherein a failure may cause loss or severe damage to equipment or property. In such cases, 'risk prevention' and 'safety' becomes important factors. Safety-compromising bugs in safety critical systems are often hard to resolve [4].

The necessity for a security system in CPS, to detect, to classify, and to analyze the attacks and an intrusion in an automated manner is becoming indispensable [5]. This paper ensures the security of the CPS by creating a stochastic model for intrusion detection that dynamically alters the structure of itself thereby making it difficult for an attacker to analyze the system. Also, it detects and classifies the attack and provides the necessary solution for the attack.

8.2 Existing Works

The existing work [6] proposes a model that has a static attack graph [7] which categorizes the attack performed over the CPS. The existing work uses a data mining approach to generate attack graphs. The existing work created an algorithm that performs the associative rule mining [8] on the Intrusion detection system datasets (Figure 8.1). The algorithm derives the predictability score of the attack and generates the ranking results of the score based on the severity of the predictability score.

The ranking results are stored for the purpose of detecting the real-time attack scenarios. The ranking results help in identifying the best match evidence for intrusion prediction. The existing system generates a candidate set for attacks sequentially based on timestamps from the intrusion detection datasets. The candidate sets are pruned based on the minimum support and confidence rate. Finally, the sequential and a static attack graph is generated from the datasets and deployed over the system.

The attack graph model was generated by using the LLDOS 1.0 and LLDOS 2.0 scenarios from the DARPA 2000 datasets with the time window as 4 minutes and a minimum support of 5%. The generated attack graph model

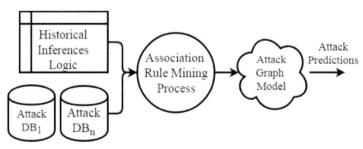

Figure 8.1: Association rule based attack graph model.

gives the predictability score of 0.933 for the detection of DDOS attacks that use fake IP addresses. The existing work [9] uses the RNN [10] for anomaly detection and classification based on the traffic density in the network (Figure 8.2). The model uses the DNS requests that have been captured within time frame. The features used to train the RNN are DNS query, APN, error flag and FQDN.

The training and testing of RNN model is performed by 10-fold cross validation. The comparison between the SVM and RNN is performed and it was found that the RNN provides higher accuracy and lower false alarm rate. The classification performance of RNN is compared with other machine learning algorithms, such as SVM, C4.5 Decision trees, Naïve Bayes and Locally-Weighted-based learning.

The Global Accuracy, Recall and Precision of the above algorithms are compared to measure the performance. For the given 5-minutes time frame, the RNN model gives the higher accuracy among the other three algorithms.

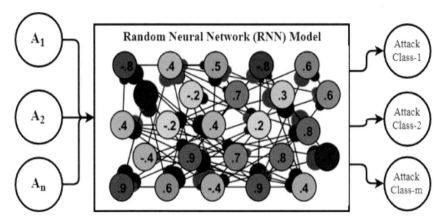

Figure 8.2: RNN-based attack graph model.

Drawbacks of the existing systems

1. The structure of the static attack graph model can be easily predicted by the attacker [9].

2. The static graph model can be generated only when the dataset contains the frequent attack scenarios [6].

3. In the RNN model, some of the anomalies may go undetected.

4. Detecting the anomalies [9] in the real-time traffic using RNN model becomes very difficult.

5. Stabilization of attack graph is not treated with much importance.

6. There is no scheduler-based recovery logic for the post-attack scenarios [6].

8.3 Proposed Work

The proposed system consists of four major stages for the identification and classification of cyber-attacks on a typical host based cyber physical system [11]. The overall stages in the proposed system are depicted in Figure 8.3.

The components of the proposed system are:

1. Neural Network based anomaly detector
2. Attack graph classification model
3. Knowledge repository on attacks
4. Recovery Logic table

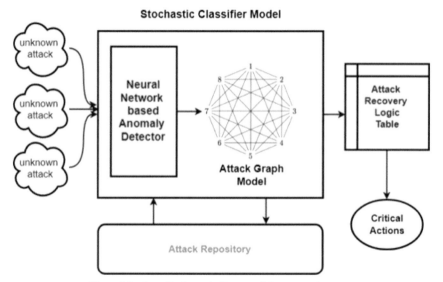

Figure 8.3: Overall schematic diagram of the proposed system.

A. *Neural Network Based Anomaly Detection*

A modified version of the MADALINE [12] neural network model (Figure 8.4) with multiple inputs and multiple outputs (MIMO) [13] is implemented in the anomaly detector module.

Input Layer

The model consists of an input layer [14], a set of hidden layers and an output layer. The input layer consists of 'n' number of neurons which varies from x_{00} to x_{0n}. Each neuron is validated with different types of protocol testing [14] on the incoming packets, such as load testing, stress testing, performance testing

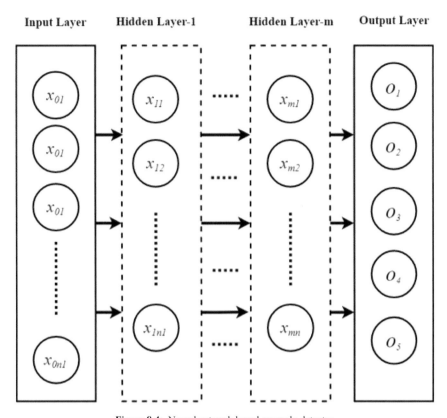

Figure 8.4: Neural network based anomaly detector.

and functional testing. Some sample test cases for the validation of packets, such as

a. operating speed of line
b. protocol conversation rate
c. negative testing
d. performance of telephone switch
e. root path cost variation
f. port blocking
g. distinct root bridge and
h. response time

are validated on the incoming packets.

Hidden Layer

The model consists of 'm' number of hidden layers [14], in which each hidden layer consists of neurons varying from x_{01} to x_{0m+1}.

$$x_{0i} \le x_{1i} \le x_{2i} \cdots\cdots \le x_{mi} \qquad (8.1)$$

The weights are chosen in such a way that the input which has satisfied the validation tests is given the higher value. The output of the input layers is multiplied with the weights summed up with other neurons and given as the input for the hidden layer.

$$y = \sum_{i=0}^{n} w_i x_i \qquad (8.2)$$

where w is the weight
     x is the input

The weight calculation process is pictorially represented in Figure 8.5.

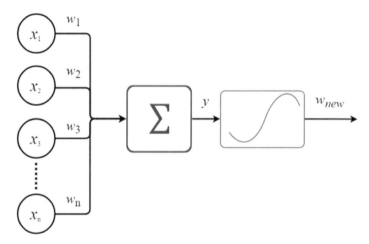

Figure 8.5: Weight calculation metrics.

The hidden layer performs different validation tests and assigns a new weight for the output which is given as input for another hidden layer. The new weight can be computed using the following equation.

$$w_i^{new} = w_i^{old} + \alpha(t - y)x_i$$

where,

w_i^{new}	is the new weight to be calculated
w_i^{old}	is the weight from the input layer
α	is the learning coefficient
t	are the target variables
y	is the intermediate computed value

The sigmoid [15] function is used as the activation function in every hidden layer. The computed y value is mapped with the threshold function which is sigmoid in every hidden layer. The default learning coefficient [15] of the MADALINE neural network is

$$\alpha = 1.7328 \qquad (8.3)$$

The learning coefficient is varied across each of the hidden layers. The variation of the learning coefficient is

$$\alpha = \pm 1\% \ P(attack_i = Pass), \quad 0 \le i \le m \qquad (8.4)$$

Output Layer

The output layer consists of five neurons $(O_1–O_5)$ which represent the following attack classes.

$$attack(x) = \begin{cases} O_1 : very\ critical \\ O_2 : critical \\ O_3 : moderate \\ O_4 : low \\ O_5 : very\ low \end{cases}$$

The output of the hidden layer directs to the classification of attack based upon the severity of the attack.

Working

The incoming packets are given into the input layer. The test cases in the input neurons are validated with the incoming packets [16]. Based on the values of the test cases, the weights are allotted for each input from the higher values to the lower values. The inputs with the allotted weights are summed up and given as input to the hidden layers. The classified values from the input layers are obtained by validating the input with the test cases.

Among 'n' input neurons, if 'a' neurons test cases fail, then (n-a) neurons are the one with attacks. The 'm' number of hidden layers proceeds with different number of validating functions and finally classifies the output in the output layer [17].

B. Attack Graph Classification Strategy

The attack graph has two types of graphs and edges which are represented as shown in Table 8.1.

Decision Nodes (DN)

The decision node in the attack graph co-relates with the attack knowledge repository and ensures that the graph traversal at each node is path consistent.

Table 8.1: Types of nodes used in the attack graph.

Nodes	
Decision Nodes (DN) (Classification decision making node)	
Class Nodes (CN) (Target Attack types)	

The order of precedence of the graph decision nodes is made linear and partially associative [18] so that the graph can be subjected to self-stabilization. The decision node follows a flow-based algorithm *(alg-1)* for classifying the type of attack.

The nodes represent the validating functions which are probabilistically correlated. The testing functions [19] used in the nodes are:

a. Penetrating Testing
b. Incident Response Testing
c. Threat detection Testing
d. Polar Testing
e. Threshold Testing
f. Correlation Test (Chi-Square)

Algorithm 1: Order Preserving Graph Traversal

```
function flowBasedTraversal(G,start,Oₓ):
    attack ← Oₓ
    ptr ← start
    while(type(ptr)≠ 'ClassNode')
        N ← getNeigh(ptr)
        P ← Φ
        for node in N:
    if(NOT marked(node))
            marked(node) ← True
        Result ← test(node)
            P.add(magn(node,result)
        end if;
end for;
Ptr ← max(P).node
    end while;
    return G[ptr]
    endfucntion;
```

The flow-based traversal algorithm [20] takes the start node, attack graph and the identified attack from the neural network-based anomaly identifier system as the inputs. For each iteration, the node which is not already visited is taken to validate the attack under test. The selected decision node is processed and a decision to select the next node is made. For optimal results [21], the ratio of number of decision nodes to number of class nodes is made as **2:1**

$$\Delta result = result - \sum \frac{1}{result(i \rightarrow j)^2} \qquad (8.5)$$

The magnitude computing function ***magn()*** returns maximum value for a class node and the optimal heuristic value (cost taken to reach any of the class nodes based upon the current node) using as in *eqn(v)*. It is certain that all paths end in a sink node and dangling paths are eliminated [22].

Algorithm 2: Magnitude Computation

---

function magn(node,result):
    y ← result* Δresult
    x ← |1 − e^{-y}|
    return (node, x)
end function;

Class Nodes (CN)

The class nodes or label nodes or target nodes are considered as the '**sink nodes**', beyond which the graph traversal is terminated. These nodes signify the final class of attacks identified. No two class nodes can be neighbors [23].

A typical complete attack graph [24] with 5 class nodes and 11 decision nodes is shown in Figure 8.6.

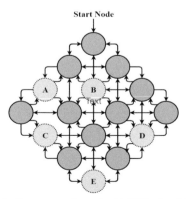

Figure 8.6: Compete attack graph with |CN| = 5 and |DN| = 11.

C. Stabilization of Attack Graphs

After each occurrence of an attack, the graph is converted into one of its isomer forms (Figure 8.7). This is done so as to ensure that the successive attacks can never learn about the behavioral characteristics [25] of the attack graph model. Formally, two graphs and with graph vertices are said to be isomorphic if there is a permutation [26].

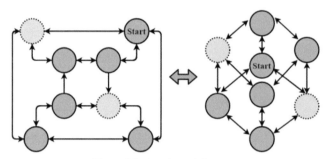

Figure 8.7: Attack graph isomers.

The isomer generation algorithm *(alg-3)* follows a stochastic approach to govern isomorphism in the graph, thereby switching a non-degenerative decision node as the start node.

The *isomer()* function is called at sporadic intervals of time in case the system is idle. The resulting node is updated as the current 'start node' of the attack graph model.

$$start \leftarrow isomer(G) \tag{8.6}$$

It is noted that, the list of all possible isomers (Isomer-Space) is computed every time because the decision and class nodes in the attack graph can be

Algorithm-3: Stochastic Isomerization

---

function isomer(G):
    m ← count(G.nodes())
    IsomerSpace[] ← Φ
    for i in range(0,m!–1):
        x ← permutate(G,i)
        IsomerSpace.add(x)
    end for;
    y ← random(0,m!–1)
    return IsomerSpace[y]
end function;

---

subjected to additions and deletions depending upon the attacks encountered in the learning phase [27].

For attack graph with higher degree of nodes, the computation of entire Isomer-Space is highly time-consuming. Hence, the time resolution strategy for up to $m!/n$ is carried out for computation of Isomer-Space in a nth degree attack graph stabilization process. The brute-force attack takes ***37.4 million years*** to identify the type of attack graph model with 256 nodes [28].

D. Recovery Logic Metrics

It is a look up table-driven solution approach for the classified attack. The approach is shown in Figure 8.8.

The Attacks are notified to a central server where the solution for the attack is mapped from the Attack Recovery Logic Table. The hash map helps identify the solution almost instantaneously [29]. The attack is subjected to n-layered evaluation in order to determine the set of actions to be done. After successful completion of each process, the Attack repository is updated.

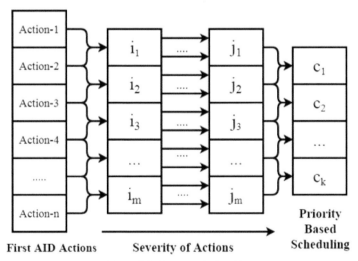

Figure 8.8: Recovery logic table.

Each time an attack is encountered, an entry is created in the attack repository to maintain the type of the attack. The entries are in the form of tuples, as follows:

$$\langle \textit{attack type} \mid \{\textit{action sequence}\} \rangle$$

Based on the severity of the attack, the priority is allocated. If the severity of the attack becomes very high, then some of the layers can be *bypassed*

[30] by increasing the priority of those attacks. The structure of the tuple after priority designation is as follows:

$$\langle attack\ type\ |\ \{action\ sequence\}\ |\ priority\rangle$$

The type of actions to be done (Table 8.2) is based on the priority of the attack. Not all the attacks use all the functions in the defined action sets. Similarly, bypass mechanism skips the unwanted layers and will help achieve faster processing capabilities [31].

Table 8.2: Types of attacks and corresponding actions taken.

S.No.	Attack Class	Priority	Action
1.	Delay attacks	7	Restart timers
2.	Unknown attack	9	Heuristic action
3.	Malicious attack	10	Counterattack
4.	Control attacks	6	Monitor devices
5.	No attacks	0	Default actions

8.4 Comparison Chart

The performance characteristics of the related and proposed works are analyzed [32] and summarized (Figure 8.9). The stabilization of the proposed model is much greater than the existing models (i.e., 87.9%).

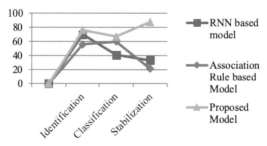

Figure 8.9: Comparison chart for identification and classification of intrusions and stabilization of attack graph models.

8.5 Conclusion

The security systems that only detect an attack will not be as useful as the system which performs necessary actions to evade the attack. Besides detecting the attack, if a system could deal with the attack, it becomes a hybrid system. This paper brings a solution for this issue, thereby proposing a hybrid system that plays an indispensable role in the security of the safety critical cyber physical systems. A hash-map-based recovery logic metric keeps track of every attack and its counter measure. The stochastic graph-based network, because of its dynamic restructuring, increases the complexity and significantly prevents external attacks. Combination of all the above methods deployed creates an integrated system with a whole novel set of capabilities that is capable of encountering the world with broad perspective of facing the problems and bringing out effective measures to solve the underlying challenges in the domain of CPS.

8.6 Future Works

The future works include:

a) Design of an **associative** attack graph model that responds to any combination of attacks

b) Parallelizing classification and detection models for the **honey pot systems** [33]

c) Design of a clock-driven priority-based scheduling algorithm for monitoring the **veracity** and **performance** of attack graphs in a multi-modeled environment [34]

d) Deployment of *bio-inspired **heuristic algorithms*** for identifying various classes of attacks with optimal cost [35]

References

[1] Robert Mitchell and Ing-Ray Chen. 2015. A hierarchical performance model for intrusion detection in cyber-physical systems. Wireless Communications and Networking Conference (WCNC), IEEE, pp. 23–40.

[2] Song Han, Miao Xie, Hsiao-Hwa Chen and Yun Ling. 2016. Intrusion detection in cyber-physical systems: techniques and challenges. IEEE Systems Journal, 8(4): 60–69, Dec. 2016.

[3] Robert Mitchell and Ing-Ray Chen. 2013. Effect of intrusion detection and response on reliability of cyber physical systems. IEEE Transactions on Reliability 62(1): 199–210, March 2013.

[4] TasukuIshigooka, Habib Saissi and Thorsten Piper. 2015. Practical use of formal verification for safety critical cyber-physical systems: a case study. Cyber-Physical Systems, Networks, and Applications (CPSNA), 2015 IEEE International Conference on 25–26 Aug. 2015, pp. 211–220.

[5] Robert Mitchell and Ing-Ray Chen. 2014. A survey of intrusion detection techniques for cyber physical systems. ACM Computing Surveys, 11: 27–56.

[6] Zhi-tang Li, Jie Lei, Li Wang and Dong Li. 2007. A data mining approach to generating network attack graph for intrusion prediction. Fourth International Conference on Fuzzy Systems and Knowledge Discovery (FSKD 2007), 4: 307–311.

[7] Mehdi Yousefi, NhamoMtetwa, Yan Zhang and Huaglory Tianfield. 2017. A novel approach for analysis of attack graph. IEEE International Conference on Intelligence and Security Informatics (ISI), pp. 7–12.

[8] Subrata Bose and Subrata Datta. 2015. Frequent pattern generation in association rule mining using weighted support. Proceedings of the 2015 Third International Conference on Computer, Communication, Control and Information Technology (C3IT), pp. 1–5.

[9] Pedro Casas, Alessandro D'Alconzo, Pierdomenico Fiadino and Christian Callegari. 2016. Detecting and diagnosing anomalies in cellular networks using random neural networks. 2016 International Wireless Communications and Mobile Computing Conference (IWCMC), pp. 351–356.

[10] Erol Gelenbe and Yongha Yin. 2016. Deep learning with random neural networks. Intelligent Systems and Networks Group, Electrical & Electronic Engineering Department, Imperial College, London.

[11] Erol Gelenbe and Yongha Yin. 2016. Deep learning with random neural networks. 2016 International Joint Conference on Neural Networks (IJCNN), pp. 1633–1638.

[12] Todd Vollmer and Milos Manic. 2014. Cyber-physical system security with deceptive virtual hosts for industrial control networks. IEEE Transactions on Industrial Informatics (Volume: 10, Issue: 2, May 2014).

[13] Jonathan Goh, Sridhar Adepu, Marcus Tan and Zi Shan Lee. 2017. Anomaly detection in cyber physical systems using recurrent neural networks. High Assurance Systems Engineering (HASE), 2017 IEEE 18th International Symposium on 12–14 Jan. 2017.

[14] Uttam Adhikari, Thomas H. Morris and Shengyi Pan. 2014. A causal event graph for cyber-power system events using synchrophasor. PES General Meeting | Conference & Exposition, 2014 IEEE (27–31 July 2014).

[15] Sergii Iarovvi, Warl M. Mohammed, Andrei Lobov and Borja Ramis Ferrer. 2016. Cyber-physical systems for open-knowledge driven manufacturing execution systems. Proceedings of the IEEE, Vol. 104, No. 5, May 2016.

[16] Teodora Snaislav, George Mois and Silviu Folea. A cloud-based cyber-physical system for environmental monitoring. Embedded Computing (MECO), 2014 3rd Mediterranean Conference on 15–19 June 2014.

[17] Wenle Zhang. 2010. MADALINE neural network for parameter estimation of LTI MIMO systems. Control Conference (CCC), 2010 29th Chinese 29–31 July 2010.

[18] Elike Hodo, Xavier Bellekens, Andrew Hamilton, Pierre-Louis Dubouilh, Ephraim Iorkyase, Christos Tachtatzis and Robert Atkinson. 2012. Threat analysis of IoT networks using artificial neural network intrusion detection system. Conference on Cloud Computing and Intelligence Systems, 01: 75–81.

[19] Harjinder Singh Lallie, Kurt Debattista and Jay Bal. 2018. An empirical evaluation of the effectiveness of attack graphs and fault trees in cyber-attack perception. IEEE Transactions on Information Forensics and Security, 13(5): 1110–1122.

[20] Sebastian Roschke, Feng Cheng and Christoph Meinel. 2013. High-quality attack graph-based IDS correlation. Logic Journal of the IGPL, 21(4): 571–591.

[21] Jon Matias, Jokin Garay, Alaitz Mendiola, Nerea Toledo and Eduardo Jacob. 2014. FlowNAC: flow-based network access control. 2014 Third European Workshop on Software Defined Networks, pp. 79–84.

[22] Zachary Hill, William M. Nichols, Mauricio Papa, John C. Hale and Peter J. Hawrylak. 2017. Verifying attack graphs through simulation. 2017 Resilience Week (RWS), pp. 64–67.

[23] Marjan Keramati. 2016. An attack graph based procedure for risk estimation of zero-day attacks. 2016 8th International Symposium on Telecommunications (IST), pp. 723–728.

[24] Yogesh Chandra, Pallaw Kumar Mishra and Chaman Prakash Arya. 2016. Attack graphs for defending cyber assets. 2016 3rd International Conference on Computing for Sustainable Global Development (INDIACom), pp. 648–653.

[25] Kirsty E. Lever, Áine MacDermott and Kashif Kifayat. 2015. Evaluating interdependencies and cascading failures using distributed attack graph generation methods for critical infrastructure defence. 2015 International Conference on Developments of E-Systems Engineering (DeSE), pp. 47–52.

[26] Shouling Ji, Prateek Mittal and Raheem Beyah. 2017. Graph data anonymization, de-anonymization attacks, and de-anonymizability quantification: a survey. IEEE Communications Surveys & Tutorials, 19(2): 1305–1326.

[27] Usman A. Zahidi. 2007. Spectral solution for detecting isomorphic graphs with nondegenerate eigenvalues. 2007 IEEE International Multitopic Conference, pp. 1–4.

[28] Muthumanickam, K. and Ilavarasan, E. 2017. Optimizing detection of malware attacks through graph-based approach. 2017 International Conference on Technical Advancements in Computers and Communications (ICTACC), pp. 87–91.

[29] Chensheng Liu, Jing Wu, Chengnian Long and Yebin Wang. 2017. Dynamic state recovery for cyber-physical systems under switching location attacks. IEEE Transactions on Control of Network Systems, 4(1): 344–349.

[30] Meng Yu, Peng Liu and Wanyu Zang. 2003. Multi-version attack recovery for workflow systems. 19th Annual Computer Security Applications Conference, 2003. Proceedings, pp. 142–150.

[31] Dong Yang, Wen-Feng Qi and Tian Tian. 2017. All-subkeys-recovery attacks on a variation of Feistel-2 block ciphers. IET Information Security, 11(5): 230–234.

[32] Pedro Casas, Alessandro D'Alconzo, PierdomenicoFiadino and Christian Callegari. 2016. Detecting and diagnosing anomalies in cellular networks using random neural networks. 2016 International Wireless Communications and Mobile Computing Conference (IWCMC), pp. 351–356.

[33] Chang-Lung Tsai, Chun-Chi Tseng and Chin-Chuan Han. 2009. Intrusive behavior analysis based on honey pot tracking and ant algorithm analysis. 43rd Annual 2009 International Carnahan Conference on Security Technology, pp. 248–252.

[34] Ming Zhang, Shuaibing Lu and Boyi Xu. 2017. An anomaly detection method based on multi-models to detect web attacks. 2017 10th International Symposium on Computational Intelligence and Design (ISCID), 2: 404–409.

[35] Zahra Sadeghi and Asadollah Shah Bahrami. 2013. Improving the speed of the network intrusion detection. The 5th Conference on Information and Knowledge Technology, pp. 88–91.

9

Active Forgery Detection in Grayscale Images using CRC-8-based Fragile Watermarking

Srilekha Paul* and *Arup Kumar Pal*

9.1 Introduction

Digital image forgery (Sencar and Memon, 2014) is an act of tampering or altering the contents of any digital image with illegal intentions. Development of powerful image processing tools and software programs have made tampering of digital images a very common and simple task. Even someone with little knowledge of images could tamper with them very easily without leaving any visible traces. In such scenarios, it becomes very important to detect whether a digital image has undergone any alteration in its contents or not. Digital image forensics (Sencar and Memon, 2014) can aid in detecting such forgeries. Image forensic techniques are basically categorized as active and passive. Active forensic approaches requires pre-processing of the original image by embedding watermarks or generating digital signatures, whereas passive forensic includes blind detection procedures. This chapter proposes a watermarking-based active forensic approach for detecting alterations in digital images.

Forgery detection using digital watermarking (Singh and Chadha, 2013) can be done in either spatial domain or transform domain. Qin et al. (2017) proposed an active forensic approach in spatial domain. This approach used

---
Department of Computer Science and Engineering, Indian Institute of Technology (Indian School of Mines), Dhanbad Jharkhand-826004, India.

Email: arupkrpal@gmail.com

* Corresponding author: srilekhapaul7@gmail.com

an overlapping block-based fragile watermarking process where watermark embedding in each block is performed in two ways. Authentication bits are embedded in certain pixels and reference bits calculated from the mean pixel values of the block are embedded in some other pixels. Watermark embedding in each block is done either in horizontal-vertical mode or in diagonal mode. Overlapping block-based strategies can produce watermarked images of satisfactory quality, but such procedures generally increase the computational costs. Trivedy and Pal (2017) proposed a non-overlapping block-based fragile watermarking technique which performs chaotic sequence generation by logistic map. The chaotic sequence is used in the formation of a key matrix which is further used for watermark embedding in image blocks. Use of such chaos-based key matrices enhances the security aspect of the procedure. Pinjari and Patil (2015) also proposed a fragile watermarking procedure, in which the watermark is generated using local binary patterns. It is a non-overlapping block-based technique, where an image is divided into 3 × 3 blocks. They performed block level watermarking by self-embedding the LBP and the mean of the blocks in the 2 least significant bits of the block pixels. Due to 2-LSB embedding, the fidelity of the watermarked image was found to be good enough. Sreenivas and Kamakshiprasad (2017) proposed a tamper detection scheme which uses the properties of Arnold Cat Map for watermark generation. It is a block-level watermarking approach which embeds watermark bits in the 3 least significant bits of the block pixels. The watermark generated by this process also contains certain recovery bits which facilitate the recovery of the tampered image at a later stage.

Transform domain-based approaches generally use various transformations, like DCT, DWT, binomial transformation, etc., for projecting the image content from spatial domain to transform domain. Azeroual and Afdel (2017) proposed a Faber-Schauder discrete wavelet transform-based fragile watermarking scheme for tamper detection and localisation. In this procedure, a watermark is generated using paramount FSDWT coefficients along with a logo. The generated watermark is embedded in the least significant bits of certain pixels in the image. Their method exhibits quite fast processing. Ghosal and Mandal (2014) performed image authentication in transform domain by using block-level binomial transformation in watermark embedding process. Further inverse-binomial transformation is used after watermark embedding to convert the watermarked blocks back to spatial domain. Qi and Xin (2015) proposed another tamper detection procedure using semi-fragile watermarking. They generated one image-dependent watermark using singular value decomposition and another image-independent watermark using Mersenne Twister algorithm. Both the watermarks are XORed to generate a new secure watermark which is embedded in the wavelet domain of randomly chosen 4 × 4 blocks. Tamper detection is done by comparing the extracted and the regenerated watermarks. Zhang et al. (2018) proposed a watermarking procedure which is capable of detecting geometric attacks efficiently. Watermark embedding is done in the composite domain of DWT and DCT. Geometric modifications are detected by comparing certain key points from the watermarked image with the feature points extracted from the tampered image using SURF (Speeded-Up Robust Features) (Bay et al., 2008). SURF exhibits better scale-invariance as compared to other similar transforms, so it helps to detect the geometric transformations easily.

Based on the above discussions, an efficient watermarking-based forgery detection procedure should have the following objectives:

- Embedded watermark should not be noticeable to the viewer.
- Watermark should not affect the quality of the original image content.
- Performing fast and accurate forgery detection.
- Obtaining low false positive rates in localisation of the forgery.

The general model of any watermarking-based forgery detection procedure is illustrated in Figure 9.1.

In the literature, we can find various fragile watermarking approaches that use error-detection codes. One such approach was proposed by (Golea, 2012); it performs pixel-level fragile watermarking using cyclic redundancy check code and RSA. In this approach, watermarked pixels were generated by calculating CRC-based checksum on 6 most significant bits from each color channels of the original pixels and eventually embedding the checksum in their remaining least significant bits. This procedure used RSA for the encryption and decryption of the generator polynomial used in the CRC encoding and decoding procedures. Another error-detection code-based image authentication procedure was proposed by (Abadi et al., 2010). In this approach, a hamming code-based block-level fragile watermarking scheme which detects tampering in medical images by utilising the error detection properties of hamming code was proposed. Error detection code-based approaches are sensitive to minute alterations in digital images, so they can be used efficiently for the purpose of forgery detection.

This chapter also proposes an error-detection code-based active forgery detection mechanism which is realised using a block-level fragile

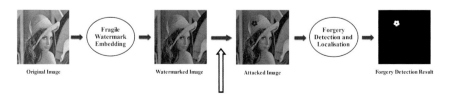

ATTACKS

Figure 9.1: Model of fragile watermarking based forgery detection process.

watermarking scheme based on CRC-8 and logistic maps. In this procedure, the image is initially divided into 2×2 non-overlapping blocks. All the pixels of a particular block are further divided into two components—significant and insignificant. CRC code is generated from the significant component of each block. The generated CRC is encrypted using a logistic map-based key sequence. The encrypted CRC code is then embedded as watermark in the insignificant component of the block. In the forgery detection phase, the embedded watermark is extracted from the received image and is decrypted to generate the syndrome values. Tamper detection results depend on the syndrome values of each block of the received image.

The upcoming portions of this chapter are organised as follows. Section 9.2 describes the pre-requisite topics of the work proposed here, including the concepts of cyclic redundancy check and logistic maps in brief. Proposed active forgery detection scheme is described in section 9.3. The experimental results are illustrated and analysed in section 9.4. Finally, the active forensic approach proposed in this chapter is concluded in section 9.5.

9.2 Preliminaries

The work proposed in this chapter needs a brief understanding of cyclic redundancy check code and logistic maps. CRC code is the basis of our watermark generation scheme, while logistic maps are used in the key generation process. These topics are described in the following subsections.

9.2.1 Cyclic Redundancy Check

Cyclic redundancy check (Baicheva and Sallam, 2007) is an efficient systematic code for error detection. CRC code is a sequence of control bits or check bits added to the data in order to detect whether any error occurred during storage or transmission. CRC is computed as the remainder of polynomial division of a data polynomial by a generator polynomial. In coding theory, CRC codewords are represented in (n, k) form where n-bit codewords are generated from k-bit data by appending $(n - k)$ parity bits. Given a k-bit message M with polynomial representation $m(x) = m_{k-1}x^{k-1} + ... + m_1x^1 + m_0$, the $(n - k)$ CRC bits can be calculated as the binary representation of the remainder polynomial $r(x) = r_{n-k-1}x^{n-k-1} + ... + r_1x^1 + r_0$, where $r(x)$ satisfies equation 9.1 with $g(x) = g_{n-k}x^{n-k} + ... + g_1x^1 + g_0$ as the generator polynomial of degree $(n - k)$.

$$r(x) = R_{g(x)}x^{n-k}m(x) \qquad (9.1)$$

Generally, the k-bit data and $(n - k)$ bit CRC are appended to form n-bit codeword as $c(x) = x^{n-k}m(x) + r(x)$. In this proposed work, we are using CRC-8 with $g(x) = x^8 + x^7 + x^6 + x^4 + x^2 + 1$ as the generator polynomial.

9.2.2 Logistic Map

Logistic map (Patidar et al., 2009) is a popular dynamic system which can be efficiently used to generate pseudo-random sequence of numbers lying between 0 and 1. Given s_0 as the initial value, the behaviour of a logistic map follows the recursive function shown in equation 9.2, where $(0 \le s_i \le 1)$ and $\alpha \in [0,4]$.

$$s_i = \begin{cases} \alpha s_0 (1 - s_0), & if \ \ i = 1 \\ \alpha s_{i-1}(1 - s_{i-1}), & otherwise \end{cases} \tag{9.2}$$

We are using logistic map to generate a pseudo-random key sequence from a given seed value $K_s = \{\alpha, s_0\}$ which is a secret key shared between both sender and receiver. Same seed value always produces same key sequence.

9.3 Proposed Work

The method proposed in this research work detects forgeries in digital grayscale images using an active forensic approach. This approach comprises mainly of two sub phases—(a) Fragile watermark embedding (b) Tamper detection and localisation. In the first phase, a watermark is embedded in the original image in order to generate a watermarked image. The second phase checks whether the watermarked image has undergone any form of forgery during transmission or storage. If any form of manipulation is detected, the procedure further localises or identifies the manipulated regions in the image. Section 9.3.1 to 9.3.6 discusses the algorithmic details of the work proposed here.

9.3.1 Fragile Watermark Embedding

The essence of the various steps involved in this proposed fragile watermarking algorithm is explained in this section. Figure 9.2 shows the overview of the entire watermark embedding algorithm.

Inputs: I: Grayscale image of size $M \times N$
             $K_s = \{\alpha, s_0\}$: Seed for generating key sequence
Output: I_W: Watermarked image

Algorithmic Steps:

Step 1: Divide I into non-overlapping blocks of size 2×2 and generate $\dfrac{MN}{4}$ blocks.

Step 2: Generate a logistic sequence $S = \left\{ s_1, s_2, \ldots s_{\frac{MN}{4}} \right\}$ with key K_s as the seed using equation 9.2 and convert it into a pseudo-random key sequence $K = \left\{ K_1, K_2, \ldots K_{\frac{MN}{4}} \right\}$ where:

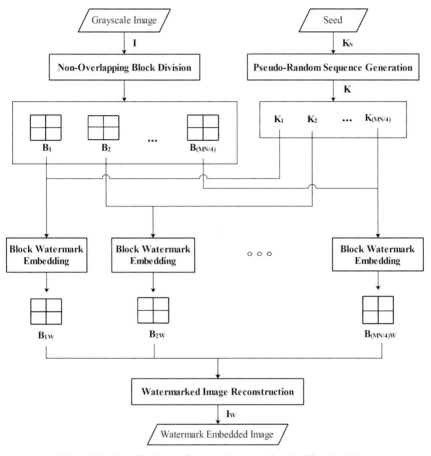

Figure 9.2: Overall scheme of proposed watermark embedding algorithm.

$$K_i = Round\,(s_i \times 255), \quad \left(1 \le i \le \frac{MN}{4}\right).$$

Step 3: Apply *Block Watermark Embedding* algorithm (9.3.2) to each block B_i with its corresponding key K_i to generate 8-bit watermark and embed it in block B_i to obtain watermarked block B_{iW} where $\left(1 \le i \le \frac{MN}{4}\right)$.

Step 4: Combine all the watermarked blocks B_{iW} to reconstruct the final watermarked image I_W and generate it as output.

9.3.2 Block Watermark Embedding

This module takes a block of original image as input, embeds an 8-bit watermark in it and generates the watermarked block as output. The schematic diagram of the entire block watermarking algorithm is shown in Figure 9.3. Figure 9.4 illustrates the block watermark embedding procedure using an example.

Inputs: B_i: Block of size 2×2
                    K_i: 8-bit key for block B_i
Output: B_{iW}: : Watermarked block of size 2×2

Algorithmic Steps:

Step 1: Extract 6 most significant bits from each pixel of block B_i and form a 24-bit data sequence D.

Step 2: Calculate 8-bit cyclic redundancy check value as $CRC_8 = Gen\_CRC(D)$.

Step 3: Encrypt CRC_8 by XORing it with the key value K_i and generate 8-bit encrypted cyclic redundancy check value as $CRC_E = CRC_8 \oplus K_i$.

Step 4: Fragment 8-bit CRC_E into four 2-bit values a, b, c and d.

Step 5: Replace 2 least significant bits from each of the four pixels of the block B_i in raster scan order, by a, b, c and d, respectively, and generate the watermarked block B_{iW} as output.

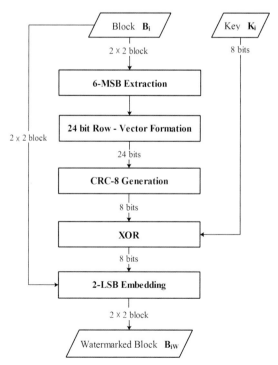

Figure 9.3: Schematic diagram of block watermark embedding algorithm.

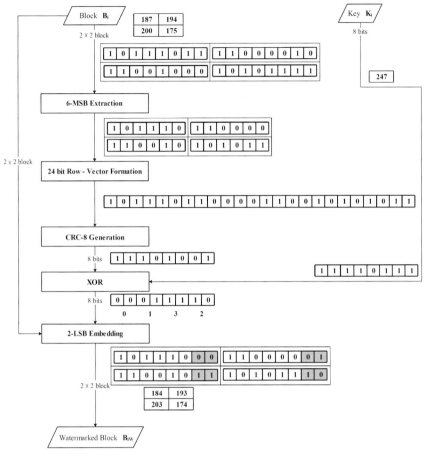

Figure 9.4: An illustrative example of the block watermark embedding procedure.

9.3.3 Generating 8-bit CRC

The function *Gen_CRC()* is designed to compute 8-bit CRC for the input data.

Inputs: D: 24-bit data
Output: CRC_8: 8-bit cyclic redundancy check code

Algorithmic Steps:

Step 1: Form the data polynomial $d(x)$ from the 24-bit input data D.

Step 2: Calculate $m(x) = x^8 d(x)$.

Step 3: Divide $m(x)$ by the generator polynomial $g(x) = x^8 + x^7 + x^6 + x^4 + x^2 + 1$ to get the remainder polynomial as $r(x) = R_{g(x)} m(x)$.

Step 4: Generate 8-bit binary representation of $r(x)$ as CRC_8.

9.3.4 Tamper Detection and Localisation

The tamper detection and localisation algorithm is responsible for analysing the received image which was earlier known to have been watermarked. It detects whether the watermarked image had undergone any form of forgery. If the received image is forged, then this algorithm also locates the forged regions. The schematic diagram of the overall tamper detection and localisation algorithm is shown in Figure 9.5.

Inputs: R: Tampered watermarked image (Grayscale) of size $M \times N$
$K_s = \{a, s_0\}$: Seed for generating key sequence
Output: I_{MAP}: Binary map image showing detected forged regions

Algorithmic Steps:

Step 1: Divide R into non-overlapping blocks of size 2×2 and generate $\dfrac{MN}{4}$ blocks.

Step 2: Generate a logistic sequence $S = \left\{ s_1, s_2, \dots s_{\frac{MN}{4}} \right\}$ with key K_s as the seed using equation 9.2 and convert it into a pseudo-random key sequence $K = \left\{ K_1, K_2, \dots K_{\frac{MN}{4}} \right\}$ where:

$$K_i = Round \, (s_i \times 255), \quad \left(1 \leq i \leq \frac{MN}{4} \right)$$

Step 3: Apply *Block Forgery Check* algorithm (9.3.5) to each block B_i with its corresponding key K_i to extract 8-bit watermark from B_i and return a binary value T_i for $\left(1 \leq i \leq \dfrac{MN}{4} \right)$ such that:

$$T_i = \begin{cases} 0, & \textit{if } B_i \textit{ is not a tampered block} \\ 1, & \textit{if } B_i \textit{ is a tampered block} \end{cases}$$

Step 4: Generate the binary map image I_{MAP} by marking the pixels corresponding to *ith* block of I_{MAP} with:

$$Color = \begin{cases} WHITE, & \textit{if } T_i = 1 \\ BLACK, & \textit{otherwise} \end{cases}$$

Step 5: Produce I_{MAP} as the output binary map image where the detected tampered blocks are marked in white. Generate the final map image by marking the white pixels of I_{MAP} as black on the original image.

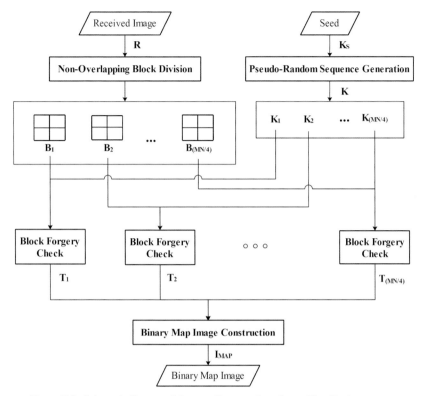

Figure 9.5: Schematic diagram of the overall tamper detection and localisation process.

9.3.5 Block Forgery Check

This module takes a block of received watermarked image as input, extracts the 8-bit CRC-based watermark from it and checks whether the block has undergone any form of tampering or not. This module calculates the CRC-8 syndrome from the data of the block. If the syndrome is non-zero, then it classifies the block as tampered. Otherwise the block is considered to be a pure block. The schematic diagram of the entire block forgery check procedure is shown in Figure 9.6. Figure 9.7 explains the concept of block forgery check module using an illustrative example.

Inputs: B_i: Block of size 2×2
             K_i: 8-bit key for block B_i
Output: T_i: Binary value

Algorithmic Steps:

Step 1: Extract 6 most significant bits from each pixel of block B_i and form a 24-bit data sequence D.

Step 2: Perform watermark extraction by extracting the 2 least significant bits from each pixel of block B_i and form a 8-bit sequence W.

Step 3: Compute the received CRC value as $CRC_R = W \oplus K_i$.

Step 4: Calculate syndrome as $SYN = Gen\_Syndrome(D, CRC_R)$.

Step 5: Generate the binary value T_i as:

$$T_i = \begin{cases} 0, & if\ SYN = 0 \\ 1, & otherwise \end{cases}$$

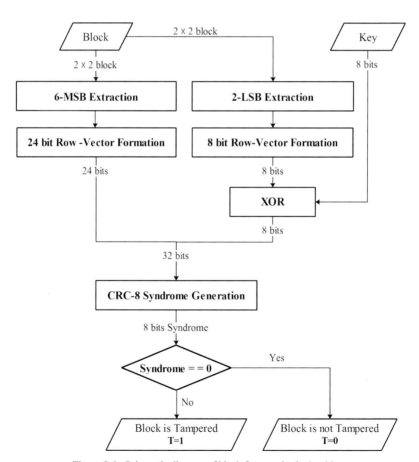

Figure 9.6: Schematic diagram of block forgery check algorithm.

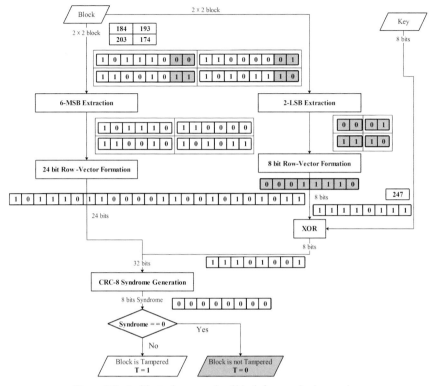

Figure 9.7: An illustrative example of block forgery check procedure.

9.3.6 Generating 8-bit Syndrome

The function *Gen_Syndrome*() is designed to compute the CRC-8 syndrome of the received data.

Inputs: *D*: 24-bit data
              CRC_R: 8-bit received CRC
Output: *SYN*: 8-bit CRC syndrome

Algorithmic Steps:

Step 1: Generate *m(x)* as the polynomial representation of 32-bit sequence *M* generated by appending *D* and CRC_R.

Step 2: Divide *m(x)* by the generator polynomial $g(x) = x^8 + x^7 + x^6 + x^4 + x^2 + 1$ to get the remainder polynomial as $r(x) = R_{g(x)}m(x)$.

Step 3: Generate 8-bit binary representation of *r(x)* as the syndrome *SYN*.

9.4 Experimental Results and Discussions

The fragile watermark embedding and forgery detection algorithms proposed in this chapter were tested on a large number of grayscale images. As representatives, Figure 9.9, Figure 9.10, Figure 9.11 and Figure 9.12 exhibit the results on test images 'Lena', 'Airplane', 'Goldhill' and 'Girl' of size, respectively, which are shown in Figure 9.8.

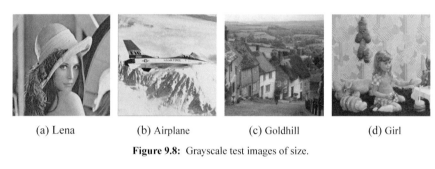

(a) Lena   (b) Airplane   (c) Goldhill   (d) Girl

Figure 9.8: Grayscale test images of size.

(a) Watermarked Image   (b) Forged Watermarked Image   (c) Binary Map Image   (d) Final Map Image

Figure 9.9: Results on test image 'Lena' of size.

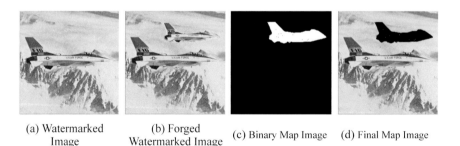

(a) Watermarked Image   (b) Forged Watermarked Image   (c) Binary Map Image   (d) Final Map Image

Figure 9.10: Results on test image 'Airplane' of size.

| (a) Watermarked Image | (b) Forged Watermarked Image | (c) Binary Map Image | (d) Final Map Image |

Figure 9.11: Results on test image 'Goldhill' of size 512 × 512.

| (a) Watermarked Image | (b) Forged Watermarked Image | (c) Binary Map Image | (d) Final Map Image |

Figure 9.12: Results on test image 'Girl' of size 512 × 512.

9.4.1 Performance Evaluation of Watermark Embedding Procedure

The performance of the watermark embedding procedure is analysed using parameters like PSNR (Peak Signal to Noise Ratio) (Tanchenko, 2014; Al-Najjar and Soong, 2012), SSIM (Structural Similarity Index) (Wang et al., 2004; Al-Najjar and Soong, 2012) and Entropy Measure. Table 9.1 shows the PSNR and SSIM values of the watermarked images with reference to the corresponding original images obtained by the proposed algorithm. Table 9.2 depicts a comparative study of proposed watermark embedding algorithm with the watermarking methods proposed by (Zhang et al., 2018; Pinjari and Patil, 2015) and (Qi and Xin, 2015) in terms of PSNR values of watermarked images for 'Lena', 'Airplane' and 'Peppers' test images. The watermarking procedure proposed by (Zhang et al., 2018) is analysed in two cases— (a) Embedding watermark of 480 bits (b) Embedding watermark of 128 bits. Comparative analysis shows that the proposed watermark embedding method produces better quality of watermarked images in terms of PSNR as compared to all the other methods in Table 9.2.

Randomness associated with the intensity values and texture of an image can be calculated using entropy measure. Entropy (Gray, 2011) of an image with K gray levels can be calculated using equation 9.3, where p_i is the probability associated with *ith* gray level.

$$Entropy = \sum_{i=0}^{K} p_i \log\left(\frac{1}{p_i}\right) \tag{9.3}$$

Entropy difference is the difference between the entropy of a processed image and original image. It is computed using equation 9.4, where $Entropy_w$ and $Entropy_o$ are the entropies of a watermarked image and its original image, respectively, while $Difference_{entropy}$ signifies the entropy difference between them.

$$Difference_{entropy} = Entropy_w - Entropy_o \tag{9.4}$$

Table 9.3 shows the entropies of the original and watermarked images along with their corresponding entropy differences for a set of standard test images. The lower the entropy difference, the higher the similarity. Analysis results depict that the watermarking method proposed here achieves significantly low entropy difference values, which implies that the watermarked images are more closer to the original images in terms of randomness increase.

Table 9.1: Analysis of PSNR and SSIM of the watermarked images.

Test Image 512 × 512	PSNR (Watermarked Image)	SSIM (Watermarked Image)
Lena	44.1627	0.9776
Airplane	44.1705	0.9790
Goldhill	44.1564	0.9866
Baboon	44.1452	0.9937
Boat	44.1233	0.9817
Peppers	44.1438	0.9814
Girl	44.1536	0.9834
Average	**44.1508**	**0.9833**

Table 9.2: Comparative analysis of PSNR of watermarked images.

Test Image 512 × 512	Proposed Method	(Zhang et al., 2018) (a) 480 bits	(Zhang et al., 2018) (b) 128 bits	(Pinjari and Patil, 2015)	(Qi and Xin, 2015)
Lena	44.1627	41.196	43.687	43.5476	41.76
Airplane	44.1705	41.157	43.781	43.5970	41.04
Peppers	44.1438	41.281	43.496	43.5313	41.24

9.4.2 *Performance Evaluation of the Forgery Detection Procedure*

The final outcome of this forgery detection scheme is formally a classification of the image blocks as tampered and pure which is further responsible for the localisation of the tampered regions when mapped on a map image.

Table 9.3: Analysis of differences in entropies of watermarked images with respect to original images.

Test Image 512 × 512	Entropy (Original Image)	Entropy (Watermarked Image)	Entropy Difference $Entropy_w - Entropy_o$
Lena	7.0880	7.0930	0.0050
Airplane	6.7025	6.7109	0.0084
Goldhill	7.4778	7.4806	0.0028
Baboon	7.3585	7.3596	0.0011
Boat	7.1238	7.1390	0.0152
Peppers	7.5715	7.5833	0.0118
Girl	7.1905	7.1970	0.0065

The performance of such classifications can be effectively evaluated using measures like false positive rate (Berrar, 2019) and accuracy (Berrar, 2019).

i) *False Positive Rate* (*FPR*): It represents the rate at which pure blocks of an image are detected as tampered.

$$FPR = \frac{FP}{FP + TN} \qquad (9.5)$$

ii) *Tamper Detection Accuracy*: It represents the extent to which the proposed method does correct detection.

$$Accuracy = \frac{TN + TP}{FP + FN + TN + TP} \qquad (9.6)$$

In equation 9.5 and equation 9.6, *FP*, *FN*, *TP* and *TN* are the number of false positives, false negatives, true positives and true negatives, respectively. Here, false positives are those image blocks that are detected as tampered but are actually pure. False negatives are those blocks of image that are actually tampered but classified as pure. True positives and true negatives are the correctly classified tampered and pure blocks, respectively. The values for both *FPR* and *Accuracy* range from 0 to 1. Low *FPR* (close to 0) indicates that the algorithm can efficiently differentiate between tampered and pure blocks of an image. High *Accuracy* values (close to 1) imply precise and accurate forgery detection results. Table 9.4 shows the performance of proposed forgery detection scheme by tabulating the tamper detection accuracy and false positive rates achieved on some standard grayscale images of size 512 × 512.

Experimental analysis shows that the forgery detection scheme proposed in this chapter, works with very high average accuracy of 0.9985 and very low average false positive rate of 0.0014. This signifies that this method is highly efficient in terms of accurate detection and localization of tampered blocks.

Table 9.4: Performance analysis of proposed algorithm in terms of tamper detection accuracy and false positive rate.

Test Image 512 × 512	Tamper Detection Accuracy	False Positive Rate
Lena	0.9991	0.0008
Airplane	0.9981	0.0019
Goldhill	0.9989	0.0010
Baboon	0.9976	0.0023
Boat	0.9992	0.0007
Peppers	0.9988	0.0011
Girl	0.9980	0.0018
Average	**0.9985**	**0.0014**

9.5 Conclusion

The active forensic scheme proposed in this chapter performs fragile watermark embedding and forgery detection very efficiently. It uses CRC-based error detection mechanism as well as encryption with logistic map-based secret key sequence, which makes the scheme more secure. In the proposed scheme, watermark is inserted block-wise, so the watermark payload is drastically reduced. Considerably high PSNR and SSIM values shows that the watermarked image retains the perceptual quality of the original image to the required extent. Watermarked images with very low entropy difference indicates that the amount of randomness added to the original image is extremely low. The proposed tamper detection scheme has achieved very high accuracy and considerably low false positive rates, which signifies that it is highly efficient in terms of accurate detection and localization of tampered blocks.

References

Abadi, M. A. M., Danyali, H. and Dehnavi, M. N. 2010. Medical image authentication based on fragile watermarking using hamming code. s.l., s.n., pp. 1–4.
Al-Najjar, Y. A. Y. and Soong, D. C. 2012. Comparison of image quality assessment: PSNR, HVS, SSIM, UIQI. Int. J. Sci. Eng. Res., 3: 1–5.
Azeroual, A. and Afdel, K. 2017. Real-time image tamper localization based on fragile watermarking and Faber-Schauder wavelet. AEU-International Journal of Electronics and Communications, 79: 207–218.
Baicheva, T. and Sallam, F. 2007. CRC codes for error control. Mathematica Balkanica, 21: 377–387.
Bashar, M., Noda, K., Ohnishi, N. and Mori, K. 2010. Exploring duplicated regions in natural images. IEEE Transactions on Image Processing.
Bay, H., Ess, A., Tuytelaars, T. and Van Gool, L. 2008. Speeded-up robust features (SURF). Computer Vision and Image Understanding, 110: 346–359.
Berrar, D. 2019. Performance measures for binary classification.

Bovik, A. C. 2010. Handbook of Image and Video Processing. s.l.:Elsevier Science.

Cao, Y., Gao, T., Fan, L. and Yang, Q. 2012. A robust detection algorithm for copy-move forgery in digital images. Forensic Science International, 214: 33–43.

Christlein, V. et al. 2012. An evaluation of popular copy-move forgery detection approaches. IEEE Transactions on Information Forensics and Security, 7: 1841–1854.

Cozzolino, D., Poggi, G. and Verdoliva, L. 2015. Efficient dense-field copy—move forgery detection. IEEE Transactions on Information Forensics and Security, 10: 2284–2297.

Florindo, J. B., Casanova, D. and Bruno, O. M. 2018. A Gaussian pyramid approach to Bouligand-Minkowski fractal descriptors. Information Sciences, 459: 36–52.

Fridrich, A. J., Soukal, B. D. and Lukáš, A. J. 2003. Detection of copy-move forgery in digital images. s.l., s.n.

Ghosal, S. K. and Mandal, J. K. 2014. Binomial transform based fragile watermarking for image authentication. Journal of Information Security and Applications, 19: 272–281.

Golea, N. E. -H. 2012. A fragile watermarking scheme based CRC checksum and public key cryptosystem for RGB color image authentication. s.l., s.n., pp. 316–325.

Gonzalez, R. C. and Woods, R. E. 2017. Digital Image Processing, Global Edition. s.l.:Pearson.

Gray, R. M. 2011. Entropy and Information Theory. s.l.:Springer Science & Business Media.

Hayat, K. and Qazi, T. 2017. Forgery detection in digital images via discrete wavelet and discrete cosine transforms. Computers & Electrical Engineering, 62: 448–458.

Huang, Y., Lu, W., Sun, W. and Long, D. 2011. Improved DCT-based detection of copy-move forgery in images. Forensic Science International, 206: 178–184.

Lin, X. et al. 2018. Recent advances in passive digital image security forensics: A brief review. Engineering, 4: 29–39.

Mahmood, T., Mehmood, Z., Shah, M. and Saba, T. 2018. A robust technique for copy-move forgery detection and localization in digital images via stationary wavelet and discrete cosine transform. Journal of Visual Communication and Image Representation, 53: 202–214.

Meena, K. B. and Tyagi, V. 2019. Image forgery detection: survey and future directions. pp. 163–194. *In*: Data, Engineering and Applications. s.l.:Springer.

Parveen, A., Khan, Z. H. and Ahmad, S. N. 2019. Block-based copy-move image forgery detection using DCT. Iran Journal of Computer Science, pp. 1–11.

Patidar, V., Sud, K. K. and Pareek, N. K. 2009. A pseudo random bit generator based on chaotic logistic map and its statistical testing. Informatica, Volume 33.

Pinjari, S. A. and Patil, N. N. 2015. A modified approach of fragile watermarking using Local Binary Pattern (LBP). s.l., s.n., pp. 1–4.

Qin, C. et al. 2017. Fragile image watermarking with pixel-wise recovery based on overlapping embedding strategy. Signal Processing, 138: 280–293.

Qi, X. and Xin, X. 2015. A singular-value-based semi-fragile watermarking scheme for image content authentication with tamper localization. Journal of Visual Communication and Image Representation, 30: 312–327.

Rao, K. R. and Yip, P. 2014. Discrete Cosine Transform: Algorithms, Advantages, Applications. s.l.:Academic press.

Schetinger, V., Iuliani, M., Piva, A. and Oliveira, M. M. 2017. Image forgery detection confronts image composition. Computers & Graphics, 68: 152–163.

Sencar, H. T. and Memon, N. 2014. Digital Image Forensics: There is More to a Picture than Meets the Eye. s.l.:Springer Publishing Company, Incorporated.

Singh, P. and Chadha, R. S. 2013. A Survey of Digital Watermarking Techniques, Applications and Attacks. s.l., s.n.

Soni, B., Das, P. K. and Thounaojam, D. M. 2017. CMFD: a detailed review of block based and key feature based techniques in image copy-move forgery detection. IET Image Processing, 12: 167–178.

Sreenivas, K. and Kamakshiprasad, V. 2017. Improved image tamper localisation using chaotic maps and self-recovery. Journal of Visual Communication and Image Representation, 49: 164–176.

Sunil, K., Jagan, D. and Shaktidev, M. 2014. DCT-PCA based method for copy-move forgery detection. s.l., s.n., pp. 577–583.

Tanchenko, A. 2014. Visual-PSNR measure of image quality. Journal of Visual Communication and Image Representation, 25: 874–878.

Tharwat, A. 2018. Classification assessment methods. Applied Computing and Informatics.

Trivedy, S. and Pal, A. K. 2017. A logistic map-based fragile watermarking scheme of digital images with tamper detection. Iranian Journal of Science and Technology, Transactions of Electrical Engineering, 41: 103–113.

Walia, S. and Kumar, K. 2018. Digital image forgery detection: a systematic scrutiny. Australian Journal of Forensic Sciences, pp. 1–39.

Wang, Z., Bovik, A. C., Sheikh, H. R. and Simoncelli, E. P. 2004. Image quality assessment: from error visibility to structural similarity. IEEE Transactions on Image Processing, 13: 600–612.

Warif, N. B. A. et al. 2016. Copy-move forgery detection: Survey, challenges and future directions. Journal of Network and Computer Applications, 75: 259–278.

Yadav, A. R., Anand, R. S., Dewal, M. L. and Gupta, S. 2015. Gaussian image pyramid based texture features for classification of microscopic images of hardwood species. Optik, 126: 5570–5578.

Zhang, W., Chen, J. and Zhang, Y. 2018. Global resynchronization-based image watermarking resilient to geometric attacks. Computers & Electrical Engineering, 67: 182–194.

Zhao, J. and Guo, J. 2013. Passive forensics for copy-move image forgery using a method based on DCT and SVD. Forensic Science International, 233: 158–166.

10

Android Malware Classification using Ensemble Classifiers

Shivi Garg[1],* and *Niyati Baliyan*[2]

10.1 Introduction

According to McAfee report [1], the amount of android malware rose by ~ 629% in quarter 1 of 2018 (i.e., more than ~ 2.9 million samples). It has been reported that 2.47 million unique mobile malware samples were collected in 2013, which depicts 197% increase over 2012 [2]. Mobile malware can be due to developmental loopholes or software vulnerabilities. Software vulnerabilities can be classified based on different technical parameters [3]. Prominent and eminent amounts of manual efforts are required in order to examine the growing number of recent malware instances. This has led to a strong interest of researchers and developers in developing techniques to automate the malware analysis process.

Majority of the mobile malware targets Android machines. This has propelled the research endeavour in Android malware analysis in the last years. Most important thing to do for malware analysis is the detection and classification of malware samples into known families. For both malware detection and family identification, light-weight and expandable techniques to handle the numbers of Android apps, both benign and malicious [4], are highly preferred. In general, static analysis techniques are computationally less expensive than emulation-based

---
[1] Department of Information Technology, Indira Gandhi Delhi Technical University for Women, Delhi, India.
[2] Computer Engineering Department, J.C. Bose University of Science and Technology YMCA, Faridabad, India.
* Corresponding author: shivi1989@gmail.com

dynamic analysis; unfortunately, various static analysis methods are easily forestalled by obfuscation, which is extremely common on Android these days. Classification of family specifically also undergo the widespread code reuse in malware, which leads to different malware families sharing code and entire modules. To address these difficulties, ensemble classifier technique is introduced for malware classification, where features are derived from a fast and expandable, yet accurate and obfuscation-resilient Android Package Kit (APKs). In this technique, four different machine learning algorithms are chosen, namely, Support Vector Machine (SVM), Ripple Down Rule Learner (RIDOR), Multilayer Perceptron (MLP), Pruning Rule-based Classification Tree (PART), based on their unique properties. Then, a combination of these is executed in a parallel manner to enhance the accuracy and efficiency.

This paper is structured as follows: Section 10.2 presents literature review where previous approaches of malware detection have been discussed in terms of their advantages and disadvantages. Section 10.3 describes the proposed methodology and the various steps involved in malware classification. Section 10.4 presents the experimental set up, different tools and machine learning techniques used to carry out this process. Section 10.5 presents the results obtained for both individual and parallel ensemble classifiers. Lastly, section 10.6 draws conclusions and future scope.

10.2 Literature Review

The following section consists of the pre-existing approaches for automatically detecting or classifying malware.

Shen et al. [5] proposed information flow analysis technique to detect mobile malware. Their approach focused on the structure of the complex flows, patterns and behaviour of both benign and malicious applications. Here, native code was not analyzed, so they could not detect malicious behaviour present in the native code. Garcia et al. [6] presented RevealDroid, a framework for Android malware detection and family identification. Supervised machine learning algorithms were used for malware family identification. They achieved an accuracy of 95% in determination of malware families. However, dataset utilized by RevealDroid poses a threat to external validity.

Cai et al. [7] designed and implemented a tool named DroidCat, which detected and categorized Android malware through systematic dynamic profiling along with supervised learning techniques. They defined 122 behavioural metrics, out of which 70 metrics were significantly different between benign and malicious apps. They achieved an accuracy of 92% with random forests. Milosevic et al. [8] employed machine learning algorithms in static analysis of Android malicious apps. APKs were first decompiled to extract static features using bag-of-words feature extraction algorithm. Feature vector was then obtained. Their approach was based on permissions and source code analysis. F-measure of 89% was achieved for permission-based classification. However, it proved to be computationally more expensive since it required de-compilation of APKs prior to analysis. FalDroid [9], an automatic system for classifying Android malware proposed and developed by Fan et al., showed common behaviour of malware in the same families through frequent subgraphs. They filtered program semantics into a function call graph representation and then assigned different weights to different sensitive APIs with TF-IDF like approach. Here, native Code was not considered. It failed to overcome advanced obfuscation like encryption and reflection. They achieved an accuracy of 94.5%.

10.3 Proposed Methodology

Different steps, as shown in Figure 10.1, involved in the malware classification are documented as follows:

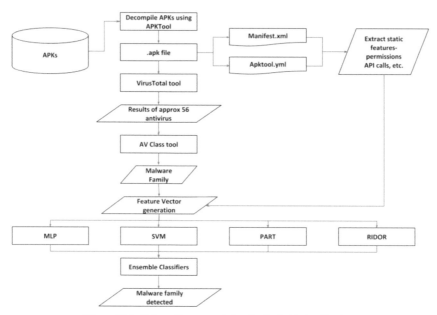

Figure 10.1: Schematic representation for Android classification.

10.3.1 Separation of Malicious Android APK

First step of classification involves separation of malicious APKs from the combined dataset. The method used for separation includes generation of MD5 hashes of the APKs [10] in order to upload them on VirusTotalAPI [11].

The results are then retrieved for each of the uploaded APKs. The evaluation results of approximately 56 anti-viruses are provided by the API. A count of anti-viruses reporting the APK as malicious is maintained. The JSON response of each APK is maintained in a separate location which is to be used for further processing.

10.3.2 Malware Family Identification

The next step after the separation of malicious APKs is running through the AVclasstool [12] with the retrieved JSON results as input. The malware family given as the result is recorded.

10.3.3 Static Feature Extraction

APK includes various static features, such as permission, version number, library used, API calls, etc. To extract the static features, reverse engineering APKTool [13] is used. This process yields Manifest.xml and APKtool.yml file. Then, a custom python script is used to extract the required features. There are 216 permissions extracted from the APKs, and represented as a binary feature vector $f = f_1, f_2,...f_n$. After the separation of malicious APKs, AVclass tool is executed with the retrieved JSON results as an input. As a result, the malware family will be recorded.

$$f_i = \begin{cases} 1, & \text{if the ith permission is present} \\ 0, & \text{otherwise} \end{cases}$$

For example, the feature vector for APKs are given by equations (10.1) and (10.2)

$$f_{airpush} = \begin{pmatrix} 0 & 1 & 1 & 0 & 0 & 0 & 0 & 0 & 0 & 1 & 0 & 0 \\ 0 & 0 & 0 & 0 & 0 & 0 & 1 & 0 & 0 & 0 & 0 & 0 \\ 0 & 0 & 0 & 0 & 0 & 0 & 0 & 0 & 0 & 0 & 0 & 0 \\ 0 & 1 & 0 & 0 & 0 & 0 & 0 & 1 & 0 & 0 & 0 \end{pmatrix} \tag{10.1}$$

$$f_{aples} = \begin{pmatrix} 1 & 1 & 0 & 0 & 0 & 1 & 0 & 0 & 0 & 0 & 0 & 0 \\ 0 & 0 & 0 & 0 & 0 & 1 & 1 & 0 & 1 & 0 & 0 & 0 \\ 1 & 0 & 0 & 0 & 0 & 0 & 0 & 0 & 0 & 1 & 0 \\ 0 & 0 & 1 & 1 & 1 & 1 & 0 & 0 & 1 & 0 & 0 & 0 \end{pmatrix} \tag{10.2}$$

10.3.4 Model Training and Evaluation

In this phase, the dataset obtained by static feature extraction and family identification is split to two parts, one part is used for training the model and the other is used to test the models. The training dataset is used for training the various machine learning algorithms, namely, SVM, RIDOR, MLP and PART. The results of individual classification of the four algorithms are compared and plotted. To further improve the efficiency, ensemble techniques are used. Various accuracy measures are used for comparison between the algorithms. The various measures:

1) Precision (P) $P = \dfrac{TP}{TP + FP}$ $\qquad$ (10.3)

2) Recall (R) $R = \dfrac{TP}{TP + FN}$ $\qquad$ (10.4)

3) Accuracy (Acc) $Acc = \dfrac{TP + TN}{(TP + FP + FN + TN)}$ $\qquad$ (10.5)

4) Error ratio (Err) $Err = 1 - Acc$ $\qquad$ (10.6)

where TP, TN, FP and FN stand for True Positive, True Negative, False Positive and False Negative, respectively.

10.4 Experimental Setup

The following section describes steps involved in this process.

10.4.1 Data Collection and Pre-processing

APKs are collected from multiple sources mentioned, as shown in Table 10.1. These collected APKs are processed and decompiled to create the dataset used for training and testing.

Table 10.1: Data set used for APK collection.

Data Set	Malicious/Benign
Android Malware Dataset (AMD) [14]	Malicious
Androzoo [15]	Benign
Google Play [16], Wandoujia app market [17]	Malicious + Benign

10.4.2 Data Filtration

For malware family identification and classification, only malicious APKs are required for further processing and implementation. The steps are as follows:

1) CSV file containing the names of different APKs is created
2) Generate MD5 hashes of all APKs present in the CSV file using a python script

3) APKs are uploaded using a python script on the VirusTotalAPI

4) Results are then retrieved using the python script. The API provides results ~ 56 anti-viruses. Count of anti-viruses is maintained for malicious APKs. JSON response of each APK is then stored in a separate file for further processing.

10.4.3 Data Classification

The results retrieved from VirusTotal are fed to the AVclass tool which then yields the malware family of each APK. The identification of the malware family classifies the APKs into 71 malware families as given by VirusTotal. The families which are identified by VirusTotal act as a class which is to be predicted using supervised machine learning.

The feature vector to be used for training the model consists of the static features extracted from the application package kit. Details of static feature extraction can be found in [18].

10.4.4 Machine Learning Techniques

A classifier algorithm maps the input data to a category in machine learning. Supervised learning is focused in our research, where the trained labelled dataset is used. The machine learning algorithms used in our methodology include: MLP, SVM, PART and RIDOR. These four algorithms are chosen because of their sparse implementations in the past researches and due to their diverse nature. Also, no one has ever used the combination of MLP, SVM, PART and RIDOR before in Android malware classification. Previous approaches of machine learning for android malware detection were proposed, however, they were not very efficient or scalable [19]. These complications ask for better yielding measures for the malware detection to abate the growth of Android malware. This is why the paper proposes a scheme to detect and classify the Android malware in the early stage using parallel machine learning classifiers and their different features. The objective of selecting only these specific classifiers is achievement of the maximum accuracy since different classifiers pose different properties, like rule-based, function-based, etc., where advantages of these combined classifiers can be seen. Simultaneous execution of the algorithms is done by assigning one core to each algorithm and then running simultaneously to obtain the higher percentage of accuracy by obtaining a single classification judgment. Furthermore, executing multiple threads in parallel on different cores may help in producing faster results. This is done for accurate malware classification, into the correct family, with least possible errors.

10.5 Results

The results obtained from the implementation of various machine learning approaches are presented in this section.

10.5.1 Classification into Various Malware Families

The application of the above methodology gave us the distribution of the APKs into 71 malware families, which forms the class label for our machine learning algorithms and is also used to train and test the model. The classification of the dataset into various malware families is shown in Figure 10.2.

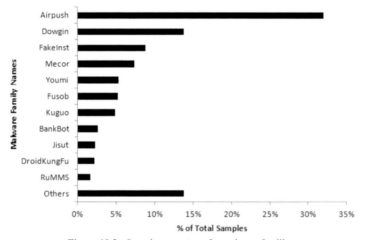

Figure 10.2: Sample percentage for malware families.

10.5.2 Results of Individual Classifiers

The first part of the evaluation considered all the algorithms individually. The results obtained by the individual execution of the algorithms are recorded and necessary representations are generated. The APKs are classified into 71 malware families and, hence, precision and recall for each family is calculated by the individual algorithms and the graphs are plotted to depict the results obtained. The following section consists of the results obtained from individual algorithms.

10.5.2.1 Multi-Layer Perceptron (MLP)

A histogram is plotted between malware families (total 71) and the precision with which they were classified using MLP classifier as shown in Figure 10.3. The red line indicates the cumulative % of families falling in different precision ranges. It has been observed that ~ 45% of total families (e.g., SimpleLocker, FakeInst, Vidro, etc.) were classified with 0.9–1.0 precision level. Post analysis, it is seen that ~ 80% of the malware families were classified with a precision range of 0.7–1.0. Also, it has been analyzed that recall level of 0.8–1.0 was obtained for ~ 52% of total families, shown in Figure 10.4. ~ 80% of the total families were classified in the recall level of 0.5–1.0.

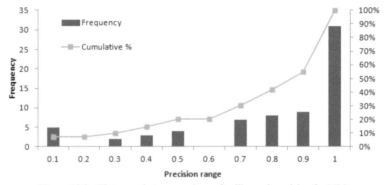

Figure 10.3: Histogram between malware families and precision for MLP.

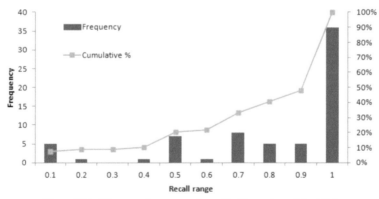

Figure 10.4: Histogram between malware families and recall for MLP.

10.5.2.2 Support Vector Machine (SVM)

A histogram is plotted between malware families (total 71) and the precision with which they were classified using SVM classifier, as shown in Figure 10.5. It has been observed that ~ 75% of total families (e.g., Airpush, Cova, FakeAV, etc.) were classified with 0.9–1.0 precision level. Post analysis, it is seen that ~ 80% of the malware families were classified with a precision

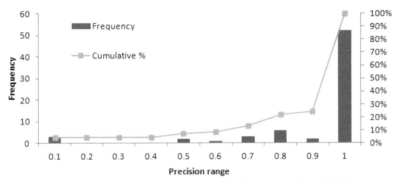

Figure 10.5: Histogram between malware families and precision for SVM.

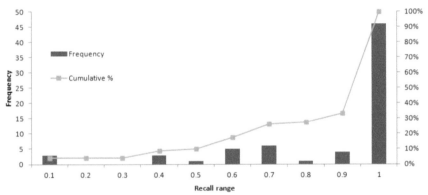

Figure 10.6: Histogram between malware families and recall for SVM.

range of 0.8–1.0. Also, it has been analyzed that recall level of 0.8–1.0 was obtained for ~ 67% of total families, as shown in Figure 10.6. ~ 80% of the total families were classified in the recall level of 0.6–1.0.

10.5.2.3 *Pruning Rule-Based Classification Tree (PART)*

A histogram is plotted between malware families (total 71) and the precision with which they were classified using PART classifier as shown in Figure 10.7. It has been observed that ~ 38% of total families (e.g., Finspy, Slembunk, FakeAV, etc.) were classified with 0.0–0.1 precision level. Post analysis, it is seen that ~ 45% of the malware families were classified with a precision range of 0.7–1.0. Also, it has been analyzed from Figure 10.8 that recall level of 0.0–0.1 was obtained for ~ 38% of total families. ~ 57% of the total families were classified in the recall level of 0.5–1.0.

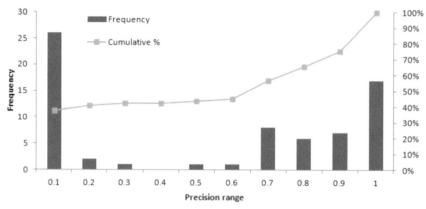

Figure 10.7: Histogram between malware families and precision for PART.

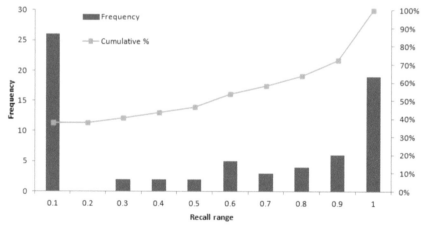

Figure 10.8: Histogram between malware families and recall for PART.

10.5.2.4 Ripple down Rule Learner (RIDOR)

A histogram is plotted between malware families (total 71) and the precision with which they were classified using RIDOR classifier as shown in Figure 10.9. It has been observed that ~ 75% of total families (e.g., AndroRAT, DroidKungFu, GoldDream, etc.) were classified with 0.9–1.0 precision level. Post analysis, it is seen that ~ 78% of the malware families were classified with a precision range of 0.8–1.0. Also, it has been analyzed from Figure 10.10 that recall level of 0.9–1.0 was obtained for ~ 67% of total families. ~ 80% of the total families were classified in the recall level of 0.6–1.0.

According to the results obtained, MLP proves to be the best algorithm for the dataset with an accuracy of 90.69% and RIDOR has the lowest accuracy of 82.6%. Figure 10.11 shows the accuracy of various algorithms.

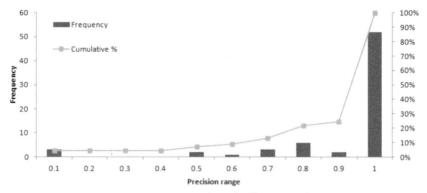

Figure 10.9: Histogram between malware families and precision for RIDOR.

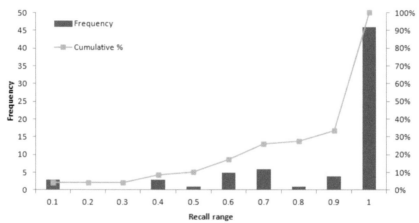

Figure 10.10: Histogram between malware families and recall for RIDOR.

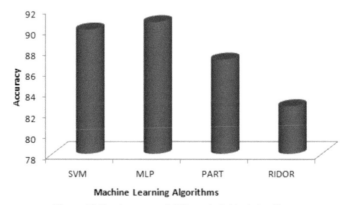

Figure 10.11: Accuracy of different individual classifiers.

10.5.3 Results of Parallel Classifiers

The second part was performed using the parallel model where the results (obtained from individual classification) were executed on various ensemble techniques. Since it is a multiclass classification problem, only two parameters were considered to judge the efficiency of the ensemble approach. These probabilities are taken from the individual classifiers. 71 malware families were detected. The two ensemble techniques used are as follows:

10.5.3.1 Maximum Vote Ensemble Technique

In maximum vote ensemble technique, predicted class is decided by the maximum vote from multiple prediction classifiers and the class with highest mode value is decided to be the final predicted class.

10.5.3.2 Averaging Ensemble Technique

In averaging ensemble technique, the average of predicting probabilities of the classifiers is taken and predicts the outcome of ensemble technique.

According to the results obtained by using different ensemble techniques, maximum vote ensemble technique is more accurate with accuracy 93.90% and Averaging ensemble technique has accuracy of 80.63%, as shown in Figure 10.12.

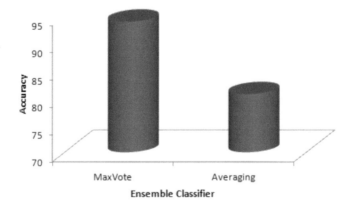

Figure 10.12: Accuracy for ensemble classifiers.

10.6 Conclusion and Future Scope

Android malware are classified using ensemble parallel classifiers in machine learning. The aforementioned work yields the feature vectors consisting of the static features of the APK, namely, permissions, libraries used, services, broadcast receivers and version number. In addition to the static features, the class of malware family which is to be predicted for a particular APK is also added to the dataset. The proposed methodology in this paper, which classifies Android malware with an accuracy of 94%, has been improved as compared to individual classifiers.

The scope of this research is limited only to the static features of APKs. This approach fails to capture the features of an APK at runtime, which sets the future scope of this work. To further improve the accuracy of our approach, dynamic feature extraction of the collected dataset is the next step.

References

[1] McAfee Labs Threats report Fourth Quarter. 2018. https://www.mcafee.com, last accessed 2018/11/21.
[2] Arora, A., Garg, S. and Peddoju, S. K. 2014. Malware detection using network traffic analysis in android based mobile devices. In Eighth International Conference on Next Generation Mobile Apps, Services and Technologies (NGMAST), pp. 66–71.
[3] Garg, S., Singh, R. K. and Mohapatra, A. K. 2019. Analysis of software vulnerability classification based on different technical parameters. Information Security Journal: A Global Perspective, 28(1-2): 1–19.
[4] Garg, S. and Baliyan, N. 2019. A novel parallel classifier scheme for vulnerability detection in android. Computers & Electrical Engineering, 77: 12–26.
[5] Shen, F. et al. 2018. Android malware detection using complex-flows. IEEE Transactions on Mobile Computing.
[6] Garcia, J. et al. 2018. Lightweight, obfuscation-resilient detection and family identification of Android malware. ACM Transactions on Software Engineering and Methodology (TOSEM), 26(3): 11.
[7] Cai, H. et al. 2016. Droidcat: Unified dynamic detection of Android malware. ReportTR-17-01.
[8] Milosevic, N. et al. 2017. Machine learning aided android malware classification. Computers & Electrical Engineering, 61: 266–274.
[9] Fan, M. et al. 2016. Frequent subgraph based familial classification of android malware. pp. 24–35. In: 27th International Symposium on Software Reliability Engineering (ISSRE).
[10] Python Software Foundation, http://www.python.org, last accessed 2018/10/16.
[11] VirusTotal Documentation, https://www.virustotal.com/en/documentation/public-api, last accessed 2018/10/16.
[12] Sebastián, M. et al. 2016. Avclass: A tool for massive malware labeling. pp. 230–253. In: International Symposium on Research in Attacks, Intrusions, and Defenses.
[13] APKTool, https://ibotpeaches.github.io/Apktool/, last accessed 2018/08/15.
[14] Wei, F. et al. 2017. Deep ground truth analysis of current android malware. pp. 252–276. In: International Conference on Detection of Intrusions and Malware, and Vulnerability Assessment.
[15] Allix, K., Bissyandé, T. F., Klein, J. and Le Traon, Y. A. 2016. Collecting millions of android apps for the research community. pp. 468–471. In: Proceedings of the 13th International Conference on Mining Software Repositories, MSR (Vol. 16).
[16] Google play store apps, https://play.google.com/store/apps, last accessed 2018/07/15.
[17] Wandoujia apps. http://www.wandoujia.com/apps, last accessed 2018/07/15.
[18] Garg, S. and Baliyan, N. 2019. Data on vulnerability detection in android. Data in Brief, 22: 1081–1087.
[19] Yan, S. et al. 2017. Field trial of machine-learning-assisted and SDN-based optical network planning with network-scale monitoring database. In: European Conference and Exhibition on Optical Communication, pp. Th-PDP.

11

Provably Secure Lightweight Key Policy Attribute-Based Encryption for Internet of Things

*K Sowjanya** and *Mou Dasgupta*

11.1 Introduction

Rapid development of the Internet of Things (IoT) provides ground for applications in diversified fields. Integration of IoT into cloud makes these applications ubiquitous, but brings challenges regarding security and privacy. Protocols at application layer of IoT determine the message passing mechanism (either secure or unsecure) at application level. Many application layer protocols [1] (like MQTT, CoAP, etc.) are deployed but they have limitations in terms of security issues of IoT. Among these, MQTT [2] is designed as lightweight and supports publish/subscribe message passing pattern. MQTT supports security in multiple layers (Network, Transport and Application), each prevents different attacks [3]. In application layer, MQTT provides user-dependent payload encryption mechanism, which is open for client implementation for encrypting application specific data. This feature of MQTT provides end-to-end encryption for application data over untrusted cloud or storage.

The sensitive data generated by IoT requires proper security and privacy preserving mechanism. One of the most effective and suitable security mechanism for cloud (or distributed) environment is Attribute Based

Department of Computer Applications, National Institute of Technology Raipur.
Email: elle.est.mou@gmail.com
* Corresponding author: sowjanya.kandisa@gmail.com

Encryption (ABE), which inherently supports the data broadcast property of IoT. With ABE, no prior secret key sharing is required, which simplifies the key management overhead in large scale applications. Primarily, ABE is categorized as CPABE (Ciphertext-Policy ABE) and KPABE (Key-Policy ABE). In KPABE, data is encrypted under user-specific attributes and the secret/decryption key is associated with the defined access policy. Likewise, in CPABE, data is encrypted under access policy and decryption is successful if a receiver possesses defined access policy satisfied attributes. Thus, ABE provides good expressive and flexible mechanism for security in the distributed environment. However, the computational overhead of bilinear pairing and exponential operations of ABE [4, 5, 6] makes it unsuitable for IoT. In this direction, this paper proposes a lightweight ECC (Elliptic Curve Cryptography)-based KPABE without bilinear pairing and exponential operations. The proposed scheme is used for payload encryption under MQTT, which provides lightweight security at the application layer of IoT.

The primary contribution of this work is to:

- Design ECC-based lightweight KPABE without bilinear pairing and exponential operations.
- Enable payload encryption using proposed KPABE for MQTT.

The organization of the paper is as follows: some background is needed to understand the proposed scheme, consequently, the related work in this area is presented in section 11.2. Section 11.3 presents the detailed description of the proposed KPABE scheme. The security analysis of the proposed security mechanism is depicted in section 11.4. Simulation and performance analysis of the proposed KPABE scheme is given in section 11.5. Finally, section 11.6 concludes the paper.

11.2 Background and Related Work

This section provides the necessary background to understand the proposed technique followed by the related work in this area. In context of this, the formal structure of KPABE, MQTT, Access Structure, complexity assumptions and security model are presented as follows. For the sake of explanation, a list of notations used in this work is given in Table 11.1.

11.3 Formal Structure of KPABE Scheme

The KPABE scheme generally consists of four algorithms, namely: *Setup, Key generation, Encryption* and *Decryption*.

Table 11.1: List of notations.

Notations	Description
q	Larger prime number.
E	Elliptic curve over the prime finite field F_q.
G_E	An additive elliptic curve group of order q.
B	Generator of group G_E.
PPM	Public parameters of the system.
SMK	System master keys of the key-authority.
Λ	Access Structure used in the proposed scheme.
H	Point to map hashing (hash in G_E)
O	Point at infinity or zero element of group G_E.
Z_q	A finite field of integers $(0, 1, 2, …, q-1)$.
Z_q^*	$Z_q^* = Z_q - \{0\}$
T_R	Computational overhead of random number generation.
T_{SM}	Computational overhead of ECC-based scalar multiplication.
T_{MI}	Computational overhead of ECC-based multiplicative inverse.
T_p	Computational overhead of bilinear pairing operation.
T_{EX}	Computational overhead of modular exponentiation.
T_{PSM}	Computational overhead of pairing based scalar multiplication.
T_{MH}	Computational overhead of hashing in G_E.
T_A	Computational overhead of modular addition.
T_M	Computational overhead of modular multiplication.

- **Setup:** This algorithm is run by an authority, generally known as *Key-Authority (KA)*. Input to this algorithm is the implicit security level of the scheme. It outputs *public parameters PPM* (announced publicly) and *system master keys SMK* (kept secret with *KA*).

- **Encryption:** This algorithm is run by the data sender. Message *M, PPM* and *set of attributes γ* are taken as input to create a *ciphertext CT*.

- **Key generation:** This algorithm is run by the *KA* to generate the decryption key corresponding to an access structure/policy by taking *MSK, access structure Λ* and the *PPM* as input.

- **Decryption:** This algorithm is run at the receiver side to reconstruct the encrypted message. It takes input: the decryption key for access structure Λ, the ciphertext *CT* encrypted under γ and *PPM*. This algorithm outputs the message *M* iff γ satisfy Λ.

11.3.1 MQTT

MQTT is one of the application layer protocols under IoT protocol stack. It is a *publish/subscribe* type message transmission protocol, mainly designed to work in a constrained environment, like IoT [2]. The principal features of MQTT are: it is lightweight, takes less bandwidth, open, easy to implement, client and broker libraries are available, and so on. These features make it suitable for a constrained environment, like IoT. In the context of security, MQTT provides authentication of devices and users at the application level by using client identifier, and username/password credentials. The protocol MQTT itself provides these features. However, the other security issues (authorization, confidentiality, integrity, etc.) are left open for broker side and/or client side implementations. One of the open features of MQTT is *payload encryption*, which may enable an additional level of security to the application-specific data. So, aside from having secure transmission, secure storage of data on any third party server (cloud) can be possible with payload encryption mechanism. Further information on this protocol can be found in the specification [2] and security aspect of MQTT can be obtained from [3].

11.3.2 Access Structure

Access structure Λ defines the access control or access scope of the users' decryption key [5]. In ABE, the users' role is defined by the set of attributes. Therefore, the access structure contains attributes that are authorized to access the secret/decryption key. Access structure can be represented with the help of access tree [5, 8]. In this access tree, attributes are associated with leaf node $u(attr(u))$ and its threshold value is given by $k_u = 1$. Each non-leaf node u of this tree is identified by its child nodes and the corresponding threshold value k_u. In this case, the value of k_u lies between 1 and the number of child nodes, i.e., $1 \leq k_u \leq num(u)$, where the number of child nodes of node u is represented by $num(u)$.

Figure 11.1 depicts one decryption example of data (encrypted under the attribute set $\{A_1, A_2, A_3\}$). Here, *AND* gate is represented using *2 of 2* and *OR* gate is represented using *1 of 2*. The number occurring before *of* is considered as threshold value, i.e., k_x. Hence, for *AND*, $k_x = 2$ and for *OR*, $k_x = 1$. From Figure 11.1, it can be observed that the *User 1* and *User 3* have the secret keys corresponding to their access tree and also attributes used for encryption satisfy these access trees. Thus, *User 1* and *User 3* successfully decrypt the data using their corresponding secret keys. However, *User 2* possesses the key corresponding to the access tree containing attributes A_2 and A_4. The attributes used for encryption do not satisfy the access tree of *User 2*. Hence, access to data for *User 2* is denied.

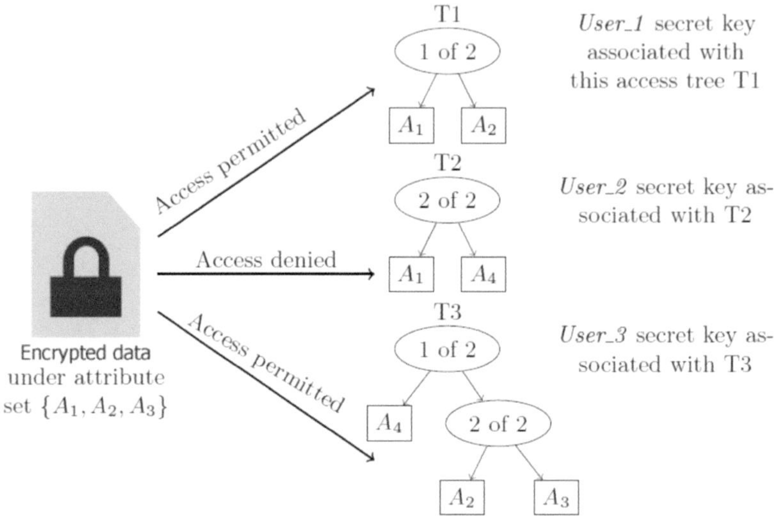

Figure 11.1: Example of KPABE decryption.

11.3.3 Complexity Assumptions

This subsection explains the strength of ECC by defining some computational problems/assumptions related to elliptic curves, which does not have any polynomial time algorithm [7]. For this, a brief introduction of ECC is presented first, followed by the assumptions.

If F_q is a prime finite field, then elliptic curve E over F_q is defined by the non-singular curve equation, i.e., $y^2 \ (mod \ q) = (x^3 + ax + b) \ mod \ q$. Here, the discriminant $4a^3 + 27b^2 \neq 0$ and $a,b,x,y \in F_q$. A group operation (addition in this case) must be defined to form a group G_E over E such that G_E forms an abelian group.

(ECDLP) Elliptic Curve Discrete Logarithm Problem

For the points $B,Q \in G_E$, where B is the generator of G_E, it is computationally impossible to find the value of $k \in Z_q^*$ (chosen at random) such that $Q = k.B$.

(ECCDH) Elliptic Curve Computational Diffie-Hellman Problem

Given generator B of G_E and $c, d \in Z_q^*$ (chosen at random), it is computationally impossible to compute $c.d.B$, given instance $(B, c. B, d. B) \in G_E$.

(ECDDH) Elliptic Curve Decisional Diffie-Hellman Problem

It is computationally impossible for a polynomial time algorithm to distinguish the two instances $(c. B, d. B, c. d. B)$ and $(c. B, d. B, z. B)$ of G_E, i.e., whether $c. d. B = z. B$ or not, where B is the generator of G_E and $c, d, z \in Z_q^*$ (chosen at random).

11.4 Security Model

The security model used for the proposed KPABE is the selective set security model [11]. This model is defined for the chosen plaintext attack, where the two messages encrypted under KPABE are indistinguishable. This model is defined using a game played among an adversary and a challenger and is given analogous to [11].

- **Initialization:** The attribute set ϑ is declared by the adversary A, which he/she wants to attack.
- **Setup:** This phase is executed by the challenger to output the public keys and the system master keys. The public keys are transferred to the adversary A and the master keys are kept secret.
- **Phase 1:** For a number of access structures Λ, the adversary A is allowed to query for obtaining the decryption key, such that $\forall$ i, $\Lambda_i(\vartheta) = 0$ (i.e., the attribute set ϑ does not satisfy the access structure Λ).
- **Challenge:** In this phase, two equal length messages M_0 and M_1 are submitted by A to the challenger. The challenger encrypts the message M_b under the attribute set ϑ, by flipping the fair binary coin $b \in \{0,1\}$.
- **Phase 2:** In this phase, the phase 1 repeated.
- **Guess:** A makes a guess b' of b.

In this game, the advantage (ε) of A is defined by

$$\varepsilon = Pr[b' = b] - \frac{1}{2}$$

11.4.1 Related Work

At first, in 2005, the concept of ABE was coined by the Sahai and Waters [4] as a variation of Identity-Based Encryption (IBE) called Fuzzy Identity-Based Encryption (FIBE). Further, in 2006, Goyal et al. [5] enhanced the concept of ABE by introducing policy-based ABE, termed as KPABE. In this scheme, the data is encrypted under a set of attributes and the decryption key is associated with the access structure. In order to provide full control over the recipients of sensitive data, Bethencourt et al. (2007) [6] introduced another policy-based ABE, i.e., Ciphertext-Policy ABE (CPABE). In this method, data is encrypted under access structure and the decryption key is embedded with a set of attributes. Later on, many variations of KPABE and CPABE are proposed to meet specific requirements. One variant of KPABE, i.e., KPABE with proxy re-encryption is designed by Ge et al. [9] in 2018. Their scheme supports monotonic access structure and the proof of the scheme is presented using adaptive model under chosen-ciphertext attack. Further, Li et al. [10]

considered one use case and accordingly proposed a KPABE scheme which is resilient to continual auxiliary input leakage. The abovementioned KPABE schemes employ bilinear pairing operations. In 2015, Yao et al. [11] proposed a lightweight KPABE without bilinear pairing operations for IoT. Their scheme is based on ECC, where the session keys are encrypted and decrypted using KPABE scheme. Afterward, in 2016, Hong and Sun [12] and Karati et al. [13] proposed without bilinear pairing ABE schemes. Their scheme does not utilize ECC and the data is directly encrypted and decrypted under their proposed ABE schemes. In the context of IoT, lightweight ABE is considered more effective as compared to the traditional ABE (comprising bilinear pairing operations). Oualha and Nguyen (2016) [14] presented lightweight CPABE using pre-computation mechanism. Authors in [15] presented the concept of integrating existing ABE with MQTT in order to enhance the security of the protocol using *payload encryption* feature of MQTT. The same approach is utilized by Thatmann et al. [16], the only difference is that, instead of using ABE directly for encrypting and decrypting data, this work uses ABE to secure encryption/decryption key. Many authors have given the security framework for MQTT. For example, Shin et al. [17] proposed the AugMQTT by incorporating AugPAKE protocol, which is secured against active attacks, passive attacks and offline dictionary attack. Authors in [18] provided a home automation system using secure MQTT. Mektoubi et al. [19] presented a secure version of MQTT using RSA and AES algorithms. They also considered Elliptic Curves for their implementation. Katsikeas et al. [20] presented the secure version of MQTT for Industrial IoT communication. They also provided justification for choosing MQTT among other application layer protocols of IoT by comparing MQTT with other protocols. In this direction, we propose a lightweight ECC-based KPABE scheme without bilinear pairing operations. Also, the proposed scheme is augmented with MQTT to provide an additional layer of security to MQTT protocol.

11.4.2 Proposed Key-Policy ABE

The proposed scheme consists of four phases, which are described below. In this proposed mechanism, the secret key in decryption phase is reconstructed under the attribute set γ using Lagrange Interpolation. Here, if each attribute in γ is associated with a random unique number in Z_q, then the Lagrange coefficient $\Delta_{i,\theta}$ is given by

$$\Delta_{i,\theta}(x) = \prod_{j \in \theta, j \neq i} \frac{x - j}{i - j} \tag{11.1}$$

where i $\in Z_q^*$ and θ is a set of numbers corresponding to each attribute in the set γ. x is a variable of the polynomial f(x) for which the Lagrange coefficient is calculated. It is also considered that the Key-Authority (KA) in this technique generates ECC based keys.

11.4.2.1 Setup

In this phase, KA defines the universal attribute set U = {1, 2, 3, ... , m}. For each attribute i ∈ U, KA chooses $a_i \in Z_q^*$ uniformly at random. Accordingly, the public key corresponding to attribute i is given by $P_{a_i} = a_i.B$. Again, KA chooses a master secret key (MSK), $s \in Z_q^*$ uniformly at random. Hence, the master public key (MPK) is P = s.B. Next, it (KA) defines two functions H_1: {ECPoint} → {0,1}* and H_2: {0,1}* → {0,1}^{m}, where m is the size of the message M and ECPoint represents the specified elliptic curve point. Thus, the system secret keys are {a_i, s} (which are kept secret by KA) and public parameters are given by {P_i, P, H} (known to all).

11.4.2.2 Encryption

In this phase, data sender chooses $r \in Z_q^*$ uniformly at random and message M is encrypted using attribute set γ as

$$CT_1 = r. B,$$

$$CT_2 = r. P_{a_i}, \forall i \in \gamma$$

and

$$CT_3 = H_2(H_1(r. P)) \oplus M$$

Hence, the ciphertext created by the data sender is given by

$$CT = \{CT_1, CT_2, CT_3\}$$

11.4.2.3 Key Generation

In this phase, KA generates and outputs a secret key in order to decrypt the message (encrypted under a set of attributes γ), iff γ satisfies Λ (access structure). For this, if T represents the access tree corresponding to the access structure Λ, then a polynomial $q_u(x)$ with degree $k_u - 1$ for each and every node u of T can be defined. For root node R of T, KA sets $q_R(0) = s$ (MSK). To define the polynomial uniquely for root node R, KA chooses $k_R - 1$ other points at random over Z_q^*. All other nodes u (except root node), KA defines $q_u(0) = q_{parent(u)}(index(u))$, here index is the number given to each node u corresponding to the ordering of its children. Like $q_R(x)$, $q_u(x)$ is defined uniquely by choosing $k_u - 1$ other points at random over Z_q^*. A share of secret key is associated, while defining the polynomial of leaf node u as

$$D_u = q_u(0) + a_i$$

where i = attr(u) and a_i is the random number chosen from Z_q^* in the previous phase (Setup). Thus, if all leaf nodes of T are processed, then we can say that the secret key is associated with T. Hence, this secret key is given by

$$D = (D_u = q_u(0) + a_i, \, i \in leaf\_nodes)$$

11.4.2.4 Decryption

This phase takes the ciphertext CT = {CT_1, CT_2, CT_3} and the decryption key $D_u = q_u(0) + a_i$, i ∈ γ. The message M is calculated using

$$M = H_2(H_1(V_R)) \oplus CT_3 \tag{11.2}$$

where V_R is the value returned by the function decryptNodeNonLeaf(D_R, CT_1, CT_2) at root node R. This function is defined recursively for each node of T. If 1 is a leaf node, then decryptNodeLeaf(D_1, CT_1, CT_2) is given by

$$\text{decryptNodeLeaf}(D_1, CT_1, CT_2) = \begin{cases} D_1.CT_1 - CT_2, & \forall i \in \gamma \\ \text{Null}, & \text{otherwise} \end{cases}$$

Here, the function decryptNodeLeaf(D_1, CT_1, CT_2) for leaf node 1 is evaluated as

$$\begin{aligned} D_1. CT_1 - CT_2 &= (q_u(0) + a_i). \, r. \, B - r. \, P_{a_i} \\ &= q_u(0). \, r. \, B + a_i. \, r. \, B - r. \, P_{a_i} \\ &= q_u(0). \, r. \, B + a_i. \, r. \, B - r. \, a_i. \, B \\ &= q_u(0). \, r. \, B \end{aligned}$$

For a non-leaf node u, decryptNodeNonLeaf(D_u, CT_1, CT_2) is calculated using Lagrange Interpolation (Equation 1) and operates on each of its child nodes v. If the set of child nodes of u is represented by C_u, then

decryptNodeNonLeaf(D_u, CT_1, CT_2) is described as

$$\text{decryptNodeNonLeaf}(D_u, CT_1, CT_2) = \sum_{v \in C_u} \Delta_{i,j}(0). \\ \text{decryptNodeNonLeaf}(D_v, CT_1, CT_2)$$

where, $\Delta_{i,j}(0)$ is the Lagrange coefficient for i = index(v), j = {index(v), i ≠ j and v ∈ C_u}.

Here, the function decryptNodeLeafNode(D_u, CT_1, CT_2) evaluates to

$$\begin{aligned} \text{decryptNodeLeafNode}(D_u, CT_1, CT_2) &= \sum_{v \in C_u} \Delta_{i,j}(0).q_v(0). \, r. \, B \\ &= \sum_{v \in C_u} \Delta_{i,j}(0). \\ &\quad q_{parent(v)}(\text{index}(v)). \, r. \, B \\ &= \sum_{v \in C_u} \Delta_{i,j}(0).q_u(i). \, r. \, B \\ &= q_u(0). \, r. \, B \end{aligned}$$

Hence, we can observe that the value of decryptNodeLeaf(D_u, CT_1, CT_2) and decryptNodeNonLeaf(D_u, CT_1, CT_2) is $q_u(0)$. r. B irrespective of whether u is leaf or non-leaf node. Therefore, the function decryptNodeNonLeaf(D_R, CT_1, CT_2) evaluates at root node R as $V_R = q_R(0)$. r. B = s. r. B = r. P

Now, by referring Equation 2, the message M is obtained as follows:

$$H_2(H_1(V_R)) \oplus CT_3 = H_2(H_1(r. P)) \oplus CT_3$$
$$= H_2(H_1(r. P)) \oplus$$
$$H_2(H_1(r. P)) \oplus M$$
$$= M$$

Hence, the proposed KPABE scheme is successful at decrypting the message M under the set of attributes γ.

11.4.3 Security Proof

The security proof of the above KPABE is described by using the security model of the section 2.5, which is a game between an Adversary/Attacker A_r and a Challenger Ch. We will prove that the proposed KPABE is secured under ECDDH by using the following theorem.

The proposed KPABE is secured under ECDDH assumption using the selective set model, iff for a polynomial time algorithm, the ECDDH assumption remains hard with non-negligible advantage.

Proof. The theorem can be proved using the reduction to absurdity method, i.e., let us assume that an attacker A_r attacks our scheme with non-negligible advantage ε. In this case, a simulator S_m with advantage ε' can be designed to break the ECDDH assumption. For this, at first the challenger Ch sets the additive group G_E over elliptic curve E and its parameters (B: Generator, q: order of G_E). After that the challenger Ch, outside S_m,s view chooses c, d, z $\in Z_q^*$ uniformly at random and flips a fair binary coin $\mu \in \{0,1\}$. Now, depending on the value μ, Ch sets the instance (C, D, Z) as:

If $\mu = 0$, Ch sets (C, D, Z) = (c. B, d. B, c. d. B) and if $\mu = 1$, Ch sets (C, D, Z) = (c. B, d. B, z. B).

- Initialization: Simulator S_m obtains the attribute set ϑ, on which the attacker A_r trying to attack. Suppose Λ is the access structure corresponding to the attribute set ϑ.
- Setup: In this step, the simulator S_m executes the Setup phase of the proposed KPABE scheme of section III and outputs the public parameters, which are in turn sent to the attacker A_r.
- S_m sets one of the system parameters as Y = C = c. B.

- Now, S_m sets the public key (Y_i) for each attribute $i \in U$ such that, if $i \in \vartheta$, then $Y_i = r_i$. B, where $r_i \in Z_q^*$ (chosen at random). Hence, in this case, the private key corresponding to each attribute is $y_i = r_i$. Otherwise, if $i \in U - \vartheta$, then S_m sets $Y_i = \alpha_i$. D = α_i. d. B. In this case, $y_i = \alpha_i$. d.

- Finally, S_m sends the public keys $\{Y, Y_i, i \in U\}$ to the attacker A_r.

In this regard, A_r does not examine any difference in setting the public and private key of each attribute and, therefore, from A_r's point of view it seems like the original KPABE scheme.

- Phase 1: In this step, the attacker A_r is allowed to make numerous queries to S_m in order to obtain secret key corresponding to any access structure Λ^*, such that ϑ does not satisfy Λ^*, i.e., $\Lambda^*(\vartheta) = 0$. For generating the secret key, the simulator S_m uses Lagrange Interpolation. For this, a polynomial $q_u(x)$ with degree $k_u - 1$ is assigned to each and every node of the access tree (as same in the proposed scheme) and also sets $q_R(0) = s$ (master secret key). Hence, the secret key corresponding to each leaf node u is given by

$$D_{Lu} = \begin{cases} q_u(0) + r_i, & \text{if attribute}(u) \in \vartheta \\ q_u(0) + \alpha_i.d, & \text{if attribute}(u) \in U - \vartheta \end{cases} \quad (11.3)$$

$\forall i = \text{attribute}(u)$

Both the terms of Equation 3 are uniformly distributed, thus in A_r's view, the D_{Lu} is identical to the key of proposed KPABE. This secret key is then sent to the attacker A_r.

- Challenge: In this step, two equal length messages (M_0, M_1) are submitted by the attacker A_r to the simulator S_m for encryption under ϑ. Now, S_m encrypts the message M_b according to the fair binary coin $b \in \{0,1\}$.

$$CT_1 = D, CT_2 = r_i. D \text{ and } CT_3 = H(Z) \oplus M_b$$

Then, $CT_B = \{CT_1, CT_2, CT_3\}$ is transmitted to A_r.

Now, for the coin $\mu \in \{0,1\}$, which has flipped by the challenger Ch raised two cases:

Case 1: Ch sets $Z = c$. d. B if $\mu = 0$. For $k \in Z_q^*$ (chosen at random) then, according to the proposed scheme: $CT_1 = k$. B, $CT_2 = k$. Y_i and $CT_3 = H(k. Y) \oplus M_b$. Hence, if the value of k is set to d, then $CT_1 = k$. B = d. B = D, $CT_2 = k$. Y_i = d. r_i. B = r_i. D and $CT_3 = H(k. Y) \oplus M_b = H(d. c. B) \oplus M_b = H(Z) \oplus M_b$.

Therefore, in A's point of view, the ciphertext CT generated by the proposed KPABE scheme is equivalent to the CT_B.

Case 2: Ch sets $Z = z$. B if $\mu = 1$. If z is assigned to k, then $CT_1 = z$. B = Z, $CT_2 = z$. r_i. B = r_i. Z and $CT_3 = H(z. c. B) \oplus M_b = H(c. Z) \oplus M_b$. Hence, from A_r,s point of view, it is completely random ciphertext.

In both the cases, A_r does not obtain any information about M_b as it is ex-ored with the hash of random elliptic curve point.

- Phase 2: In this step, the simulator S_m and the attacker A_r repeats Phase 1.
- Guess: In this last step, the attacker A_r sends a guess of b, i.e., b' to the simulator S_m. Accordingly, S_m outputs $\mu' = 0$ if b' = b, to indicate (C, D, Z) = (c. B, d. B, c. d. B). Otherwise, if b' $\neq$ b, then S_m outputs $\mu' = 1$, i.e., (C, D, Z) = (c. B, d. B, z. B).

Now, according to the game, when $\mu = 1$, from the attacker A_r,s point of view, the ciphertext is completely random, thus, we get

$$Pr[\mu = 1 \,|\, b' \neq b] = \frac{1}{2} \tag{11.4}$$

Also, the simulator S_m outputs $\mu' = 1$ when b' $\neq$ b, so we get

$$Pr[\mu' = \mu \,|\, \mu = 1] = \frac{1}{2} \tag{11.5}$$

For $\mu = 0$, from the A_r,s point of view, it gets the valid ciphertext, hence, according to the game, A_r has advantage ε. Thus, we get

$$Pr[\mu = 0 \,|\, b = b\,] = -+\varepsilon \tag{11.6}$$

And again for the simulator S_m, we get

$$Pr[\mu' = \mu \,|\, \mu = 0] = \frac{1}{2} + \varepsilon \tag{11.7}$$

Finally, the overall advantage of the simulator S_m according to the specified security model is Pr[b' = b] – 1/2 and is given by Equation 5 and Equation 7 as (1/2Pr[$\mu' = \mu|\mu = 1$] + 1/2Pr[$\mu' = \mu|\mu = 0$]) – 1/2, i.e., (1/2.1/2 + 1/2(1/2 + ε)) – 1/2. Thus, the overall gain of the simulator S_m turns out to be ε/2. This proves that the ECDDH game remains hard with advantage ε/2, which conflicts our assumption that attacker A_r attacks our scheme.

Hence, based on the above security proof, we can state that the proposed MQTT protocol is secured under chosen plaintext attack, as the decryption of a message is based on the intractability assumption of ECDDH problem.

11.5 Simulation and Performance Analysis of Proposed KPABE

The proposed KPABE scheme is simulated in MQTT payload encryption. In MQTT specification [2], payload encryption is not defined, thus, it is entirely application specific. This type of encryption provides end-to-end encryption for data over untrusted environment. For example, if an adversary has obtained an MQTT packet (stored on trusted broker, but may get compromised), then the adversary is not able to decrypt the data without having the key for decryption. The proposed KPABE is simulated under the payload encryption of MQTT, assuming the broker side mechanism is already present. Simulation is done using open source Java-based Eclipse Paho client [21] and HiveMQ public broker [22].

The performance analysis of the proposed scheme is done in terms of computation time required for all the operations of KPABE phases. For the sake of comparison, we have considered the following: (1) Standard elliptic curve secp160r1, i.e., 160-bit ECC (which provides security strength comparable to 1024-bit RSA). (2) Pairing-based ABE is considered equivalent to RSA, because both employ modular exponentiation. (3) All the schemes considered for comparison have same number of attributes for encryption. (4) Only arithmetic operations (ECC-based operations, pairing based operations, modular exponentiation, etc.) are considered in comparing computation overhead (excluding random number generation and Lagrange coefficient calculation). Table 11.2 depicts the comparison of computation overhead of the proposed KPABE with existing schemes. Also, the minimum time (in milliseconds) taken by each phase is presented for n = 30 and K = 10. For this, we have considered the work [13], where the standard time taken by various cryptographic operations are given and also depicted in Table 11.3.

Table 11.2: Comparison of computation overhead in Milliseconds (n: number of attributes in universal attribute set, k: number of attributes used for encryption).

Scheme	Setup	Key generation	Encryption	Decryption	Total time
SRSB [15]	$2T_R + 4T_{EX}$ $+ T_P$	$T_R(k+1) +$ $k(T_{MH} + 2T_{EX})$	$T_{PSM} + T_P + T_{EX}$ $+ n(2T_{EX} + T_{MH})$	$2kT_P + 3kT_{EX}$ $+ 2kT_{MH}$	
	$\approx 41.28\ ms$	$\approx 136.6\ ms$	$\approx 409.8\ ms$	$\approx 620.3\ ms$	$\approx 1207.98\ ms$
TZFK [16]	$(n+1)T_R +$ $nT_{EX} + T_P$	$k(T_{EX} + T_{PSM})$	$T_R + (k+1)T_{EX}$ $+ T_{PSM}$	$kT_{EX} + kT_P$	
	$\approx 179.34\ ms$	$\approx 116.9\ ms$	$\approx 64.79\ ms$	$\approx 253.4\ ms$	$\approx 614.43\ ms$
XZY [11]	$(n+1)T_R +$ $(n+1)T_{SM}$	$k(T_{SM} + T_{MI})$	$kT_{SM} + T_R$	$k(T_{MI} + T_{SM})$	
	$\approx 68.51\ ms$	$\approx 47.1\ ms$	$\approx 22.1\ ms$	$\approx 47.1\ ms$	$\approx 184.81\ ms$
DLL [23]	$(n+1)T_R +$ $(n+1)T_{SM}$	$k(T_M)$	$(3k+1)T_{SM}$ $+ T_R$	$(k+v)T_{SM}$	
	$\approx 68.51\ ms$	$\approx 2.35\ ms$	$\approx 68.51\ ms$	$\approx 44.20\ ms$	$\approx 183.57\ ms$
Proposed KPABE scheme	$(n+1)T_R +$ $(n+1)T_{SM}$	$k(T_A)$	$T_R + (k+2)T_{SM}$ $+ T_{MH}$	$k(T_{SM}) + T_{MH}$	
	$\approx 68.51\ ms$	$\approx 17.99\ ms$	$\approx 29.56\ ms$	$\approx 29.14\ ms$	$\approx 145.20\ ms$

Table 11.3: Execution time for cryptographic operations.

Operation	T_{EX}	T_P	T_{PSM}	T_{SM}	T_{MI}	T_{MH}	T_A	T_M
Time (ms)	5.31	20.04	6.38	2.21	2.5	3.04	1.7	≤ 0.22

From Table 11.1, it can be observed that the setup time taken by our scheme is equivalent to the schemes [11, 23], as these are ECC-based schemes. Next, the key generation phase of our scheme takes significantly less time as compared to all the other schemes because our scheme employs only scalar addition to generate the keys. Encryption phase of our scheme takes slightly more time as compared to [11] because of the extra overhead of hashing. Finally, the decryption phase of the proposed scheme takes comparatively less time than all the other mentioned schemes. Hence, it can be observed that the total time taken by the proposed KPABE as compared to the other related schemes is significantly less.

11.6 Conclusion

We have designed a lightweight ECC-based KPABE without bilinear pairing and exponential operations. The proposed security scheme is secured under ECDDH assumption using selective set model. The proposed KPABE is compared with the other ABE schemes. The result shows that the computation overhead of our KPABE is comparatively less than other existing ABE schemes. Further, we have simulated the proposed KPABE scheme in MQTT payload encryption feature.

In the future, we are planning to deploy the proposed secure MQTT protocol and evaluate the performance in real platform of IoT.

References

[1] Yassein, M. B., Shatnawi, M. Q. and Al-zoubi, D. 2016. Application layer protocols for the Internet of Things: A survey. IEEE International Conference on Engineering and MIS (ICEMIS), pp. 1–4, Agadir, Morocco.

[2] Banks, A. and Gupta, R. (eds.). 2014. MQTT Version 3.1.1 OASIS Standard, http://docs.oasis-open.org/mqtt/mqtt/v3.1.1/os/mqtt-v3.1.1-os.pdf, last accessed 2017/11/16.

[3] MQTT Security Fundamentals, https://www.hivemq.com/blog/introducing-the-mqtt-security-fundamentals, last accessed 2017/11/16.

[4] Sahai, A. and Waters, B. 2005. Fuzzy identity-based encryption. EUROCRYPT'05 Proceedings of the 24th Annual International Conference on Theory and Applications of Cryptographic Techniques, pp. 457–473, Aarhus, Denmark.

[5] Goyal, V., Pandey, O., Sahai, A. and Waters, B. 2006. Attribute-based encryption for fine-grained access control of encrypted data. CCS'06, Proceedings of the 13th ACM conference on Computer and communications security, pp. 89–98, Alexandria, Virginia, USA.

[6] Bethencourt, J., Sahai, A. and Waters, B. 2007. Ciphertext-policy attribute-based encryption. Proceedings of IEEE Symposium on Security and Privacy, SP'07, IEEE Computer Society, pp. 321–334, Washington, DC, USA.

[7] Ray, S., Biswas, G. P. and Dasgupta, M. 2016. Secure multi-purpose mobile-banking using elliptic curve cryptography. Springer: Wireless Personal Communications, 90(3): 1331–1354.

[8] Touati, L. and Challal, Y. 2016. Collaborative KP-ABE for cloud-based Internet of Things applications. IEEE International Conference on Communications (ICC), pp. 1–7, Kuala Lumpur, Malaysia.

[9] Ge, C., Susilo, W., Fang, L., Wang, J. and Shi, Y. 2018. A CCA-secure key-policy attribute-based proxy re-encryption in the adaptive corruption model for dropbox data sharing system. Designs, Codes and Cryptography, Springer, 86(11): 2587–2603.

[10] Li, J., Yu, Q., Zhang, Y. and Shen, J. 2019. Key-policy attribute-based encryption against continual auxiliary input leakage. Information Sciences, 470: 175–188.

[11] Yao, X., Chen, Z. and Tian, Y. 2015. A lightweight attribute-based encryption scheme for the Internet of Things, Elsevier: Future Generation Computer Systems, 49(C): 104–112.

[12] Hong, H. and Sun, Z. 2016. High efficient key-insulated attribute based encryption scheme without bilinear pairing operations. SpringerPlus: SpringerOpen Journal, pp. 1–12.

[13] Karati, A., Amin, R. and Biswas, G. P. 2016. Provably secure threshold-based abe scheme without bilinear map. Arabian Journal for Science and Engineering, Springer, 41(8): 3201–3213.

[14] Oualha, N. and Nguyen, K. T. 2016. Lightweight attribute-based encryption for the Internet of Things. IEEE 25th International Conference on Computer Communication and Networks (ICCCN), pp. 1–6, Waikoloa, HI, USA.

[15] Singh, M., Rajan, M. A., Shivraj, V. L. and Balamuralidhar, P. 2015. Secure MQTT for Internet of Things (IoT). IEEE Fifth International Conference on Communication Systems and Network Technologies, pp. 746–751, Gwalior, India.

[16] Thatmann, D., Zickau, S., Förster, A. and Küpper, A. 2015. Applying attribute-based encryption on publish subscribe messaging patterns for the Internet of Things. IEEE International Conference on Data Science and Data Intensive Systems, pp. 556–563, Sydney, NSW, Australia.

[17] Shin, S., Kobara, K., Chuang, C. and Huang, W. 2016. A security framework for MQTT. IEEE Conference on Communications and Network Security (CNS), pp. 432–436, Philadelphia, PA, USA.

[18] Upadhyay, Y., Borole, A. and Dileepan, D. 2016. MQTT based secured home automation system. IEEE Symposium on Colossal Data Analysis and Networking (CDAN), pp. 1–4, Indore, India.

[19] Mektoubi, A., Hassani, H. L., Belhadaoui, H., Rifi, M. and Zakari, A. 2016. New approach for securing communication over MQTT protocol A comparison between RSA and Elliptic Curve. IEEE Third International Conference on Systems of Collaboration (SysCo), pp. 1–6, Casablanca, Morocco.

[20] Katsikeas, S., Fysarakis, K., Miaoudakis, A., Bemten, A. V., Askoxylakis, I., Papaefstathiou, I. and Plemenos, A. 2017. Lightweight and secure industrial IoT communications via the MQ telemetry transport protocol. IEEE Symposium on Computers and Communications (ISCC), pp. 1193–1200, Heraklion, Greece.

[21] Eclipse paho Homepage, https://www.eclipse.org/paho/clients/java/, last accessed 2018/09/10.

[22] HIVEMQ Homepage, https://www.hivemq.com/try-out/, last accessed 2018/09/10.

[23] Ding, S., Li, C. and Li, H. 2018. A novel efficient pairing-free CP-ABE based on elliptic curve cryptography for IoT. IEEE Access: Security and Trusted Computing for Industrial Internet of Things, 6: 27336–27345.

12

An Improved Two Factor Authentication Scheme for TMIS Based on Dual Biometrics

Aashish Kumar,[1,]* *Preeti Chandrakar*[1] and *Rifaqat Ali*[2]

12.1 Introduction

With the advancement of IT and its impact on various areas, security has become a point of major concern. Every sector has a few components which are of utmost importance and whose failure can lead to bitter consequences. Security is one such crucial aspect. In this chapter, we have tried to introduce advancement in a system similar to Telecare Medical Information Systems (TMIS). The security in TMIS is important because it involves dealing with user's critical data and, thus, appropriate technological advancements should be considered so as to avoid any data breach. Nowadays, almost every service has made its presence felt on smartphones and elsewhere, and thus, it has become important to keep the scalability of protocols into consideration. In this chapter, the proposed protocol takes into account both of the above needs.

Previously, there have been numerous works in the domain of security and this segment has been agile in addressing the shortcomings and bringing in the improvements readily. The very first authentication scheme was brought before the world by Lamport (1981) [1] and used password for authentication. Following this, a series of remote authentication protocols with enhanced

[1] National Institute of Technology, Raipur, 492010, India.
  Email: pchandrakar.cs@nitrr.ac.in
[2] National Institute of Technology, Hamirpur, 177005, India.
  Email: rifaqatali27@gmail.com
* Corresponding author: aashish2096@gmail.com

security capability and added features were also introduced. Some of the work included the use of two or three-factors for authentication, like password, smart-cards and also biometrics.

Islam and Khan (2014) [4] developed a two-factor improved authentication scheme for TMIS which aimed to bring an improvement for Xu et al. (2014) [6]. The scheme addressed the failure in features such as mutual authentication and password updation. Chaudhry et al. (2015) [9] then proposed an improvement to Islam and Khan (2014) [4] which suffered a vulnerability to user and server impersonation attacks. It also made an improvement to the algorithm, thereby aiming to resist further attacks.

Liu et al. (2016) [13] brought an improvement to Zhang and Zhou's (2015) [15] scheme which failed to resist offline password guessing attacks and even failed to provide revocation of lost/stolen smart-card. Liu et al. (2016) [13] scheme dealt with addressing the drawbacks by improvement in updation of password phase and also lost smart-card revocation.

Wazid et al. (2016) [17] analyzed the security pitfalls of Amin and Biswas' (2015) [20] protocol and proposed a scheme that was capable of handling insider attack and offline password guessing attack, at the same time improving the computation costs involved. Then, Chaudhry et al. (2016) [22] also devised a three-factor encryption scheme for TMIS for multi-server architecture. Their scheme was an improvement to Amin et al.'s (2015) [24] which addressed the shortcomings as well as vulnerability to lost smart card and stolen verifier attack with improved computation.

Chandrakar and Om (2018) [25] proposed another improvement to Amin and Biswas' (2015) [20] protocol which claimed to be secure from most of the vulnerabilities but was found to suffer from attacks such as user impersonation attack, online and offline password guessing attacks, privileged insider attack, and known session key temporary information attack. The scheme was based on the three-factor remote authentication scheme. Both formal and informal analysis indicates that the designed protocol shields against the attacks with improved computation only. In the above-addressed scheme, a lot of dependency is laid over smart-card. This dependency hinders scaling to different platforms (laptops, smart phones, etc.), at the same time addressing the need to eliminate security loopholes. The upcoming works should be capable enough to address the security loopholes and at the same time improve the performance and capability.

It might be clear from the view projected till now that most of the schemes discussed earlier fail to meet the recent requirement, which comes in the name of making the solution portable, scalable at the same time keeping the seamless service secure. In an attempt to address the latest requirements, an approach is presented which would be efficient enough to handle most of the critical shortcomings. This chapter introduces a smart-cardless approach which brings in the existing features of security protocols with major improvements, such as forget password phase, damaged biometric phase handling and making the application of protocol scalable to any device, such as smartphones, laptops, etc. The chapter has been organized as follows: Section 12.2 explains about the proposed protocol, section 12.3 deals with the informal security analysis, section 12.4 leads to verification with BAN Logic, section 12.5 details about the performance comparison of the algorithm and finally, we arrive at a conclusion in section 12.6.

Table 12.1: Used notation.

Symbol	Definition
U_i	User
S	Server
ID	User ID
PW	User password
B_i	User biometric fingerprint
B_j	User biometric facial capture
x	Secret key
h(.)	Hash Function
T	Current timestamp

12.2 The Proposed Protocol

To address the issue of over dependence on the smart-card, the proposed algorithm comprises four phases, namely, Registration, Login, Authentication and Recovery, which are described further.

12.2.1 Registration Phase

For a new user to avail the services, an initial registration has to be done. This consists of forwarding the user credentials to the server and the server replying when the credentials match.

Step 1: The system takes in ID, PW from the user. Next are the biometric inputs, consisting of B_i (fingerprint) and B_j (facial capture). The inputs ID and PW are processed as $ID_i = h(ID)$ and $PW_i = h(PW)$. Taking the biometrics, fuzzy extractor computes $Gen(B_i) = (R_i, P_i)$ for fingerprint and $Gen(B_j) = (R_j, P_j)$ for image, respectively. These obtained values are extended to derive parameters such as $C_1 = h(R_i)$ and $C_2 = h(R_j)$. A parameter K equals $P_i \oplus h(ID_i \| PW_i)$. The user U then sends the message $\{ID_i, PW_i, C_1, C_2, K\}$ through the reliable channel to S.

Step 2: After receiving the message the server computes $G_i = h(ID_i \| PW_i)$, $P_{i'} = K \oplus G_i$, $R_n = R \oplus G_i$, $A_i = h(G_i \| P_{i'} \| R)$, $x = h(P_{i'} \| C_2)$, $Y_i = h(x).P$, $U_i = Y_i + h(C_1 \| R)*P$, $V_i = h(A_i \| C_1)$ and $W = h(V_i \| PW_i) \oplus x$.

Step 3: Two blocks being framed, namely, $B_1 = \{V_i, U_i, K, R_n, C_1, W\}$, $B_2 = \{C_2, P_j\}$, and encryption of the two blocks with the respective keys $ENC_{h(IDi)}(B_1)$ and $ENC_{(h(Pi' \| C1)}(B_2)$.

Step 4: Server maintaining a store of IDi received during registration, which is then kept in a database.

12.2.2 Log-in Phase

Post registration, when the user logs in to the system, the following steps are performed.

Step 1: The system takes user U_i input ID and PW and makes a request to the server for the B_1 where the request key is $h(ID)$. If a match of $h(ID)$ is successful, then the block is returned, otherwise the request is denied. On receiving, the block is then decrypted with the key $h(h(ID))$. The parameters obtained after decryption are $\{V_i, U_i, K, R_n, C_1, W\}$.

Step 2: Computations are performed $G_i^* = h(ID_i \| PW_i)$, $P_i^* = K \oplus G_i^*$, and biometric input B_i^* taken and B_i^* taken into deterministic reproduction procedure $Rep(B_i^*,P_i^*) = R_i^*$ and further computes $C_1^* = h(R_i^*)$. If $C_1 == C_1^*$ holds, then proceed to the next step, otherwise quit.

Step 3: After the successful match computation of $R^* = R_n \oplus G_i^*$, $A_i^* = h(G_i^* \| P_i^* \| R^*)$, $Y_i^* = U_i - h(C_1 \| R^*).P$, $V_i^* = h(A_i^* \| C_1^*)$. If $V_i^* != V_i$ exit, otherwise perform other computation in the next step.

Step 4: Next computation is Nonce N_i, $M_i = N_i.P$, $Y_i' = h(W \oplus h(V_i^* \| PW_i)).P$, $E_i = N_i .Y_i'$, $D_i = h((h(ID_i) \| Y_i' \| E_i)$, $Q_i = D_i \oplus h(C_1^*)$, $F = h(W \oplus h(V_i^* \| PW_i)) \oplus h(T_i \| h(ID_i))$, and send messages $\{D_i, M_i, T_i, F, Q_i\}$ to the server through the channel.

12.2.3 Authentication Phase

The phase where the mutual authentication is achieved among the U_i and Server S.

Step 1: If $T_j - T_i > \Delta T$ then reject, otherwise perform next computations $h(x') = F \oplus h(T_i \| h(ID_i))$, $E_i^* = h(x').M_i$, $Y_i' = h(x').P$, $D_i^* = h(h(ID_i) \| Y_i' \| E_i^*)$. If $D_i != D_i^*$ reject, otherwise compute Nonce N_j, $J_i = N_j.Y_i'.h(T_j')$, $I_k = (Q_i \oplus D_i^*)$, $H_i = N_j \oplus h(T_j' \| h(ID_i^*) \| I_k)$, $L_i = h(J_i \| I_k)$ and send the message $\{H_i, L_i, T_j'\}$ over the channel.

Step 2: Checking for the time interval of the message being received and, if $T_i' - T_j' > \Delta T$ then reject, otherwise computing $N_j^* = H_i \oplus h(T_j' \| h(ID_i')) \| h(C_1))$, $J_i^* = (N_j^*) * (Y_i^*) * h(T_i')$, $L_i^* = h(J_i^* \| h(C_1))$. Comparing if $L_i \mathrel{!=} L_i^*$ rejects, otherwise compute $SK = h(J_i^* \| h(C_1) \| h(ID_i) \| T_c)$ and $Z_i = h(SK \| Y_i^*)$ share the message $\{Z_i, T_c\}$.

Step 3: Again, checking for the time interval of receipt of message, if $T_j^* - T_c > \Delta T$ reject, otherwise compute $SK' = h(J_i^* \| Q_i \oplus D_i \| h(ID_i) \| T_c)$, $Z_i' = h(SK' \| Y_i^*)$. Comparing if $Z_i' \mathrel{!=} Z_i$ rejects, otherwise the session is encrypted and secure.

12.2.4 Recovery Phase

It is the special phase which offers flexibility regarding the password change, biometric update and forgot password phase handling.

12.2.4.1 Reset & Biometric Updates

Step 1: Perform the series of steps from Step 1–3 of the login phase and continue the further procedure as stated and, if the match is a success, then $DEC_{h(C1\|Pi*)}B_2$. Input facial biometric Rem $(B_j^*, P_j) = R_j^*$. If $h(R_j^*) \mathrel{!=} C_2$ then reject, otherwise proceed to next Step 2 for password change and Step 3 for biometric update.

Step 2: Take the new password PW_j. After input, compute $PW_{new} = h(PW_j)$, $G_{new} = h(ID_i \| PW_{new})$, $K_{new} = K \oplus G \oplus G_{new}$, $R_{n-new} = R_n \oplus h(ID_i \| PW_j) \oplus h(ID_i \| PW_{new})$, $P_i^* = K_{new} \oplus G_{new}$, $A_{i-new} = h(G_{new} \| P_i^* \| R)$, $V_{new} = h(A_{new} \| C_1)$. After that, replace $\{G, R_n, K, A_i, V_i\}$ with $\{G_{new}, R_{n-new}, K_{new}, A_{i-new}, V_{new}\}$ and changes are to be reflected in block B_1 at S.

Step 3: Almost similar to the above steps. An input of the new biometric is taken and successive computations follow. New Biometric B_k, $Gen(B_k) = R_{i-new}, P_{i-new}, h(R_{i-new}) = C_{1\,new}, K_{new} = K \oplus P_i \oplus P_{i\,new}, A_{i\,new} = h(G_i \| P_{i\,new} \| R)$, $U_{i\,new} = Y_i + h(C_{1\,new} \| R)*P, V_{i\,new} = h(A_{i\,new} \| C_{1\,new})$ and finally replace values $\{C_1, K, A_i, U_i, V_i\}$ with $\{C_{1\,new}, K_{new}, U_{i\,new}, V_{i\,new}\}$ in block B_1 and the changes are reflected in B_1 at S.

12.2.4.2 Forgot Password

Step 1: Take the input ID and perform the computations as $ID_i = h(ID)$ and find $DEC_{h(IDi)} \Rightarrow B_1$, $Rep(B_i^*, P_i) = R_i^{**}$. Compare if $(h(R_i^{**}) \mathrel{!=} C_1)$ rejects, otherwise move to the next step.

Step 2: Find $DEC_{h(Ci \| Pi)} \Rightarrow B_2$. Input facial biometric B_j^* and find Rem $(B_j^*, P_j) = R_j^*$. If $(h(R_j^*) \mathrel{!=} C_2)$ then reject, otherwise find $G_{new}, R_{new}, K_{new}, A_{i\,new}$ as per the definitions defined in the registration phase. Set $G = G_{new}$ and other terms subsequently and replace the same in block B_1 at S.

12.3 Informal Security Analysis

Proposition 3.1. Resistance to extract ID and Password PW from the block B_1 $\{V_i, U_i, K, R_n, C_1, W\}$ by the attacker even if the data of B_1 is revealed.

Proof: From the definition of the terms where $V_i = h(A_i \| C_1)$, $W = h(V_i \| PW_i)$ $\oplus x$, $U_i = Y_i + h(C_1 \| R) * P$, $x = h(P_i' \| C_2)$, $A_i = h(G_i \| P_i' \| R)$, $G_i = h(ID_i \| PW_i)$, $P_i' = K \oplus G_i$, $R_n = R \oplus G_i$ and $Y_i = h(x).P$.

1. From the parameter G_i, there isn't any scope for retrieval of ID and PW password because of the one-way hash function.
2. From the parameter A_i's definition, it is clear that there exists a dependency over G_i discussed earlier along with the added parameters as $\{R, P_i'\}$ would be necessary extract. R and P_i' both show dependency over G whose chances of getting disclosed are minimal.
3. For the parameter W, there exists a greater dependency among $\{V_i, PW_i, x\}$ which further makes extraction probability next to zero.
4. For the case when the request for block B_1 is made, $h(ID_i)$ is used as the key to make a match knowing the extraction of ID is possible as it is enclosed by dual hash functions such as $h(ID_i) = h(h(ID_i))$. So, our proposed scheme is secure against identity and password guessing attacks. Hence, ID and PW cannot be derived.

Proposition 3.2. Resistance to extract the secret key x from the block of data B_1 $\{V_i, U_i, K, R_n, C_1, W\}$ by the attacker even if the B_1 data is revealed.

Proof: Secret key involving parameters being $W = h(V_i \| PW_i) \oplus x$, $Y_i = h(x).P$, $x = h(P_i' \| C_2)$, $U_i = Y_i + h(C_1 \| R)*P$, $A_i = h(G_i \| P_i' \| R)$, $R_n = R \oplus G_i$. Assuming that the user knows the ID and PW and then tries to extract the secret key x.

1. Parameter U_i depending on the value Y_i and R. It can be seen that secret key cannot be extracted because of the elliptic curve discrete logarithm problem (ECDLP).
2. From the parameter W, there exists a dependency on V_i and PW_i. V_i requires additional parameters P_i' and A_i, which again is a random value, and guessing random numbers is a difficult task in itself.

From the above discussion, it can be concluded that x cannot be derived.

Proposition 3.3. Resistance to derive secret 'x' from message parameters $\{D_i, M_i, T_i, F, H_i, L_i, Q_i\}$.

Proof : The definition of respective message parameters are $W = h(V_i \| PW_i)$ $\oplus x$, $F = h(W \oplus h(V_i^* \| PW_i)) \oplus h(T_i \| h(ID_i))$, $H_i = N_j \oplus h(Tj' \| h(IDi^*) \| Ik)$, $L_i = h(J_i \| Ik)$. The intermediate terms which were used are defined as $I_k = (Q_i \oplus D_i)$, $J_i = N_j . Yi'.h(Tj')$ and $Y_i = h(x).P$ respectively.

1. Taking the message parameter F, from the above definitions we could derive h(x') as $F \oplus h(T_i \| h(ID_i))$. The expression shows a dependency on the value $h(ID_i)$ which as per Proposition 3.1 cannot be obtained. If by any chance the value of ID is revealed then computing the value of x from the hash function h(x') will be impossible due to one way hash function.

2. From the definition of message parameter L_i there exists a dependency on values of J_j and I_k. Parameter I_k could be derived from parameter Q_i and D_j as $I_k = (Q_i \oplus D_j)$. J_j shows dependency on N_j and Y_i where $N_i = H_i \oplus h(T_i' \| h(ID_i) \| I_k)$ and $Y_i = h(x').P$ so J_j turns out to be $H_i \oplus h(Ti' \| h(ID_i) \| I_k).h(x).P.h(Ti')$. So putting everything together we have L_i as $h((H_i \oplus h(Tj' \| h(ID_i) \| I_k).h(x').P.h(Tj')) \| I_k)$. The computation of the expression would not be possible due to ECDLP and the dependency on value $h(ID_i)$ which again as per Proposition 3.1 cannot be obtained.

So, resistance is obtained and the secret key is secure.

Proposition 3.4. Resistance to replay attack.

Proof: After capturing the message $\{D_i, M_i, T_i, F, Q_i\}$, availing the services and then retransmitting again after sometime, the server would know that the message is a duplicate because of the random nonce being used which is unique for each session. So, the protocol shields against the replay attack.

Proposition 3.5. Resistance to privilege insider attack.

Proof: It is possible for User U_i to use the same password to access multiple servers and the knowledge of the same could bring out the loss of confidential info. In our protocol there's no direct sharing of a user's password across the channel and even the parameters are secured by that of hash functions. Even if the direct password is known it won't be easy enough to log into the server as the biometrics are used as the next step for authentication.

So, the protocol secured against the privilege insider attack.

Proposition 3.6. Resistance to impersonation attack.

Proof: Trapping the communication message and transmitting with modifications trying to impersonate legal user or server. This being possible with that of extracting the parameters from block B_1. How the system prevents the attack is justified below.

1. For framing a new login message such as that of $\{D_i, M_i, T_i, F, H_i, L_i, Qi\}$ to impersonate a legal user and generate the following parameter $\{N_i, ID_i, x, C_1, PW_i\}$ is required to be present. It is known that the ID_i, PW_i, x is not derivable from proposition 3.1 and 3.2. Subsequently, N_i and C_1 couldn't be derived and so the chance for user impersonation is negative.

2. Coming to that server sending the message $\{H_i, L_i, T_j'\}$ which requires the received message $\{D_i, M_i, T_i, F, H_i, L_i, Qi\}$ along with that of ID_i required which is not possible to obtain as that of Proposition 3.1.

Proposition 3.7. Resistance from the known key attack.

Proof: Even if the session key (SK) is disclosed to that of the attacker it is not possible to derive or obtain the past or the future session keys using the current session key $SK = h(J_i^* \| h(C_1) \| h(ID_i) \| T_c)$, $J_i^* = (N_j^*) * (Y_i^*) * h(T_j')$. The session key being calculated using that of the random nonce Ni which unique for each session so future or the past session keys couldn't be computed. Also, deriving the additional parameters is a task that is difficult to perform, as described earlier.

Proposition 3.8. Resistance from Denial of Service attack.

Proof: Sometimes due to hardware's inefficiency, the legitimate user is denied access, leading to a DoS attack. This system uses fuzzy extractor functions to deal with the hardware drawback and ensure that no legal user is denied the access if the credentials are legitimate.

Proposition 3.9. Resistance from extract random nonce N_i and N_j extraction from the intercepted message across the channel.

Proof: From the message segment shared as login message $\{D_i, M_i, T_i, F, H_i, L_i, Qi\}$ from user and reply message $\{H_i, L_i, Tj'\}$ from the server end.

1. From the parameter $M_i = N_i * P$, the extraction of the random nonce cannot be retrieved because of ECDLP.

2. From the parameter $D_i = h((h(ID_i) \| Y_i^* \| E_i)$, where $E_i = N_i.Y_i^*$ and $Y_i^* = h(W \oplus h(V_i^* \| PW_i)).P$, the extraction cannot be a success as the parameter being protected by that of hash function and deriving the same seems a typical task.

3. From the parameter $H_i = N_j \oplus h(T_j' \| h(ID_i^*) \| (Q_i \oplus D_i^*))$ the prior requirement for extraction being $\{Q_i, D_i^*$ and $h(ID_i)\}$. These variables could be known by intercepting login messages but $h(ID_i)$ cannot be derived, as discussed in Proposition 3.1.

4. Again from $L_i = h(J_i \| E_i)$ the parameters being protected by hash function and where $E_i = N_i . Y_i^*$ and $J_i^* = N_j . Y_i^* . h(T_j')$ and these cannot be derived because of ECDLP.

Proposition 3.10. Efficient password and biometric update phase along with forget password handling phase.

Proof:

1. For the password and biometric update phase, there exists three stage checks for making progress. First, after the legitimate ID and PW are entered, there is a biometric check for C_1 match followed by match of $V_i = h(A_i \| C_1)$. Failure of any would terminate the session. The final

check comes in the form of B_j facial biometric match. If successful, new parameters are accepted and replaced at proper positions.

2. For the forget password case there exists two phases of check, both involving biometric check and, on success, new parameters are accepted and replaced at proper positions. The system is efficient in dealing with password, biometric update and forgot password phase.

12.4 Authentication Proof Based on BAN Logic

In this section, we verify the given protocol by means of BAN logic [27] which is a system based out of belief with logic. It is a technique that helps in determining if the information shared across the channel is reliable and at the same time shielded from threats. If the verification is made correctly, then the scheme would be successful in keeping the system secure. The following steps are performed to prove our scheme.

Step 1: The goals for proving the scheme as per BAN Logic's procedure being—

Goal 1: $U_i \mid\equiv (U_i \overset{SK}{\leftrightarrow} S)$
Goal 2: $U_i \mid\equiv S \mid\equiv (U_i \overset{SK}{\leftrightarrow} S)$
Goal 3: $S \mid\equiv (S \overset{SK}{\leftrightarrow} U_i)$
Goal 4: $S \mid\equiv U_i \mid\equiv (S \overset{SK}{\leftrightarrow} U_i)$

Step 2: The protocol being transformed in idealized form

Message 1: $U_i \rightarrow S : M_i, F, Q_i, D_i : < Y_i, E_i > h(ID_i)$
Message 2: $S \rightarrow U_i : H_i, L_i : < I_k > J_i$

Step 3: Few assumptions about the initial state to proceed with the analysis with BAN Logic

R1: $Ui \mid\equiv \#\{Y_i,E_i\}$
R2: $S \mid\equiv \#\{Y_i,E_i\}$
R3: $S \mid\equiv (S \overset{h(IDi)}{\leftrightarrow} U_i)$
R4: $Ui \mid\equiv (U_i \overset{Ji}{\leftrightarrow} S)$
R5: $S \mid\equiv Ui \Rightarrow \{Y_i,E_i\}$
R6: $Ui \mid\equiv S \Rightarrow \{I_k\}$

Step 4:

Message 1, leads to following info being known
D1: $S \lhd M_i, F, Q_i, D_i : < Y_i, E_i > h(ID_i)$
With D1, R3, and the message-meaning rule, it derives
D2: $S\mid \equiv U_i\mid \sim \{E_i,Y_i\}$
From D2, R2, and the nonce-verification rule, we derive
D3: $S\mid \equiv U_i\mid \equiv \{E_i,Y_i\}$

With jurisdiction rule, D3, and R5, it can be concluded
D4: $S| \equiv \{Y_i, E_i\}$
Now, from D3, R2, and the session key rule it obtains
D5: $S| \equiv (S_i{}^{SK} \leftrightarrow U_i)$ **Goal 3**
Using the nonce-verification rule, D5, and R2, we conclude
D6: $S| \equiv U_i| \equiv (S{}^{SK} \leftrightarrow U_i)$ **Goal 4**
From Message 2, the following info is known
D7: $U_i \lhd H_i, L_i: <I_k> J_i$
From D7, R4, and the message-meaning rule, we derive
D8: $U_i| \equiv S| \sim I_k$
Again, with nonce-verification rule, D8 and R1, we derive
D9: $U_i| \equiv S| \equiv I_k$
With jurisdiction-rule, R6 and D9, we derive
D10: $U_i| \equiv I_k$
Again, the session-key rule and from D9, R1, we could obtain
D11: $U_i| \equiv (U_i{}^{SK} \leftrightarrow S)$ **Goal 1**
Also from the nonce-verification-rule and D11, R1 we conclude that
D12: $U_i| \equiv S| \equiv (U_i{}^{SK} \leftrightarrow S)$ **Goal 2**

12.5 Performance Comparison

The performance measure of any scheme which performs the authentication
is done by comparison of computation cost, communication and storage cost,
which are the most important factors to consider. For implementation of
any service, security from attacks is an essential entity to consider. We take
into consideration the five protocols for comparison and use the short hands
mentioned in Table 12.2.

In Table 12.3, the analysis of the protocol's cost and the comparison with
the few other protocols is made. For knowledge about memory requirements
for processing and storage, we assume the length of ID, PW, hash function to
be of 160 bits each and elliptic curve point requires 320 bits and encryption
or decryption operations deliver 512 bits long output. In proposed protocol B_1
$\{V_i, U_i, K, R_n, C_1, W\} = \{160 + 320 + 160 + 160 + 160 + 160 = 1120$ bits$\}$ and

Table 12.2: Protocol short hands.

Protocol	Abbreviation
Chaudhry et al. [22]	CH
Islam and Khan [4]	IK
Wazid et al. [17]	WZ
Liu et al. [13]	LU
Chaudhry et al. [9]	CD

Table 12.3: Performance comparison of the proposed protocol with other protocols.

Performance Parameter	CH	IK	WZ	LU	CD	Proposed
Storage (bits)	1184	960	1152	1312	1440	1440
Communication (bits)	1984	1120	1760	1984	1280	1280
Computation Time	$23T_h +$ $8T_s + 7T_{pm}$	$10T_h +$ $3T_m$	$28T_h + 6T_{pm}$ $+ 4T_s + 4T_{pa}$ $+ 2T_{fe}$	$6T_{pm} +$ $4T_s +$ $11T_h$	$12T_h +$ $6T_{pm}$	$35T_h +$ $11T_{pm} +$ $2T_s + 2T_{fe}$
Time (seconds)	0.52265	0.1942	0.5969	0.41875	0.63675	0.989725

B_2 {C2, P_j} = {160 + 160 = 320 bits}, total storage requirement being (1120 + 320) = 1440 bits and consecutively schemes such as CH, IK, WZ, LU and CD take up {1184, 960, 1152, 1312, 1440 bits}, respectively, for storage.

On the communication front, it comes out to be M_1 {D_i, M_i, T_i, F, Q_i} = 800 bits, M_2 {H_i, L_i} = 320 bits, M_3 {SK} = 160 bits, which collectively sums out to be 1280 bits in total. The other schemes, such as CH, IK, WZ, LU and CD, require about {1984, 1120, 1760, 1984, 1280, 1280 bits}, respectively, for communication.

The calculation for the computation cost and estimated time is presented here. In the table above, T_h, T_s, T_{pm} and T_{fe} represent hash function, symmetric key encryption, point multiplication and fuzzy extractor operation time, respectively, and the corresponding values are (0.0005, 0.0087, 0.063075, 0.063075 sec). Our scheme requires $12T_h + 2T_{pm} + 2T_s$ for registration and $24T_h + 10T_{pm} + 1T_s$ for login and authentication, so time computation adds up to 35* 0.0005 + 12 * 0.063075 + 3*0.0087 + 3*0.0087 = 0.989725 sec and

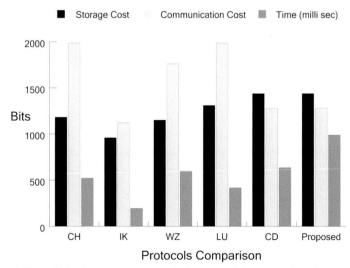

Figure 12.1: Storage cost, communication cost and time comparison chart.

for the similar algorithm is calculated in the similar manner. The calculated running time for schemes such as CH, IK, WZ, LU, CD are {0.52265, 0.1942, 0.5969, 0.41875, 0.63675 seconds}, respectively.

In Table 12.4, security property comparison of the previously proposed protocol is made with our proposed protocol. It is found that the proposed scheme provides security features, such as mutual authentication, user anonymity and perfect forward secrecy, and provides security against replay attack, impersonation attack, privilege insider attack, offline password guessing attack, as well as having the added features of no smart-card dependency, biometric update and forget password phase, which are missing from most of the protocols proposed earlier.

Table 12.4: Protocols comparison with other protocols based on functionality and features.

Security Property/feature	CH	IK	WZ	LU	CD	Proposed
Mutual Authentication	Yes	Yes	Yes	Yes	Yes	Yes
User/Patient anonymity	Yes	Yes	Yes	Yes	Yes	Yes
Perfect forward secrecy	Yes	Yes	Yes	Yes	Yes	Yes
Replay Attack	Yes	Yes	Yes	Yes	Yes	Yes
Impersonation Attack	Yes	No	Yes	Yes	Yes	Yes
Privilege Insider Attack	Yes	Yes	Yes	Yes	Yes	Yes
Offline Password Guessing	Yes	Yes	Yes	Yes	Yes	Yes
Denial of Service	No	-	Yes	No	-	Yes
Smart-card dependency	Yes	Yes	Yes	Yes	Yes	No
Biometric Update phase	No	-	Yes	Yes	-	Yes
Forgot Password phase	No	No	No	No	No	Yes

12.6 Conclusion

In this chapter, a two-factor dual biometric-based protocol which provides mutual authentication using ECC is proposed. The scheme is verified from BAN Logic, at the same time, the security analysis ensures the security properties are enabled with utmost priority. In the analysis part, the timing requirement and computational operations performed appear to be on the higher side, but with this compromise our system provides better functionality and platform flexibility in comparison with existing schemes. In future, the work could be extended on enhancement of the algorithm and try optimizing the same with reduced computation and time incurred to achieve the same.

References

[1] Lamport, L. 1981. Password authentication with insecure communication. Communications of the ACM, 24(11): 770–772.

[2] Chandrakar, P. and Om, H. 2017. A secure and robust anonymous three-factor remote user authentication scheme for multi-server environment using ECC. Computer Communications, 110: 26–34.

[3] Ali, R., Pal, A. K., Kumari, S., Karuppiah, M. and Conti, M. 2018. A secure user authentication and key-agreement scheme using wireless sensor networks for agriculture monitoring. Future Generation Computer Systems, 84: 200–215.

[4] Islam, S. H. and Khan, M. K. 2014. Cryptanalysis and improvement of authentication and key agreement protocols for telecare medicine information systems. Journal of Medical Systems, 38(10): 135.

[5] Ali, R. and Pal, A. K. 2018. An efficient three factor based authentication scheme in multi server environment using ECC. International Journal of Communication Systems, 31(4): e3484.

[6] Xu, X., Jin, Z. P., Zhang, H. and Zhu, P. 2014. A dynamic ID-based authentication scheme based on ECC for telecare medicine information systems. In Applied Mechanics and Materials. Trans Tech Publications Ltd. 457: 861–866

[7] Ali, R. and Pal, A. K. 2017. A secure and robust three-factor based authentication scheme using RSA cryptosystem. International Journal of Business Data Communications and Networking (IJBDCN), 13(1): 74–84.

[8] Chandrakar, P. 2019. A secure remote user authentication protocol for healthcare monitoring using wireless medical sensor networks. International Journal of Ambient Computing and Intelligence (IJACI), 10(1): 96–116.

[9] Heydari, M., Sadough, S. M. S., Chaudhry, S. A., Farash, M. S. and Aref, M. R. 2015. An improved authentication scheme for electronic payment systems in global mobility networks. Information Technology and Control, 44(4): 387–403.

[10] Chandrakar, P. and Om, H. 2018. An extended ECC based anonymity preserving 3 factor remote authentication scheme usable in TMIS. International Journal of Communication Systems, 31(8): e3540.

[11] Islam, S. H. and Khan, M. K. 2014. Cryptanalysis and improvement of authentication and key agreement protocols for telecare medicine information systems. Journal of Medical Systems, 38(10): 135.

[12] Chandrakar, P. and Om, H. 2017. Cryptanalysis and improvement of a biometric based remote user authentication protocol usable in a multi server environment. Transactions on Emerging Telecommunications Technologies, 28(12): e3200.

[13] Liu, W., Xie, Q., Wang, S. and Hu, B. 2016. An improved authenticated key agreement protocol for telecare medicine information system. Springer Plus, 5(1): 555.

[14] Chandrakar, P. 2019. A secure remote user authentication protocol for healthcare monitoring using wireless medical sensor networks. International Journal of Ambient Computing and Intelligence (IJACI), 10(1): 96–116.

[15] Zhang, L. and Zhu, S. 2015. Robust ECC-based authenticated key agreement scheme with privacy protection for telecare medicine information systems. Journal of Medical Systems, 39(5): 49.

[16] Chandrakar, P. and Om, H. 2018. An efficient two-factor remote user authentication and session key agreement scheme using rabin cryptosystem. Arabian Journal for Science and Engineering, 43(2): 661–673.

[17] Wazid, M., Das, A. K., Kumari, S., Li, X. and Wu, F. 2016. Design of an efficient and provably secure anonymity preserving three factor user authentication and key agreement scheme for TMIS. Security and Communication Networks, 9(13): 1983–2001.

[18] Chandrakar, P. and Om, H. 2017. Cryptanalysis and security enhancement of three-factor remote user authentication scheme for multi-server environment. International Journal of Business Data Communications and Networking (IJB- DCN), 13(1): 85–101.

[19] Ali, R. and Pal, A. K. 2017. Three-factor-based confidentiality-preserving remote user authentication scheme in multi-server environment. Arabian Journal for Science and Engineering, 42(8): 3655–3672.

[20] Amin, R. and Biswas, G. P. 2015. A novel user authentication and key agreement protocol for accessing multi-medical server usable in TMIS. Journal of Medical Systems, 39(3): 33.

[21] Chandrakar, P. and Om, H. 2017. Cryptanalysis and extended three-factor remote user authentication scheme in multi-server environment. Arabian Journal for Science and Engineering, 42(2): 765–786.

[22] Chaudhry, S. A., Khan, M. T., Khan, M. K. and Shon, T. 2016. A multi server biometric authentication scheme for TMIS using elliptic curve cryptography. Journal of Medical Systems, 40(11): 230.

[23] Chandrakar, P. and Om, H. 2015. RSA based two-factor remote user authentication scheme with user anonymity. Procedia Computer Science, 70: 318–324.

[24] Amin, R., Islam, S. H., Biswas, G. P., Khan, M. K. and Kumar, N. 2015. An efficient and practical smart card based anonymity preserving user authentication scheme for TMIS using elliptic curve cryptography. Journal of Medical Systems, 39(11): 180.

[25] Chandrakar, P. and Om, H. 2018. An extended ECC based anonymity preserving 3 factor remote authentication scheme usable in TMIS. International Journal of Communication Systems, 31(8): e3540.

[26] Chandrakar, P. and Om, H. (2015, November). A secure two-factor mutual authentication and session key agreement protocol using Elliptic curve cryptography. In 2015 IEEE International Conference on Computer Graphics, Vision and Information Security (CGVIS) (pp. 175–180). IEEE.

[27] Burrows, M., Abadi, M. and Needham, R. 1990. A logic of authentication. ACM Trans Comput Syst., 8(1): 18–36.

13

Identifying and Mitigating Against XSS Attacks in Web Applications

Shashidhara R[1,*] and *R Madhusudhan*[2]

13.1 Introduction

XSS is a dominant security issue faced by application developers of the web. It's one of the topmost vulnerabilities that an adversary exploits to duplicate dangerous content to a victim's website. Cross-Site Scripting is a malevolent attack that has increased rapidly in prominence since the exponential growth of social networks like Twitter, Facebook, Instagram, etc. These applications are enabling the web users to transfer a malicious information into the web [5]. The impact of malicious vector injection into web application is often difficult to quantify because end users may unintentionally execute malicious strings when they follow untrusted links in web pages written by an adversary, through instant messages and any other web-based applications capable of interpreting JavaScript code. Current approaches of defending against XSS attacks mainly hinges on effective detection and prevention of real time XSS vulnerabilities from the web applications.

13.1.1 Motivations and Contributions

Cross-site scripting attacks occur almost daily. Recently, the famous social networking sites like Twitter, Facebook and Google have fallen victim to

[1] School of Engineering and Applied Sciences, Bennett University Greater Noida, Uttar Pradesh India.
[2] Department of Mathematical and Computational Science, National Institute of Technology Karnataka, Surathkal, India.
 Email: madurk96@gmail.com
* Corresponding author: eemailshashi@gmail.com

these attacks [5]. Furthermore, cross-site scripting deficiencies were found in the universal search engine of UK parliament website in 2014, Yahoo website in 2013, PayPal website in 2012, Hotmail website in 2011, Justin.tv website in 2009, Orkut website in 2008, and many more [2].

The contributions to this article include:

- Our center of interest on exploiting and testing various XSS vulnerabilities by inserting real-world malevolent XSS vectors into vulnerable web applications.
- This article presents a detailed survey on the discovery, identification and mitigation of XSS attacks in web applications.
- To mitigate XSS vulnerability in the web applications, a novel technique comprising of dynamic analysis approaches which successfully identifies the malicious XSS vectors has been presented.
- In addition, we have focused on initiating a client side cross-site scripting attack discovery and mitigation technique, known as Secure XSS layer, on browser JavaScript engine using spider monkey to filter malicious scripts.
- We have estimated the accuracy and performance of the proposed framework using sensitivity and F-measure, which is very high and acceptable in contrast to the existing client side XSS filters.

The paper is organized as follows: Section 13.2 covers related work, including XSS detection and prevention mechanisms. Section 13.3 defines the mechanism to identify XSS vulnerabilities. Section 13.4 describes the proposed secure XSS layer to eliminate XSS attacks in the web. Section 13.5 demonstrates the implementation details and performance analysis of the proposed approach. Section 13.6 concludes the article.

13.2 Related Work

For several years, there has been a lot of research going on at industries and institutes to identify and defend against XSS attacks. However, research is still on to discover an effective solution to mitigate XSS vulnerabilities in web applications.

In 2006, Kirda et al. [10] proposed a tool called Noxes, a client mechanism for defending against XSS vulnerabilities. This tool introduces a firewall to defend the users from scripting attacks. Basically, it receives the HTTP requests, then decides whether script will be allowed or blocked based on the rules introduced by the firewall.

In addition, Saxena et al. [15] proposed input validation vulnerabilities on the web applications, which commonly occur due to the usage of untrusted data which is not validated. The work introduced by Saxena et al. [15] is unable to handle the complexity of sanitization errors.

A general approach to detecting XSS vulnerability from web applications can be found in 2012 [4]. This approach exploits fault injection and is based on a dynamic analysis of web applications in order to discover the presence of XSS vulnerabilities. Later, Shahriar et al. [16] come up with an approach to identify XSS vulnerabilities using static analysis technique. Moreover, their technique produces false positive and false negative results.

Rattipong and Bunyatnoparat [14] proposed a technique is called rewriting of cookies. The approach changes the cookie values in order to detect XSS attacks.

In 2014, Toma and Islam [19] proposed a dynamic analysis approach, in order to detect stored XSS vulnerabilities on server side. However, this approach only deals with stored XSS attacks. In 2015, Gupta and Gupta [5] described cross-site scripting exploitation, discovery and prevention. In addition, they also presented 11 major XSS attack incidents from previous years. Their analysis and state-of-the-art techniques led to the conclusion that cross-site scripting is very dangerous for web-based applications.

Therefore, this vulnerability needs to be mitigated. In addition, Gupta et al. [6] describe a proxy-based approach to prevent XSS attacks, which intercepts the http queries in input to a server page. In this way, it is possible to simulate XSS attacks in order to verify if a web page is vulnerable or not. This approach requires knowledge of all potentially vulnerable of the application. Therefore, this approach has been used only for web applications implemented with a specific language.

In 2016, Nagapal et al. [13] presented a security engine to counter XSS attacks in PHP-based applications. The proposed technique protects against non-persistent cross-site scripting attacks for composite applications, which are not mitigated by previous mechanisms.

Later, Mitropoulos et al. [12] proposed an approach to counter XSS attacks based on fingerprints. A demerit of this mechanism is that when an identifier element is modified, a new valid script generation step is required, which greatly increases the complexity.

In 2017, the authors in [11] presented methods and tools used to remove XSS vulnerabilities from PHP web applications. Very recently, Gupta et al. [7] proposed a context-aware sanitization and DOM tree generator framework to use against DOM-based attacks in cloud environments.

13.2.1 Research Gaps

The existing XSS defensive approaches have the following limitations:

1. Most of the existing XSS defensive approaches are unable to provide safe input handling and encoding mechanisms at client as well as server-side of web-based applications.

2. An automated process is essential to differentiate between JavaScript and the malicious script.

3. There is no proper defensive solution that can detect and prevent all XSS attacks, such as reflected, stored and encoding attacks.

4. A Secure XSS defensive algorithm must possess a list of malicious scripts and domains in order to avoid the rate of false positive and negatives.

5. In existing approaches, effective policy checks are not implemented to increase XSS detection speed and mitigation process.

In order to find XSS attacks in the web environments, a novel idea that consists of static-dynamic analysis mechanisms which successfully identify the malicious XSS vectors has been presented. We use a training-based generic XSS detector to filter the malicious scripts on browser JavaScript engine, which successfully deals with all static, dynamic and external scripts. After a training phase, the automated secure XSS layer is responsible for tracking all incoming and outgoing Scripts using the white-list and block-list scripts stored in the generic XSS detector. If an unknown script is found, the generic XSS detector raises the alarm to signal an XSS attack.

The proposed approach is capable to defend against all types of XSS attack with low false positive rate.

13.3 Identifying XSS Vulnerabilities

In this section, we are presenting an approach to mitigate XSS vulnerabilities in web-based environments using static and dynamic analysis.

Static analysis is the process of identifying whether a given web page is vulnerable to cross-site scripting [3]. In addition, dynamic analysis approach is able to verify whether a given web application with vulnerable page assessed by static analysis approach is actually vulnerable [3].

13.3.1 Assessing the Vulnerability of a Web Page

To identify XSS vulnerability of a web page, we make use of the Control-Flow Graph (CFG) suggested by Lucca et al. [3]. In CFG, a node will be labeled as Input (v), where v is the input variable. Input nodes are commonly interconnected with statements performing reading of the value of a query string, cookie, input of the user information from web forms, or reading any data from a file. In a similar manner, a node will be marked as Output (O). In a web application, output nodes are those incorporated with statements writing a cookie, a file or a database field.

Figure 13.1 represents CFG Graph for describing binary encoding attack for stealing cookie information.

A given web page is vulnerable if there exists is a variable v, two input nodes (v) and output nodes (v), in such a way that all paths in a CFG are leaving input (v) reach the output (v), being definition-clear path [3].

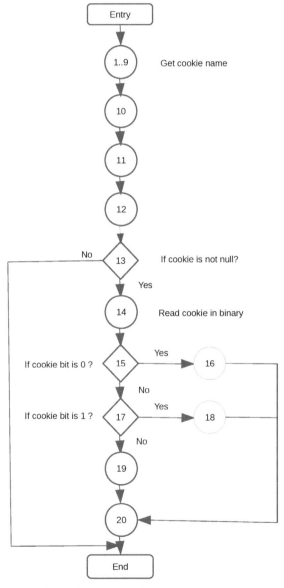

Figure 13.1: CFG for binary encoding attack.

A web page containing input information that doesn't have an effect on output is known as an invulnerable web page, with respect to a given input.

Consider a web page P associated with a variable v, two CFG nodes are I (input node) and O (output node). Let us initiate the subsequent predicates to define a set of rules for identifying the vulnerabilities of a given web page P:

1. A (v): There exists a pathway between Input (I) and Output (O) nodes of the control flow graph.

2. B (v): Output node post-dominates Input node (O post-dominance I, if and only if all paths from I to an exit block must pass through O).

3. C (v): Each path between Input node (I) and Output node (O) is a def-clear path.

The above rules are used to distinguish the vulnerability of a web page by the subsequent conditions. A vulnerable web page is labelled as V and the web page which is not vulnerable is labelled as NV.

1. Vulnerable (V) ∃ $v \in P$: $B(v)$ *AND* $C(v)$ => P is exposed vulnerability with respect to a given variable v => P.

2. Not Vulnerable (NV) ∃ $v \in P$: $NOT(A(v))$ => P is not exposed to vulnerability with respect to a given variable v of web page P.

Algorithm 1: Identifying Vulnerability of Web Application

1: **for** each vulnerable page P of the Web Application do
2: **for** each input field I of page P causing vulnerability do
3: Define a set S of XSS attack strings
4: **for** each s ∈ S do
5: **EXECUTE** server page P with
6: input field I = s
7: Check for the attack consequences
8: **if** ∃ v P : NOT (A(v)) then
9: P is not vulnerable with respect to a variable v
10: **else**
11: P is vulnerable with respect to v
12: **end if**
13: **for** each test-case T from test-suite do
14: **EXECUTE** test-case T
15: **end for**
16: **end for**
17: **end for**
18: **end for**

13.3.2 Assessing a Web Application Vulnerability

Server pages may not transfer output information directly to the browser, rather to another server page or to a storage device like a database [3]. In this scenario, if any external components receiving the malicious string from output of the server page are validated, web applications are accordingly protected from attacks. With this regard, the vulnerabilities of a given web page do not imply vulnerability of the web application.

Consider that the stored XSS attack of the Guest book application depends on Guest.php, which is a server page and cache the user entered information into a database. On vulnerability of a server page that is Guestbook.php, transfer the user information retrieved from database to the user. If database has a sanitization technique, web applications may not be vulnerable to the stored XSS attacks. Therefore, identifying vulnerabilities of a web application depends not only on the server pages, but also the external software components that are connected to the server pages which are to be considered.

The algorithm 1 defines the proposed web application testing strategy to identify the XSS vulnerabilities in web-based environments. Stored XSS attacks are more difficult to detect, since the attack vectors have to insert malevolent content that will not be directly transferred to the user but will be cached in a device permanently. After an attack has been accomplished, all web applications that interpret the information from a persistent device should be exercised in order to detect attack consequences.

13.4 Mitigating XSS Attacks

Here, we demonstrate the proposed mechanism to defend against XSS attacks in web-based environments.

13.4.1 The Proposed Approach to Mitigate XSS Attacks

The proposed approach involves a secure XSS interception layer placed in the client's browser. The proposed layer is responsible for discovering all malicious strings that reach a client browser from all paths. Later, the secure XSS layer compares the received scripts with a list of valid scripts that are already created by an administrator for the site being accessed, the received strings not in browser list are discarded from execution and protecting the system. The proposed layer generic XSS detector uses an identifier while comparing the strings. The identifiers represent the specific elements and context of script execution in the browser.

To defend against XSS attacks, the proposed approach makes use of training phase, where every benevolent script is promoted by an identifier [12].

After a training phase, the automated secure XSS layer is responsible for tracking all incoming and outgoing scripts using the white-list and block-list of scripts stored in the generic XSS detector. If an uncovered string is found, the generic XSS detector raises the XSS attack alarm.

Algorithm 2: Secure XSS Layer Algorithm

1: **for** each script reaches the browser do
2: Generate corresponding Script Identifiers
3: **if** Training Phase then
4: Register the Script identifiers
5: **else**
6: Validate the Script identifiers
7: **end if**
8: **if** Are the Identifiers valid then
9: **EXECUTE** the script
10: **else**
11: Prevent script execution
12: Raise an alarm to web admin to notify the attack
13: **end if**
14: **end for**

To mitigate the XSS attacks, we propose a secure XSS layer algorithm, which consists of the following steps:

1. An identifier generation is the first phase of secure XSS layer algorithm. In this phase, the proposed layer makes use of training approach that contains all trusted static, dynamic and external JavaScript. Accordingly, all benign scripts are mapped into identifiers, also known as script identifiers.

2. All generated script identifiers are stored in the backup table.

3. During script execution phase, the secure XSS layer verifies whether the corresponding script identifier is present in the backup table.

4. If the script exists in the table, then it will be treated as benign script. In this phase, it also checks whether the script parameters refer to an unexpected URL.

5. If no similar script identifier is originating and any unauthorized URL identifier is found, then a user browser is under attack. In this scenario, the proposed layer can stop any further execution and forwards an alarm to the user to notify them of an XSS attack.

13.5 Implementation and Performance Analysis

This section demonstrates the implementation details and performance analysis of the secure web application approach.

13.5.1 Implementation

The proposed approach is implemented as an integrated module in the browser engine. Further, we instrumented that API methods are entry points to the JavaScript engine, which either takes input script as a string or executes the input statement that was already complied by the JavaScript engine. The processing of script and document location is accomplished by the parser. The web browser makes use of line number and codebases, then passes the script location within a document to API methods as the parameter. We can differentiate between external and internal scripts by examining the location of a script. To accumulate valid script identifiers, we designed an identifier generation module.

13.5.2 Experimental Evaluation

In order to analyze the effectiveness of our algorithm, we have taken a few vulnerable web-based applications into account. The experiment involves the installation of vulnerable web applications and attacking for real world cross-site scripting threats.

Initially, we applied the identifier generation module to the downloaded vulnerable application. Then, we changed to execution phase and performed several XSS attacks by vulnerability type of the applications. Deficiencies like improper verification of HTTP requests and absence of sanitization force us to perform cookie stealing and redirect attacks. Especially, the phpMyFAQ vulnerable application is unable to sanitize URLs, paving the way to insert malicious JavaScript to steal cookies of the mobile browser.

In addition, we selected a few vulnerable applications, like eBay.com and nydailynews.com, from the XSSed.com archive. Initially, we applied the proposed secure layer in the context of web environment to search for XSS attacks. Further, we attempted various attack vectors to verify stored and other XSS threats that use an eval function. The proposed layer successfully detected and blocked all of the vulnerabilities.

13.5.3 Performance Analysis using F-Measure

F-Measure is a mean of Sensitivity and Specificity. XSS detection performance is measured by the subsequent metrics [12]:

- **Sensitivity:** The possibility that the cross-site scripting attacks have been seized.
- **Specificity:** Possibility that the normal interaction will not be identified.

- **True-Positives (TP):** A cross-site scripting attack that raises an alarm to notify the web administrator.
- **True-Negatives (TN):** This is an event but not a cross-site scripting attack, which does not raise an alarm.
- **False-Positives (FP):** This is an event but not a cross-site scripting attack, which raises an alarm.
- **False-Negatives (FN):** It's an event that is a cross-site scripting attack but doesn't raise an alarm.

Table 13.1 outlines the detail performance analysis of the proposed XSS approach on various web-based environments. We analyzed results of the proposed web application approach on various parameters (number of malicious strings inserted, True Positives, Negatives, False Positives, Negatives). We can notice that the Highest number of TPs are encountered in Humhub, Jcart and phpMyFAQ. Furthermore, in all web applications the observed rate of false negatives and positives are acceptable. We can observe from Table 1 that the performance of the proposed approach is nearly 95% as the maximum rate of F Measure is 0.95.

Furthermore, we have collected various XSS attack strings from XSS cheat sheet and tested on injection points of Damm Vulnerable Web Application. By identifying entry points of the web application like document.write (), we are able to find scripts that reach the JavaScript engine. In the proposed approach, the unwanted scripts are eliminated from the identifiers list in order to reduce computation overhead.

In addition, Table 13.2 summarizes the functionality comparison of the proposed approach with related works. The proposed mechanism is able to prevent all major XSS attack vectors from web-based environments. Further, the proposed XSS defensive mechanism will be useful for mitigation of various attacks from web applications, cloud-based and mobile cloud-based environments.

Table 13.1: Computation of F measure.

Application	No. of Malicious String Injected	True Positive	False Positive	True Negative	False Negative	Sensitivity (SE)	F: Measure
WordPress	120	107	4	6	3	0.972	0.916
Joomla	150	105	5	7	3	0.972	0.933
Jcart	120	111	3	4	2	0.982	0.958
phpMyFAQ	120	108	4	6	2	0.981	0.955
Humhub	120	114	2	3	1	0.991	0.975

Table 13.2: Functionality comparison.

Schemes	Implementation Location	Stored XSS attack detection	Reflected XSS attack detection	DOM-based XSS attack detection	Other Sophisticated attacks
Kirda et al. [10]	Client	√	√	×	×
Bisht et al. [1]	Client	√	√	×	×
Zhang et al. [22]	Client	×	√	√	×
Johns et al. [9]	Server or proxy	×	√	×	√
Shar and Tan [16]	Server or proxy	√	√	×	√
Toma and Islam [19]	Server	√	×	×	×
Hydara et al. [8]	Client	√	√	×	√
Wurzinger et al. [21]	Server	√	√	√	×
Louw et al. [18]	Server	√	√	×	×
Gunday et al. [20]	Server	√	√	×	×
Proposed scheme	Client	√	√	√	√

13.6 Conclusion

In order to identify and mitigate XSS attack vectors in web-based environments, a novel approach which successfully identifies and prevents XSS attack strings from injection points has been presented. In the proposed approach, we designed the secure XSS framework in order to deal with malicious strings that reach the client browser from all routes. In order to implement secure XSS defensive framework, we wrapped all entry points of the browser engine to execute the scripts based on the identifiers which are stored in the backup table. The script identifiers in the auxiliary table can be added with trusted elements, making the framework more robust.

In order to assess the effectiveness of the proposed approach, a number of web applications implemented with scripting languages, such as PHP and ASP, have been submitted to the vulnerability analysis. This approach has been preliminarily tested to prevent vulnerabilities in open source web-based applications,

An experimental result shows that the proposed framework is able to find the injection of malicious attack strings with acceptable false negative and false positives.

References

[1] Bisht, P. and Venkatakrishnan, V. 2008. XSS-guard: precise dynamic prevention of cross-site scripting attacks. pp. 23–43. *In*: International Conference on Detection of Intrusions and Malware, and Vulnerability Assessment. Springer.
[2] Chaudhary, P., Gupta, B. and Gupta, S. 2016. Cross-site scripting (XSS) worms in online social network (OSN): Taxonomy and defensive mechanisms. pp. 2131–2136. *In*: Computing

for Sustainable Global Development (INDIACom), 2016 3rd International Conference on IEEE.

[3] Di Lucca, G. A., Fasolino, A. R., Mastoianni, M. and Tramontana, P. 2004. Identifying cross site scripting vulnerabilities in web applications. pp. 71–80. *In*: Web Site Evolution, Sixth IEEE International Workshop on (WSE'04). IEEE.

[4] Duchene, F., Groz, R., Rawat, S. and Richier, J. L. 2012. XSS vulnerability detection using model inference assisted evolutionary fuzzing. pp. 815–817. *In*: Software Testing, Verification and Validation (ICST), 2012 IEEE Fifth International Conference on IEEE.

[5] Gupta, S. and Gupta, B. 2015. Cross-site scripting (XSS) attacks and defense mechanisms: classification and state-of-the-art. International Journal of System Assurance Engineering and Management, pp. 1–19.

[6] Gupta, S. and Gupta, B. 2016. XSS-safe: a server-side approach to detect and mitigate cross-site scripting (XSS) attacks in javascript code. Arabian Journal for Science and Engineering, 41(3): 897–920.

[7] Gupta, S., Gupta, B. and Chaudhary, P. 2018. Hunting for dom-based XSS vulnerabilities in mobile cloud based online social network. Future Generation Computer Systems, 79: 319–336.

[8] Hydara, I., Sultan, A. B. M., Zulzalil, H. and Admodisastro, N. 2014. An approach for cross-site scripting detection and removal based on genetic algorithms. *In*: The Ninth International Conference on Software Engineering Advances ICSEA.

[9] Johns, M. 2006. Sessionsafe: Implementing XSS immune session handling. pp. 444–460. *In*: European Symposium on Research in Computer Security. Springer.

[10] Kirda, E., Kruegel, C., Vigna, G. and Jovanovic, N. 2006. Noxes: a client-side solution for mitigating cross-site scripting attacks. pp. 330–337. *In*: Proceedings of the 2006 ACM Symposium on Applied Computing. ACM.

[11] Marashdih, A. W. and Zaaba, Z. F. 2017. Cross site scripting: Removing approaches in web application. Procedia Computer Science, 124: 647–655.

[12] Mitropoulos, D., Stroggylos, K., Spinellis, D. and Keromytis, A. D. 2016. How to train your browser: Preventing XSS attacks using contextual script fingerprints. ACM Transactions on Privacy and Security (TOPS), 19(1): 2.

[13] Nagpal, B., Chauhan, N. and Singh, N. 2017. Secsix: security engine for csrf, sql injection and XSS attacks. International Journal of System Assurance Engineering and Management, pp. 1–14.

[14] Putthacharoen, R. and Bunyatnoparat, P. 2011. Protecting cookies from cross site script attacks using dynamic cookies rewriting technique. pp. 1090–1094. *In*: Advanced Communication Technology (ICACT), 2011 13th International Conference on IEEE.

[15] Saxena, P., Hanna, S., Poosankam, P. and Song, D. 2010. Flax: Systematic discovery of client-side validation vulnerabilities in rich web applications. *In*: NDss.

[16] Shar, L. K. and Tan, H. B. K. 2012. Automated removal of cross site scripting vulnerabilities in web applications. Information and Software Technology, 54(5): 467–478.

[17] Shar, L. K., Tan, H. B. K. and Briand, L. C. 2013. Mining sql injection and cross site scripting vulnerabilities using hybrid program analysis. pp. 642–651. *In*: Proceedings of the 2013 International Conference on Software Engineering. IEEE Press.

[18] Ter Louw, M. and Venkatakrishnan, V. 2009. Blueprint: Robust prevention of cross-site scripting attacks for existing browsers. pp. 331–346. *In*: 2009 30th IEEE Symposium on Security and Privacy. IEEE.

[19] Toma, T. R. and Islam, M. S. 2014. An efficient mechanism of generating call graph for javascript using dynamic analysis in web application. pp. 1–6. *In*: Informatics, Electronics & Vision (ICIEV), 2014 International Conference on IEEE.

[20] Van Gundy, M. and Chen, H. 2012. Noncespaces: Using randomization to defeat cross-site scripting attacks. Computers & Security, 31(4): 612–628.
[21] Wurzinger, P., Platzer, C., Ludl, C., Kirda, E. and Kruegel, C. 2009. Swap: Mitigating XSS attacks using a reverse proxy. pp. 33–39. *In*: Proceedings of the 2009 ICSE Workshop on Software Engineering for Secure Systems. IEEE Computer Society.
[22] Zhang, X. h. and Wang, Z. j. 2010. Notice of retraction a static analysis tool for detecting web application injection vulnerabilities for asp program. pp. 1–5. *In*: e-Business and Information System Security (EBISS), 2010 2nd International Conference on IEEE.

14

Secure Image Parameters Comparison for DES, AES and Rubik's Cube Encryption Algorithms

*Krishna Dharavathu** and *M S Anuradha*

14.1 Introduction

Today, data security is the need of the hour. It is necessary for us to keep our information safe from the reach of intruders without authorized access, to maintain confidentiality and the integrity of the sender and receiver. Also, with the drastic increase in the number of cyber-attacks happening across the world, cybersecurity is now a concern of not only individuals but also governments. Many technologies are emerging offering solutions to vulnerabilities in the computer world. Researchers were motivated about this issue to protect multimedia information with new novel encryption techniques.

Cryptography means keeping the information secret, hidden or concealed—the efficient transmission of image and security based on cryptography. Encryption can be defined as a method of protecting the information from unwanted access or attacks by converting it into a non-recognizable form [1]. It mainly involves in the scrambling of data contents, such as text, image, audio, video, etc., resulting in a new form of data which is unreadable during transmission [2]. The encrypted data is called the ciphertext, and the unencrypted information is called plaintext data. The process of recovering the plaintext data from ciphertext is called decryption [3]. Many authors proposed several image encryption algorithms based on chaotic to protect the multimedia information against cryptographic attacks. The chaotic-based

Dept. of ECE, AUCE (A), Andhra University-Visakhapatnam.
* Corresponding author: krishnadharavath4u@gmail.com

algorithms have some drawbacks, such as small key space, low-performance speed and limited security [4]. In this paper, we compared the statistical analysis tests of the Data Encryption Standard (DES), Advanced Encryption Standard (AES) and Rubik's cube encryption algorithm. The Rubik's cube encryption algorithm uses huge key size, greater security to protect the safety of encrypted images from exhaustive attack, statistic attack, and differential attack. The details of DES and AES algorithms are found in [5–9].

The rest of the paper is organized as follows: Section 14.2 discusses the Rubik's Cube Encryption Algorithm. Section 14.3 discusses Statistical Analysis tests. Section 14.4 presents the Simulation Results and Discussions, and finally, conclusions are made in section 14.5.

14.2 Rubik's Cube Algorithm

The initial idea developed for the use of Rubik's cube principle in image cryptosystems. Pixels in individual rows or columns (or a block of pixels) of an image are permutated, and circular shifts are applied in any possible direction. In one of the original approaches, inherent features of an image (i.e., pixels) are used to determine the number of circular shifts in their direction or both [10]. Firstly, the pixel values within each row or column are added together. Then, the obtained value is used in establishing the path for circular shifts. The circular transformations to be performed in the algorithm are given by two randomly generated vectors (one vector associated with rows and the other associated with the columns). Through an inclusive assessment of the efficacy of the propound approach, the reality is that the propound cryptosystem has a reasonable security level [11].

Rubik's cube principle is used to disturb the order of the pixels existing in the original image. This process alters the position of the pixels. Here, two randomly generated keys (discussed in the steps below), which are concealed, are used. Using these two hidden keys, the circular shift is applied to each row and column of the image. XOR operation was done between odd rows and columns with two secret keys. Thereby, using flipped concealed keys, bitwise XOR operation is applied to the even rows and columns of the image. To revamp the security of the image, these steps can repeat N number of times. The steps involved in the encryption algorithm are as follows:

Step 1: Initially, two random vectors V_R and V_C of respective lengths P and Q are generated. Elements $V_R(i)$ and $VC(j)$ each take random value of the set $A = \{0, 1, 2, \ldots 2^p - 1\}$.

Step 2: To determine the number of counts, initialize value of the counter *count* at 0 and final value is $count_{max}$.

Step 3: Increase the counter value by one: *count* = *count* + 1.

Step 4: For each row i of image I_0,

a. To determine the sum of all elements in the row i, the total sum is denoted by $\rho(i)$

$$\rho(i) = \sum_{j=1}^{Q} I_0(i, j) \quad i = 1, 2, \ldots P \tag{14.1}$$

b. Modulo 2 of $\rho(i)$ is performed and is denoted by $P_{\alpha(i)}$,

c. Row i is left or right, circular-shifted by $V_R(i)$ positions by using the following process:

$$\text{If } P_{\alpha(i)} = \begin{cases} 0 & \rightarrow \text{right circular shift} \\ \text{else} & \rightarrow \text{left circular shift} \end{cases}$$

Step 5: For each column j of image I_0,

a. To determine the sum of all elements in the column j, this sum is denoted by $\gamma(j)$,

$$\gamma(j) = \sum_{i=1}^{P} I_0(i, j) \quad j = 1, 2, \ldots Q, \tag{14.2}$$

b. Modulo 2 of $\gamma(j)$ is performed and is denoted by $P_{\gamma(j)}$.

c. Column j is down or up, circular-shifted by $V_C(i)$ positions, according to the following:

$$\text{If } P_{\gamma(j)} = \begin{cases} 0 & \rightarrow \text{up circular shift} \\ \text{else} & \rightarrow \text{down circular shift} \end{cases}$$

The muddled image will be generated by using step 4 and 5, and is denoted by I_{MUD}.

Step 6: Using vector V_C, the bitwise XOR operator is applied to each row of muddled image I_{SCR} using the following expressions:

$$I_1(2i - 1, j) = I_{MUD}(2i - 1, j) \oplus V_C(j)$$

$$I_1(2i, j) = I_{MUD}(2i, j) \oplus rot180(V_C(j)) \tag{14.3}$$

In the above equation, $\oplus$ denotes bitwise XOR operator and rot180 (V_C) denotes the flipped vector of V_C from left to right, respectively.

Step 7: Using vector V_R, the bitwise XOR operator is applied to each column of image I_1 using:

$$I_{ENC}(i, 2j - 1) = I_1(i, 2j - 1) \oplus V_R(j)$$

$$I_{ENC}(i, 2j) = I_1(i, 2j) \oplus rot180(V_R(j)) \tag{14.4}$$

where rot 180 V_R denotes the left to right flip of vector V_R.

Step 8: Finally, when the value of *count* = *count*$_{max}$, then encrypted image I_{ENC} is created and encryption process is done; otherwise, the algorithm loops to step 3.

The decryption is the reverse process of the encryption algorithm. Full details regarding Rubik's Cube algorithm and its implementation can be found in references [12–14].

14.3 Statistical Analysis Test Parameters

Statistical analysis tests are used to quantify the quality of encryption techniques. The quality of the encrypted images is measured by using metrics, namely, Histograms, Number of Pixel Changing Rate (NPCR), Unified (UACI), Entropy, Correlation Co-efficient Visual inspection and Speed Test.

14.3.1 Histogram

The histogram of an image generally indicates pixel intensity values. An 8-bit grayscale image has 256 different intensities and histogram symbolically shows the intensity distribution of 256 levels. It is one of the important performance metrics which will measure the encryption quality of an algorithm. Uniformity in the histogram of an encrypted image makes an encryption scheme stronger against different attacks [15].

14.3.2 NPCR and UACI

The number of changing pixel rate (NPCR) and unified averaged changed intensity (UACI) are the two most common quantities used for evaluating the resistance against differential attacks for image encryption schemes. NPCR indicates the percentage of different pixels between two images [10, 15]. Mathematically,

$$NPCR = \frac{\sum_{i=1}^{P}\sum_{j=1}^{Q}D(i,j)}{P \times Q} \times 100\% \qquad (14.5)$$

The second parameter is the Unified average changing intensity (UACI), which measures the average intensity of differences in pixels between two images [29]. Let $I_0(i,j)$ and $I_{ENC}(i,j)$ be the pixel values of original and encrypted images, I_0 and I_{ENC} at the ith pixel row and jth pixel column, respectively [3]. Mathematically UACI values between two images, whose plain text images are slightly different, can be defined as,

$$UACI = \left[\sum_{i=1}^{P}\sum_{j=1}^{Q} \frac{|I_0(i,j) - I_{ENC}(i,j)|}{255} \right] \times \frac{100\%}{P \times Q} \qquad (14.6)$$

To access the performances of an perfect image encryption algorithm, NPCR values must as large as possible, and UACI values must be around 33% [10].

14.3.3 Entropy

In the image encryption algorithm, the concept of entropy analysis was introduced by Edward [16]. Consider for a grayscale image of size 256 × 256, and it has 256 levels, if each level of gray is assumed to be equiprobable, then, theoretically, the value of the entropy of this image is equal to 8-bits. Generally, the encryption algorithms of images should give an encrypted image having equiprobable gray levels [10]. The information entropy can be used to measure the randomness of the image, as provided in the following equation [17].

$$H(X) = -\sum_{i=1}^{n} P_r(x_i) \log_2 P_r(x_i) \tag{14.7}$$

$$P_r(X = x_i) = \frac{1}{F} \tag{14.8}$$

where X denotes the test image, x_i is ith possible value in X, $P_r(x_i)$ is the probability of $X = x_i$ and F denotes the number of allowed intensity sequences associated with the image format [15].

14.3.4 Correlation Coefficients

The correlation coefficient is an important parameter to judge the encryption quality of an image. The correlation coefficient measures the relationship between two adjacent variables or pixels in a specific direction. In general, the pixels in the original image are strongly correlated with adjacent pixels in horizontal, vertical or diagonal directions. A good encryption scheme conceals all attributes of plaintext image and makes encrypted data entirely random and highly uncorrelated. The correlation coefficient between two adjacent pixels is given in the following equation [10, 15].

$$r = \frac{\text{cov}(x, y)}{\sqrt{D(x)}\sqrt{D(y)}} \tag{14.9}$$

where

$$D(x) = \frac{1}{N}\sum_{i=1}^{N}(x_i - \overline{x})^2$$

$$D(y) = \frac{1}{N}\sum_{i=1}^{N}(y_i - \overline{y})^2$$

$$\text{cov}(x, y) = \sum_{i=1}^{N} (x_i - \overline{x})(y_i - \overline{y})$$

where N is the total number of pairs (x_i, y_i) obtained from the images, and $\overline{x}$ and $\overline{y}$ are the mean values of x_i and y_i, respectively [18]. For example, if the value of correlation coefficient assumes one then the encryption process totally fails because the encrypted image and plaintext image are same. When correlation coefficient is -1, then encrypted image data is negative of plaintext image data [2].

14.4 Simulation Results and Discussion

The statistical analysis tests are performed on three different images, which are available in .TIF, .JPG and .GIF formats and have pixel sizes 256×256. The statistical analysis, like histograms, number of pixel changing rate (NPCR), unified averaged changed intensity (UACI), correlation coefficient and entropy tests, is conducted to judge the efficiency and care of the image encryption algorithms.

The histogram represents the distribution of intensity levels in an image. In cryptography uniform, tonal distribution gives better security [19]. Figures 14.1 to 14.9 illustrate the original cameraman, checkerboard and MRI images along with their encrypted versions of Rubik's cube, DES and AES algorithms. It is observed from histograms that the tonal distribution is uniform in all three algorithms, viz., DES, AES and Rubik's Cube, thereby indicating that these encryption algorithms are very powerful. It observed that

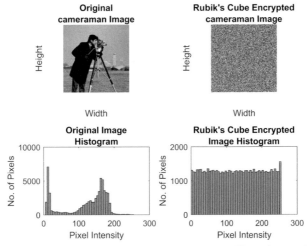

Figure 14.1: Original Cameraman Image and Rubik's Cube encrypted image images along with their Histogram distribution.

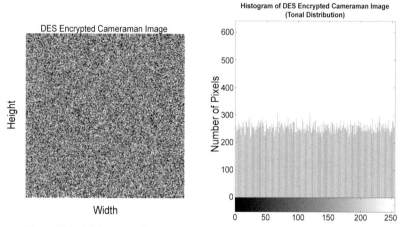

Figure 14.2: DES encrypted cameraman image along with its histogram distribution.

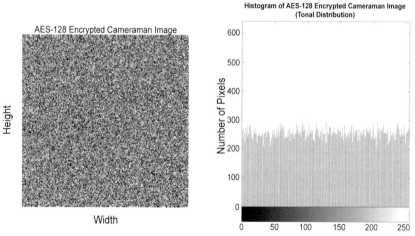

Figure 14.3: AES encrypted cameraman image along with its histogram distribution.

the histogram of an original image is random when compared to that of an encrypted image which is uniform in nature.

To verify the effect of a one-pixel change, experiments were performed on Cameraman, Checkerboard and MRI images. Simulation results are presented in Table 14.1. In encryption algorithm, NPCR values must be as large as possible, and UACI values must be around 33%. From the table, it is clear that DES has better diffusion characteristics than AES and Rubik's Cube Encryption algorithms.

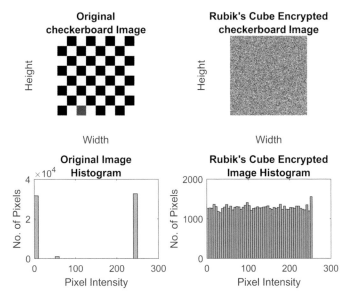

Figure 14.4: Original checkerboard image and Rubik's Cube encrypted images along with their histogram distribution.

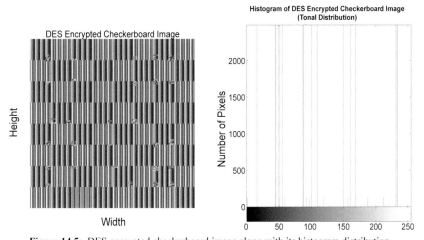

Figure 14.5: DES encrypted checkerboard image along with its histogram distribution.

Entropy tests performed on Cameraman image, Checkerboard and MRI images. Simulation results for entropy tests presented in Table 14.2. From the Table, for Rubik's cube, the value of entropy is very close to the theoretical value of 8-bits in the case all the three images. It means that information aperature is negligible and Rubik's Cube encryption algorithm is more secure against entropy attack. But AES and DES have less entropy compared to

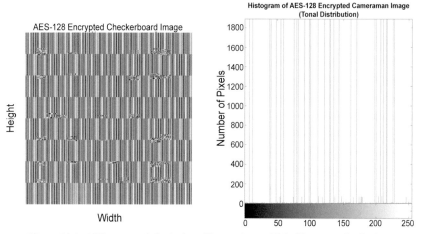

Figure 14.6: AES encrypted checkerboard image along with its histogram distribution.

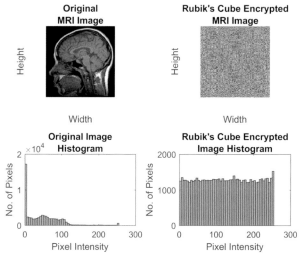

Figure 14.7: Original MRI Image and Rubik's Cube encrypted images along with their Histogram distribution.

Rubik's Cube algorithm in the case of Checkerboard image. The value of entropy for an original image without encryption algorithm is decidedly less, i.e., approximately 7-bits, 2-bits and 6-bits of Cameraman image, Checkerboard and MRI images as compared to encryption techniques.

Correlation is a measure that finds the degree of similarity between two adjacent variables, as discussed in the early section. Here, we present correlation coefficient analysis on AES, DES and Rubik's Cube Encryption

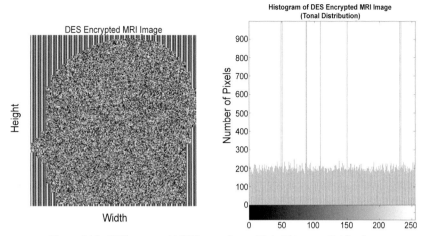

Figure 14.8: DES encrypted MRI image along with its histogram distribution.

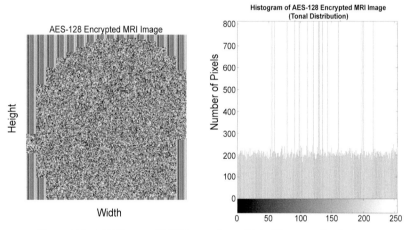

Figure 14.9: AES Encrypted MRI Image along with its Histogram distribution.

Table 14.1: NPCR and UACI tests.

	NPCR			UACI		
Image	**AES**	**DES**	**Rubik's Cube**	**AES**	**DES**	**Rubik's Cube**
Cameraman	99.59	99.60	99.60	31.06	31.17	31.12
Checkerboard	99.88	99.99	99.62	48.34	51.48	47.60
MRI	99.68	99.75	99.60	38.73	38.26	38.40

Table 14.2: Entropy test.

Image	Entropy			
	Original Image	Encrypted Image		
		AES	DES	Rubik's Cube
Camera Man	7.0097	7.9969	7.9973	7.9974
Checkerboard	1.1404	5.1565	4.2570	7.9957
MRI	6.2522	7.7482	7.5610	7.9969

Table 14.3: Correlation coefficient between adjacent pairs of pixels.

Image Name	Name of Encryption Algorithm	Original Image Correlation			Encrypted Image Correlation		
		Horizontal	*Vertical*	*Diagonal*	*Horizontal*	*Vertical*	*Diagonal*
Cameraman (.TIF)	AES	0.9261	0.9781	0.8956	0.1960	0.0163	−0.0371
	DES	0.9261	0.9781	0.8956	−0.8030	0.996	0.0039
	Rubik's Cube	0.9261	0.9781	0.8956	−0.0047	0.0411	−0.0664
Checkerboard (.JPG)	AES	1	1	0.1000	−1	1	−0.3837
	DES	1	1	0.1000	1	1	0.2400
	Rubik's Cube	1	1	0.1000	−0.0018	0.0402	0.1395
MRI (.GIF)	AES	NaN	0.9467	0.8497	0.1960	0.0163	−0.0371
	DES	NaN	0.9467	0.8497	−0.8030	0.0996	0.0039
	Rubik's Cube	NaN	0.9467	0.8497	−0.0047	0.0411	−0.0664

algorithms. Tests performed on Cameraman image. The size of the image was 256 × 256 pixels—the values of correlation coefficients given in Table 14.3.

Figures 14.10, 14.11 and 14.12 shows the horizontal, vertical and diagonal correlation for AES, DES and Rubik's Cube algorithms. When cameraman image was encrypted using AES, correlation coefficients are 0.0163 and –0.037 in vertical and diagonal directions, respectively. However, the correlation coefficient in a horizontal direction is 0.1960, which implies that image encrypted by AES has a high correlation in a horizontal direction. When cameraman image was encrypted using DES, correlation coefficients are –0.8030 and 0.0039 in horizontal and diagonal direction, respectively. However, the correlation coefficient in a vertical direction is 0.996, which implies that image encrypted by the DES has a high correlation in a vertical direction. The ciphertext images obtained using the Rubik's Cube encryption algorithm has values of the correlation coefficient are very close to zero in all directions, which means that the adjacent pixels (horizontal, vertical and diagonal directions) are very weakly correlated. However, the AES technique

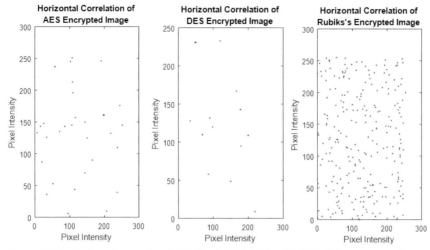

Figure 14.10: Horizontal correlation distribution in AES, DES and Rubik's Cube cameraman image.

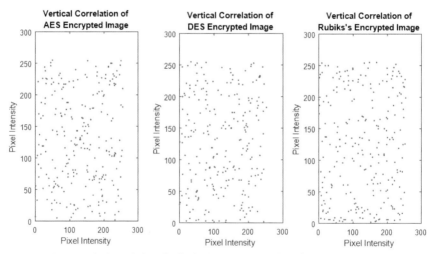

Figure 14.11: Vertical correlation distribution in AES, DES and Rubik's Cube cameraman image.

gives a high correlation in the horizontal direction and DES technique gives high relationship in the vertical direction.

Another critical parameter for security considerations in the design of image encryption techniques is the actual algorithm processing time, especially for real-time multimedia applications. A traditional encryption scheme generally requires long processing time and high computing power [3]. The proposed encryption algorithm [19–21] is high-speed compared to other algorithms. Table 14.4 illustrates the performance of DES, AES and

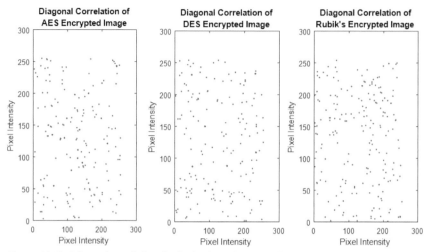

Figure 14.12: Diagonal correlation distribution in AES, DES and Rubik's Cube cameraman image.

Table 14.4: Speed test.

Encryption Technique	Encryption Time	Decryption Time
DES	510.212967 seconds	510.212967 seconds
AES	52.084214 seconds	52.084214 seconds
Rubik's Cube	0.600838 seconds	0.600838 seconds

Rubik's Cube encryption algorithm using original Cameraman image with size 256 × 256 pixels. These algorithms were performed using the MATLAB simulation platform. Table 14.4 concluded that the Rubik's Cube encryption algorithm execution time is decidedly less than the DES and AES algorithms.

14.5 Conclusion

In this paper, some statistical analysis tests were presented to form the groundwork for assessing image encryption algorithms. DES, AES and Rubik's Cube schemes were compared to each other. The paltry of the observations for all the three algorithms were those metrics which are examined in the simulation results part. In NPCR and UACI was very high for DES. In correlation coefficient analysis, the image encrypted by DES has vertical direction, and AES correlates with the horizontal direction while Rubik's cube encrypted image has very little correlation in all directions. A lower value of correlation gives higher security. Entropy values for AES and DES are less, compared to Rubik's Cube. The execution time for DES and AES are high compared to Rubik's Cube algorithm. Finally, we conclude that the Rubik's Cube encryption algorithm gives superior performance and more security compared to DES and AES.

References

[1] Stallings, W. 2006. Cryptography and network security: principles and practice. Prentice Hall, vol. 2006.
[2] Jawad Ahmad and Fawad Ahmed. 2010. Efficiency analysis and security evaluation of image encryption schemes. International Journal of Video & Image Processing and Network Security IJVIPNS-IJENS, Vol. 12, No. 04.
[3] Schneier, B. 1996. Applied Cryptography. John Wiley & Sons, Inc., USA.
[4] Li Zhang, Xiaolin Tian and Shaowei Xia. 2011. A scrambling algorithm of image encryption based on Rubik's Cube rotation and logistic sequence. 2011 International Conference on Multimedia and Signal Processing, 978-0-7695-4356-7/11 $26.00 © 2011 IEEE.
[5] Coppersmith, D. 1994. The data encryption standard (DES) and its strength against attacks. IBM Journal of Research and Development, 38(3): 243–250.
[6] Yun-Peng, Z., Wei, Shui-Ping, C., Zheng-Jun, Z., Xuan, N. and Wei-Di, D. 2009. Digital image encryption algorithm based on chaos and improved DES. In IEEE International Conference on Systems, Man and Cybernetics.
[7] Sai Srinivas, N. S. and Akramuddin, M. D. 2016. FPGA based hardware implementation of AES Rijndael Algorithm for Encryption and Decryption. In 2016 International Conference on Electrical, Electronics, and Optimization Techniques (ICEEOT), Chennai, India, March 2016, pp. 1769–1776.
[8] AES (Advanced Encryption Standard), FIPS-197 (Federal Information Processing Standard), November 26, 2001, FIPS Publications.
[9] Xinmiao Zhang, Student Member, IEEE and Keshab K. Parhi, Fellow, IEEE. 2004. High-speed VLSI architectures for the AES algorithm. IEEE Transactions on Very Large Scale Integration (VLSI) Systems, 12(09): 957–967, September 2004.
[10] KhaledLoukhaoukha, Jena-Yves Chouinard and AbdellahBerdai. 2012. A secure image encryption algorithm based on Rubik's Cube principle. Journal of Electrical and Computer Engineering, Hindawi Publishing Corporation, Volume 2012, Article ID 173931, 13 pages.
[11] KhaledLoukoukha, MakramNabti and Khalil Zebbiche. 2013. An efficient image encryption algorithm based on blocks permutation and Rubik's cube principle for iris images. 2013 8th International Workshop on Systems, Signal Processing and their Applications (WoSSPA), 978-1-4673-5540-7/13/$31.00 ©2013 IEEE.
[12] Adrian-Viorel Diaconu and Khaled Loukhaoukha. 2013. An improved secure image encryption algorithm based on Rubik's Cube principle and digital chaotic cipher. Hindawi Publishing Corporation, Mathematical Problems in Engineering, Volume 2013, Article ID 848392, 10 pages.
[13] Padma Priya Praveen Kumar, Aswin, G. and Naveen Bharathi, S. 2014. Rubik's Cube blend with logistic map on RGB: Away for image encryption. Research Journal of Information Technology, 6(3): 207–215, Academic Journals Inc.
[14] Ester Yen and Li-Hsien Lin. 2009. Rubik's cube watermark technology for grayscale images. Expert Systems with Applications, 37(2010): 4033–4039, Elsevier Ltd. All rights reserved.
[15] Wu, Y., Noonan, J. P., Yang, G. and Jin, H. 2012. Image encryption using the two-dimensional logistic chaotic map. Journal of Electronic Imaging, 21(1): 013014.
[16] Edward, O. 2003. Chaos in Dynamical Systems. Cambridge University Press, Cambridge, UK, 2nd edition.
[17] Gray, R. 2010. Entropy and Information Theory. Springer Verlag.

[18] Huang, C. K., Liao, C. W., Hsu, S. L. and Jeng, Y. C. Implementation of gray image encryption with pixel shuffling and gray-level encryption by single chaotic system. Springer, Telecomm syst, June, 2011.

[19] Krishna Dharavathu and Dr. Anuradha, M. S. 2017. Image transmission and hiding through OFDM system with different Encrypted schemes. International Journal on Future Revolution in Computer Science and Communication Engineering, Vol. 3, Issue: 9.

[20] Dharavathu, K. and Mosa, A. 2020. Secure image transmission through crypto-OFDM system using Rubik's Cube algorithm over an AWGN channel. Int. J. Commun. Syst., e4369. https://doi.org/10.1002/dac.4369.

[21] Krishna Dharavathu and Satya Anuradha Mosa. 2020. Efficient transmission of an encrypted image through a MIMO-OFDM system with different encryption schemes. ISSN 1557-2064, Sens. Imaging, 21(1): 1–31. DOI:10.1007/s11220-020-0275-6.

15

Cloud Based Security Analysis in Body Area Network for Health Care Applications

Dharmendra Dangi,* Dheeraj Dixit and *Amit Bhagat*

15.1 Introduction

Body Area Networks (BANs) allow the collection of physiological data for various purposes, especially in support of medical decisions and improved medical care, through wired or wireless interaction between various types of systems, such as wearable and embedded sensors, smartphones, tablets, and external servers [1]. Data collected by Body Area Networks are deemed sensitive, and a range of safety standards need to be addressed. When unauthorized individuals obtain access to these data, patients may have different effects because of the tampering of their health information. Modified data can lead to wrong medical decisions, like injecting an incorrect dose of insulin, which may cause a major issue in the body of the patient. This study discusses numerous ideas dealing with health in BAN environments. The chapter will discuss the various proposals in the area of security in Body Area Networks by covering the security specification details and the different types of BAN components. The first part will cover the authentication, confidentiality, integrity, etc. [2]. Concerning security issues, the next part will cover the BAN components that include calculation of physiological data with sensors and actuators [3]. Personal servers, smartphones, and tablets are used for forwarding the data, and lastly, we can use external devices and cloud

Maulana Azad National Institute of Technology, Bhopal, India.
* Corresponding author: dangi28dharmendra06@gmail.com

servers to store the data. It has been found that most of the work related to BAN architecture focuses on one or two components, such as sensors and actuators. However, there are a very small number of literatures available which cover the security of entire BAN architecture.

To build a security proposal for the entire BAN architecture, we must consider the majority of the components, like cloud services and external servers, and we even have to cover the auxiliary devices, such as gateways and access points. It is a well known fact that security solutions which are available for sensors and actuators cannot be applied to the external servers and cloud services. So, we have to develop separate security solutions for the data forwarding and data storing approach. Key management will play a crucial role in providing security solutions for both approaches [4]. In some methods, keys are generated with the help of data collected by the sensors but in case of personal or external server keys cannot be generated automatically. In the remaining section of the chapter, first, we will discuss the different components of BAN architecture, and later on, the discussion will move to the security aspects of BANs.

15.2 Architecture of Body Area Network (BAN)

Wireless N/W of wearable computing systems are a BAN (body area network) or WBAN (wireless body area network). Such gadgets may be mounted in a specific location on the human body or floor. A greater emphasis on wireless networking was the increasing interest of wearable devices, such as glasses and watches. To refer to wireless network infrastructure used for wearable's, the term BAN (body area networks) has been invented [5]. These networks main purpose is to forward data generated by wearable devices to wireless internet or WLAN [6]. Wearables can, in some cases, share the data directly.

15.2.1 Components

A standard body area network requires active sign monitoring sensors, movement sensors to better locate the position of the person observed and some form of contact, relay movement readings to care providers, or healthcare professionals. A standard BAN pack provides Sensors and actuators, personal servers, auxiliary network devices, channels, external servers, and cloud services. Physiological sensors, like SpO2 and ECG sensors, and other sensors, like BP, PDA, and EEG sensors, are also under development [7].

a. Sensors and actuators – Sensors are embedded or wearable instruments that monitor human biological and developmental functions. Actuators are machines performing specific tasks; for example, an intramuscular injection, electric toothbrush, etc. Sensors and actuators can be part of one device; for example, Implantable Medical Devices (IMD) has sensors, actuators, and even a CPU. Figure 15.1 displays many sensors: electroencephalography (EEG), electrocardiography (ECG), blood pressure, and sensor motion.

b. Personal servers – These computer devices collect sensor data, temporarily store it, and forward it to stakeholders like a patient's medical team or relatives. Depending on a patient's movement restrictions, different devices can be used as personal servers; personal computers or notebooks can function with patients with mobility restrictions, whereas tablets or smartphones are more suited for physically active users. Figure 15.1 shows two devices that can act as personal servers: tablets and laptops.

c. Auxiliary network devices and channels – Access points, gateways, and cellular towers are considered as auxiliary network devices that allow communication between devices. Mostly, data transmission is wireless as most potential personal servers have Wi-Fi antennas or use wireless networks, such as smartphones and tablets. A BAN can also include wired communications, like, for example, a hospital-deployed computer. Figure 15.1 displays the following entry points, a gateway, and a cellular tower.

d. External servers – External servers are small and large computing machines that capture and store information from many personal servers belonging to patients [8]. External servers that hold records for a majority of patients and records may have various data types, such as papers, medical images, or videos. Therefore, high-speed storage and processing facilities are attractive.

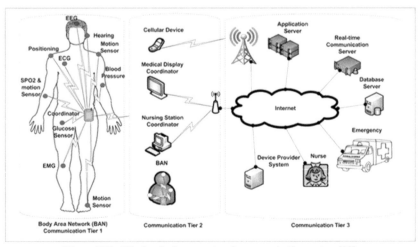

Figure 15.1: Wireless body area network communication system [10].

e. Cloud – Cloud computing systems offer free storage and computational tools in various contexts [9]. For example, hospitals with high numbers of patients may use cloud storage. Cloud systems may be used to analyze data for various reasons, such as analyzing illness and behavior or building statistical models.

15.3 Challenges

Problems with this technology may include:

- **Data quality** – Data produced and obtained by BANs that play a major role in patient care. The quality of this data must be of high authorities to ensure that the decisions taken are based on the best possible knowledge.

- **Data management** – As BANs produce vast quantities of data, it is important to monitor and preserve these datasets.

- **Sensor validation** – Ubiquitous sensing systems are subject to inherent connectivity and hardware limitations, including poor network links, interference, and restricted power reserves. This can lead to transmitting incorrect datasets to the care provider. Especially in a healthcare environment, validating all sensor readings is of utmost importance. It significantly reduces false alarm generation and recognizes possible hardware and software design vulnerabilities.

- **Data consistency** – It easily captures and interprets data on various devices and wireless patient records. Inside body area networks, critical patient databases can be distributed across a variety of nodes and interconnected Computers or devices. If a physician's smartphone does not carry all recognized details, the overall quality of care can degrade.

- **Security** – Keeping WBAN transmission safe and accurate takes a lot of effort. It should be assured that patient "safe" data is obtained only from the committed WBAN system of each patient and is not mixed with other patient data. Furthermore, WBAN created data must have safe, restricted access. While privacy is a major concern in several systems, WBANs did limited research in this field. Since WBANs are resource-constrained in terms of resources, storage, transmission rate, and memory speed, the proposed security solutions may not apply to WBANs. WBAN's security specifications are privacy, confidentiality, honesty, and data freshness along with availability and safe management. The IEEE 802.15.6 specification, WBAN's new version, sought to protect WBAN. Nonetheless, it has some security issues [11].

- **Interoperability** – WBAN systems should ensure seamless data sharing through standards such as Bluetooth, ZigBee, etc., in order to facilitate connectivity of information and plug and play devices [12]. The systems should also be scalable, ensure effective network migration, and provide uninterrupted connectivity.

- **Network devices** – WBAN sensors should be low in size, compact in form factor, lightweight, power-efficient, simple to use, and reconfigurable. Therefore, storage systems need to enable remote storage and display of patient data, as well as Internet access to online retrieval and analysis resources.

- **Power vs. accuracy** – The activation strategy of sensors will be calculated to maximize the trade-off between the BAN's power usage versus the risk of misclassification of the patient's health status. High power usage also leads to more reliable measurements of patient safety and vice versa.

- **Privacy invasion** – People might consider WBAN technology a potential threat to freedom if applications go beyond "secure" medical use. Social recognition will be crucial to seek a broader application.

- **Interference** – The wireless connection used for body sensors will reduce interference and improve the coexistence of sensor node devices with other environmental network devices. This is especially important for large-scale WBAN implementation.

- **Cost** – Today's customers demand high-functional low-cost health monitoring solutions. WBAN implementations need to be cost-optimized to appeal to health-conscious consumers.

- **Constant monitoring** – Consumers may need specific monitoring rates, such as those at risk of cardiovascular disease who may want their WBANs to work continuously, while those at risk of falls may only need WBANs to track them while walking or driving. The monitoring level affects the amount of energy needed and BAN's life cycle until the energy supply is depleted.

- **Constrained deployment** – Wearable, lightweight, and non-intrusive WBAN. This does not alter the everyday activities of the individual. Ultimately, the system should be transparent to the user, i.e., it should execute its monitoring activities without the user knowing it.

- **Consistent performance** – WBAN will perform consistently. Sensor measurements should be precise and balanced, even when the WBAN is turned off and turned on again. Wireless communications should be reliable and operate in various user environments.

15.4 BAN Architecture Security Aspect and Solutions

To ensure the protection, privacy, data integrity, and confidentiality of the records at all times, BAN systems require certain security measures. Unique security operations that ensure all such features [18] must be enforced by a supporting BAN infrastructure. Data protection and privacy are the two main features of each BAN program. Safety means that, as data is transmitted, retrieved, processed, and securely stored, it is protected against unauthorized users. Data security, on the other hand, includes the power to monitor the processing and use of personal data. For example, a patient may demand that his information not be exchanged by insurance undertakings that might use this information to restrict his or her coverage.

More precisely, the data inside the BAN program is highly sensitive, which can lead to many effects on the individual, such as loss of work, public embarrassment, and mental illness if leaked through the unauthorized staff. Another example is the physical capture of the node and information as the intruder's access information; therefore incorrect information would be transmitted to the physician which could lead to a patient's death.

Someone may use the medical records of the victim to find personal rivalries with the patient. To protect this sensitive and vital information from unauthorized access, more attention should, therefore, be taken.

Figure 15.2 and Figure 15.3 demonstrates a secure data collection system and various networking points, including the end where data can be collected only

Figure 15.2: Wireless mode communication.

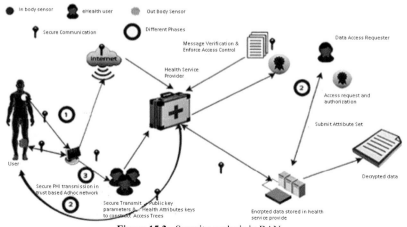

Figure 15.3: Security analysis in BAN.

by an authorized individual and utilizing decryption for personal identification. The following are the key security and confidentiality criteria to guarantee the protection of the BAN program and its thorough acceptance by its users.

15.4.1 Confidentiality

In BAN architecture, data confidentiality refers to the security of sensitive data, and this is considered to be one of the most important issues. Since BAN nodes in medical circumstances are required to transmit sensitive and private information about the state of the patient's well-being, they must, therefore, protect their data from unauthorized, life-threatening access. During the transmission, this critical and transported data can be "overheard" which can harm the patient, the provider, or the device itself. The encryption of this sensitive data can be more discrete by offering a shared key on a protected communication channel between protected BAN nodes and their coordinators. To perform confidentiality, there are two important processes: one is a data encryption and the other one is key generation. Cryptography is the most popular method for providing confidentiality in network security. However, implementing encryption algorithms for BAN is always challenging because of the capacity, memory, and processing limitations and limited sensor and actuator communication ranges [13]. Another problem is that data must be readily available in certain situations, in case of a medical emergency, for example. When patient data is encrypted and the key is not available, a patient cannot be handled properly. Given sensor and actuator constraints, most approaches search for effective encryption techniques. Secret key encryption and elliptic curve cryptography are the most studied algorithms. To produce the encryption keys. Physiological values and channel characteristics are also considered as important factors.

15.4.1.1 Data Encryption and Key Distribution

It has been discussed in the above section that in most of the approaches to maintain confidentiality, two approaches are widely used, i.e., secret key encryption and elliptic curve cryptography. Let's discuss them one by one in detail.

i. Secret Key Cryptography – Secret key cryptography or symmetric key algorithms are better suited than asymmetric key algorithms for BAN architectures, as they use shortened key lengths requiring shorter random numbers and fewer computational resources and energy [14]. However, symmetric encryption and decryption are quicker and safer for emergencies, where someone needs to recover data as quickly as possible. Secret key algorithms, on the other hand, have to solve the key distribution problem.

ii. ECC (Elliptic Curve Cryptography) – ECC has acquainted an interest in work since 2010. BAN architectures are equipped with ECC since small keys are used. The 160-bit ECC key is as powerful as a 1024-bit RSA key [15]. The 2048 RSA key corresponds to an ECC key of 224 according to the NIST [16] Using protocols like Diffie-Hellman, ECC keys can be distributed. These keys may also be used for authentication digital signatures [17]. Nonetheless, ECC implementations have to deal with unresolved issues, such as the development of a random private keys generator and initial parameter distribution [54].

15.4.1.2 Key Distribution

More than half of the research projects choose an appropriate key algorithm in BAN environments to provide secret keys. Considering this, two of the most famous algorithms are Diffie-Hellman and Fuzzy Vaults.

i. Diffie-Hellman: When it comes to the key sharing approach then Diffie-Hellman is the widely used algorithm [18]. Most of the research papers adapt the algorithm to ECC for the generation of a shared secret key using the public information created by the keys with an elliptical curve. Two devices must agree on the curve parameters to use Diffie-Hellman with ECC and each system uses these parameters. Firstly it computes a random number that acts as a private key and then it computes the point in the curve. Later on, this is the public key that will be formed by multiplying the point with the private key. The mutual key is the private key of a device multiplied by the public key of the other device.

ii. Fuzzy Vault: In this approach a user X is using a set of values $Set_x = (x_1, x_2, x_3, ...x_n)$ to conceal a hidden key (K_x). Another person, Y, has a further set of $Set_y = (y_1, y_2, y_3, ...y_n)$ values. The secret key K_x can be obtained by user Y, if appropriate Set_y values correlate with Set_x values [19]. Fuzzy vaults are used in BANs for the distribution of hidden keys with Physiological Values (PVs) and channel functionality. Some suggestions use PVs to build an injection-controlled vault which protects a secret key. The authors used channel features for the development of the fuzzy vault sets in [20] and [21]. An enhanced fuzzy vault system is also used for access control and they are ideal because they can deal with slight errors when calculating PVs and the channel characteristics; users may determine some, though not all values.

15.4.1.3 Other Algorithms

Other primary distribution algorithms are used in the rest of the proposals. The most commonly used protocol is the distribution centers with a node responsible to distribute keys to other computers and there are also other proprietary protocols [22]. The ISAKMP (Internet Security Association and Key Management Protocol) also supports the implementation of key exchange processes and the development of encrypted links between two endpoints [23]. While ISAKMP can be used as a security mechanism within BAN scenarios, an early study showed that the implementation of this protocol increases bandwidth and power consumption [24].

15.4.1.4 Agreement of the Key

Some proposals use a predefined algorithm using physiological and channel values and create a shared closed key [25]. Keys will be produced, not distributed. Some main agreement solutions often provide notification to a patient of a big deal procedure in the network; the generation of a short vibration is an example [26].

15.4.2 Access Control

Access control must ensure access to the data obtained, distributed and stored data by BAN devices are accessible only to approved entities; users, processes, or devices. Two conditions need to be met to ensure access control: authentication and permission.

15.4.2.1 Authentication

Data authentication can be essential for medical and non-medical applications. Therefore, BAN nodes have to be able to confirm that the information is sent from a proven trust center rather than from an imposter. The messages authentication code (MAC) is determined with network and coordinator nodes for all data by sharing the undisclosed key. Calculating the MAC code correctly ensures a trustworthy node for the Network Manager.

The authentication protocols exist in most of the proposals related to accessibility. Such protocols can function together or independently from the main agreement protocol. For example, some authors suggest that the sensor should be implanted or physically connected to a patient and authenticated as a part of the BAN to authenticate it, using PVs, channel features, or system recognition [27]. New methods are, therefore, designed to measure PV without physical contact with the user. In one example, two approaches to recover HRV from human face videos were implemented by the author [28]. In the other one, a Doppler microwave for the measurement of heart- and breathing rates through the thoroughfare of a heartbeat [14]. While such techniques are currently not commonly used, they indicate that proximity-based authentication can not suffice in the future.

15.4.2.2 Permission

Access to medical details of a patient under predefined access rules is limited by permission requirements. In a hospital, for example, multiple BANs will track patients who store all data on the same server. Nevertheless, the information of all the patients should not be received by all physicians and nurses, only physicians who have a direct connection with the patient should have access to his information. A BAN must create approval processes to only send data to approved agencies, such as the medical team of a patient. Therefore, the approved agency should have access only to the necessary information; for instance, physicians should have access to all the patient details, but a pharmacist should only have access to drug prescriptions. In a multiple user BAN architecture [29], therefore, role-based access control is required. The approach suggests that behavioral profiles should be developed based on patterns of access to and from BAN apps. Access requests are only permitted, which are in line with the profiles. A permission mechanism can carry out mitigation techniques to handle conflicting requests, including passive actions, such as alerting, or aggressive actions, such as signal jamming to avoid data access [30].

An alternative solution builds behavior profiles based on locations and times. For different locations, such as rooms for consultations and hospitals, consumers, including doctors and nurses, can only have access to information at specific times [31]. Another solution uses attribute-based access policies. A minimum threshold is set for the authorization 'p' and a collection of attributes is assigned to each user. When a user has a 'p' from n attributes, he or she has access to a piece of BAN personal server information [32]. In conclusion, other proposals use additional devices to carry out authentication tasks; another system can be used as a proxy for sensors and personal servers communications and can require or reject requests for access to them [33]. As regards intra-BAN components and communications, the authentication and permission of sensors and actuators by proximity is one method. Only devices that are nearby or in physical contact with the human body are allowed to obtain information from the sensors.

15.4.3　Integrity of the Data

The quality and accuracy of the data refers to the steps taken to safeguard the content of a document and the step is defined as data integrity. This refers both to individual messages and to communications streams [13]. The security of data does not preclude external changes as it can be illegally changed if data is transmitted to the vulnerable BAN as an opponent that can easily manipulate patient information before entering the network coordinator. Setting up some packets, modifying data inside a packet, and passing the packet to the PS can be done to alter them. This detection and alteration can, in extreme cases, lead to serious health problems and even death. Accordingly, when using authentication protocols it is important that the information is not available and that the future adversary changes it.

A BAN would avoid replay attacks as well as unauthorized detection of alterations. Old packets that seek to make servers think certain packets are true, likely generating false alerts or failing to generate alarms, are resented to opponents when replaying attacks. Personal and external servers will determine the freshness of data in order to avoid replay attacks, a property that indicates that the data obtained is recent and arrives when expected. The proposals examined use hash functions and session identifiers to promote confidentiality and prevent replay attacks.

15.4.4 Freshness of the Data

Data freshness strategies can efficiently ensure that the quality and confidentiality of data is shielded from the data being captured and manipulated by the adversary, so that the BAN coordinator is confused. It ensures the non-recycling of old data and relevant frameworks. There are currently two forms of freshness: strong freshness guarantees time delay besides the ordering of frame, and weak freshness is limited to the ordering of frames but does not guarantee any time span. For synchronization, high freshness is used when a light is transmitted to the BAN coordinator and low freshness is used for low-duty BAN nodes.

15.4.5 Data Availability

The provision for protection in a BAN ensures that data and devices are accessible whenever possible. When required, and in emergencies, the doctors, nurses and paramedics shall have physiological and medical information. If a network is insufficient to transfer packets, servers cannot receive data on time [34]. If other elements, such as sensors and servers, are compromised, information cannot be produced or obtained. Only a few of the works in question are using protocols to avoid usable attacks, such as Denial-of-Service (DoS) attacks. Two ways of detecting and mitigating the attacks have been suggested. In the first, adaptive network profiles, authors create normal behavior profiles based on various network features, such as QoS (Quality of Service), traffic patterns, and power consumption [35].

The network is monitored continuously to detect abnormal behavior; if an atypical activity, such as a QoS decline or an increase in energy consumption, is observed, corrective actions are taken. The second method is to control high energy usage tasks. Data transmission tasks in energy consumption are especially costly and doS attacks tend to rapidly drain the sensor resources [36]. Authors create procedures based on proximity in order to prevent DoS attacks which send high amounts of data; the sensors only share information with devices close to the human body. Data transmission happens in controlled environments only in specific scenarios, which reduces energy consumption.

Since a system of this kind contains important, highly sensitive, and life-saving data, it is of the essence that the network is at all times accessible for use by patients in emergencies [34]. In case of loss of availability, it is necessary to switch the operations to another BAN.

15.4.6 Privacy Rules and Compliance Requirements

It is a global problem to protect private health records. A major privacy measure is to create rules/policies under which the patient's confidential information is available to protect the privacy of the patient [37]. Within the safety legislature, numerous laws and acts are enrolled. There are numerous sets of privacy rules/policies worldwide. A collection of guidelines is given for physicians, health care providers, and hospitals by the American Health Insurance Portability and Accountability Act (HIPAA) in order to make sure that the health and medical records of a patient are secure [13]. HIPAA offers comprehensive measures to secure medical data for administrative or correspondence purposes. The legislation allows for civil and criminal penalties, including a fine of 250,000 dollars, and/or 10 years imprisonment if a provider shares private money benefit information.

15.5 Role of Cloud Computing as a BAN Component

Given that BANs manage medical information and that there are requirements for data security, such as the Health Insurance Portability and Transparency Act (HIPAA), BANs should follow standards and legislation. Because of these criteria, cloud computing can be problematic in health-related facilities, as the security and storage of patient information partly depend on third-party networks and legislation.

Cloud storage applications are not currently widely included in BANs but are starting to emerge [38]. Many of the ventures reviewed found cloud computing for medical studies. Such programs concentrate on maintaining the contact network among external and cloud servers and protecting information stored in the cloud. There were several suggestions that the cloud presented for the privacy of a patient's medical records as a supporting resource. Certain writers protect a BAN-cloud contact channel. Another idea discusses the need for cloud authorization; different users will have access to various information according to their positions. Nonetheless, we need further research to learn how to help permission and validation to allow patients access to Cloud-based records.

Most of the proposals are based on sensors and the projects are based on the safety of sensors and personal servers, this is the main theme, despite the fairly new role that software can play as part of BANs. On either side, it's not a very well-examined topic to know how to completely protect external servers and cloud providers from a BAN and storing medical data.

- Authorization: Some works consider this subject. One research proposes the introduction of roles-based permission to personal servers [39], while another proposes to use profiles to allow profiles access to sensor data based on information such as proximity [40].

- Data Correction: None of the works reviewed suggest software quality testing systems. As stated previously, the software is the key reason for medical devices to be recalled, according to the Food and Drug Administration (FDA) [41]. This arises because of bad program design, upgrading, and checking procedures. Therefore, the development of secure and appropriate applications tends to require methodologies and frameworks.

- Comprehensive approach: Many of the proposals studied deal with the protection of one or two BAN components, but not with the remaining components. Neither of the works analyzed comprehensively examines the entire system taking into account all components' features and specifications. This perspective is required because depending on the part in which the data is collected does not affect the security requirements.

The importance of the BANs in healthcare is unmistakable, but the amount of data collected by these sensing devices is massive and calls for more computational, memory, powerful communication, mass stock facilities, energy efficient processing performance, real-time monitoring and data analysis. Cloud computing provides good progress in the use of the above resources as Internet services. Today, the IT professionals are increasing the scope and application of BANs' tools into cloud computing. This extension is known as sensor-cloud infrastructure (S-CI). Figure 15.4 illustrates a typical S-CI for patient physiological parameters (PPP) surveillance and access.

S-CI collects large numbers of patient information from BANs and sends it to cloud servers for optimization, real-time access, saving and processing capabilities. Thanks to the distributed world, the protection of patient data and safety are also more difficult. This section will review and organize the current S-CI techniques so that the research community can approach Patient Data Privacy and Security (PDPS) vulnerabilities, drawbacks and the need for further work in the field. Substantially, a lot of studies have used the patient physical parameters (PPPs). However, other studies concern their datasets such as medical data, personal health information (PHIs) or Electronic Medical Records, not including those that are PPP.

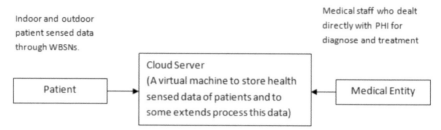

Figure 15.4: S-CI (sensor-cloud infrastructure) for PPPs monitoring.

The use and meaning of S-CI can no longer be denied in the field of healthcare. A wide variety of apps are now available on the commercial level: ubiquitous healthcare, Google health, Microsoft Health Vault, etc. However, the distributed Software world opens new challenges for data privacy and safety for patients: data integrity, confidentiality, patient data management, restriction of access, audit control, availability, scalability, data security, network security, source authentication, and so on. Almedar et al. [42] reviewed literature in 2010 to demonstrate the current state of affairs in wireless sensor technology, how health conditions for home patients are improved and how issues for future growth are taken into consideration.

Two studies have also been published in 2012. Kumar et al. [34] examined the research to explore security and privacy problems in the medical sensor-based app while Ameen et al. [43] reviewed wireless network literature and brought up major social implications, such as security and privacy concerns. Alamri et al. [44] also researched the sensor cloud architecture in a number of different applications in 2013 and talked about emerging possibilities for dealing with more complex real-world scenarios by S-CI. No comprehensive and organized trial to resolve the privacy and protection of patient data is currently available.

15.6 Basic Concepts and Terms

Within this section, some essential concepts and terminologies concerning patient data privacy and safety will be addressed within S-CI.

15.6.1 UBUNTU Web

Cloud computing is the general definition of a third party Internet-based infrastructure. This is true of a public cloud, but there is another type of cloud that is known as private cloud computing, whereby a company or organization runs its own private cloud. The UBUNTU cloud is a cloud-based technology that allows a company to build a private cloud. UBUNTU permits a centralized resource pool on a local network behind the firewall. This technology offers the main benefits: (1) improved server usage; (2) the delivery in a short space of time of new cloud images; (3) public cloud spills (e.g., Amazon EC2), increased flexibility and also reduced construction and maintenance costs [45].

15.6.2 IaaS Platform for Amazon EC2

Amazon Elastic Compute Cloud EC2 is a Web service from Amazon that provides self-service access to Internet software, servers and storage resources. Amazon EC2 offers scalability, pay-per-use capacity and an elastic scale [46].

15.6.3 System of Eucalyptus

Eucalyptus is a free open source software for developing Amazon's web services (AWS) that is compatible with the hybrid and private cloud computing environment. Eucalyptus is "Elastic Utility Computing Architecture Linking Your Programs to useful Systems." Eucalyptus makes storage faster, and dynamically pools computing and network energy. In March 2012, Eucalyptus announced that AWS would enter into a formal agreement. It focuses primarily upon providing (1) a vehicle to broaden the cloud computing utility model; (2) a technology experiments vehicle and public cloud testing platform prior to purchasing original software; (3) a homogenized public cloud IT environment; and (4) a simple open source community (i.e., Linux) platform [47].

15.6.4 Cloud Data Management System SNIA

A standard for data storage in the cloud SNIA cloud data management interface. This framework proposed an interface for data cloud storage management and access. The Cloud Data Management System is generally appropriate, providing a structure for data access, data management, data object description, access control and cloud-based logging specifications. This standard, however, does not have security and privacy specifications [48].

15.6.5 Social Place

According to Zhang et al. [49], the Social Place (SP), a completely designed local portal for storage and efficient communication, has been pre-implemented. With cloud-aided BANs, the PHDA scheme proposed uses these social spots to capture external PPPs. Total L numbers of SP are at intersections or 'roads' that patients frequently travel. These locations are based on their conduct. SP collects PPPs from the patient through cloud-aided BANs directly sensed data. SPs will finally upload the aggregated data to cloud servers.

15.6.6 Virtual Cloud Server

A virtual Cloud server (CS) stores large numbers of health-sensitive data from data storage for patients. The standard includes an interface for data cloud storage management and access. The "cloud data management system," includes a platform for accessing data, data management processes, data objects descriptions, access control and cloud logging, is widely appropriate. This standard, however, lacks safety and privacy specifications [50].

15.6.7 Patient (Indoor and Outdoor)

The word "outdoor," means those patients who are equipped with Wireless Body Sensor (WBS) devices for the monitoring of health and transmission of PPPs via the CS through social spots or social networks (as discussed below). The 'Indoor' patients are the one which consist of WBSs and controlled within the home, hospitals and so on. Private hand held devices or laptops relay PPPs to CS [51].

15.6.8 Trusting Authority (TA)

A trustworthy authority is a powerful and rich storeroom. In the initialization phase, a TA boots the whole system. According to Zhang et al. [49], a TA in the real world is a certified hospital that manages health data. In the PHDA scheme, a TA originally produces a hidden key for authorized users and more licensing certificates. After permission of legitimate users and aggregation of health data, a TA can decrypt diagnostic data. Furthermore, a TA repels malicious PHDA app attacks. In ESPAC, a TA generates key parameters in community and confidential. A TA is able to take responsibility to issue keys, delete, upgrade and approve individuals according to their positions and characteristics.

In order to store the distributed storage server, the TA maintains an index table to store its role. Lounis et al. [52] introduced an HA (healthcare authority) as a TA in their health data management scheme. An HA produces a hidden HKp key and creates an ACp control system for encrypting health data.

15.6.9 Medical Body

Medical body include personnel directly involved in PPPs and PHI for diagnosis and treatment for patients, such as physicians, nurses and health care workers. These companies mainly access PHI for certain operations or for secondary use by third parties.

15.6.10 Cloud Computing Encryption Technology

The trouble-free monitoring and promotion of untrusted servers attract a wide variety of users. A CS can leak any unidentified entities with information. Thus, all data must be ciphertext transmitted to ensure confidentiality and integrity of data against non-trustworthy cloud service providers (CSPs). Three security techniques used and used in cloud computing are set out as follows.

i. The data are transmitted by an authenticated entity and symmetric codes are a basic and trustworthy method for secure online transmission and are known as the "Private Key Cryptography". A private key arbitrarily preserves words or letter mixes linked as a secret key to specifically alter the message. For instance, allowing the password to be 123, and an algorithm advances the password for encryption by five places, the new password is 456, obviously easy to hack, as is the 123 password. The technique of encryption may be used as a 'stream cipher' or as a block cipher which is directly commensurate with the amount of data encrypted or decrypted over time. A "stream cipher", while a "block cipher" processed a certain amount of information, was encrypted by character at one time. "Data Encryption Standards (AES)", "Advanced Encryption Standard (DES)", and traditional symmetric encryption algorithms are based on private key cryptography [53].

ii. The asymmetric method, or just "public key cryptography", uses two paired keys together to encrypt and decrypt messages, in order to keep them protected throughout transmission. This approach is considered to be better than symmetric encryption when thinking about data transmission for large companies or organizations. Microsoft says, "You mustn't worry about the Internet passing public keys (the keys should be public)". Asymmetric coding is, nevertheless, slower than symmetrical coding. It requires much more computing power to encrypt and decrypt the message's content.

iii. Hash encryption is called the generation of special fixed-length passwords for a letter, signature or collection of data. Hash functions are used to secure the data in this kind of encryption. The main advantage of this technique is that a completely new hash function is created by the slightest alteration of details, which is extremely difficult to crack and when the message is encrypted it cannot be read or modified by the process: "And if the potential attacker might get a hash, he or she will not have to be able to locate the contents of the original with a decryption tool". Some common Hash algorithms are Secure Hash Algorithms (SHA) and Message Digest 5 [54].

15.7 Conclusion

In this chapter, we have discussed the security analysis in Body Area Network (BAN) with different types of security aspects and solutions. Later on, cloud computing approach is used as the BAN component and some of the security aspects with cloud computing were also mentioned in the chapter. A comprehensive literature review on the privacy and protection of patients in S-CI has been studied in this chapter. So far, we can see clearly that a lot of mobile healthcare and e-health approaches are introduced, and that there is a lot of room for research into health data management and collection of data. Throughout this area, however, there is an absence of standard infrastructure, compliance with policy regulations, standard databases, patient behavior, encrypted medical terms search, data exchange, data reporting, emergencies, and data management for multiple accesses. This is the case with S-CI in terms of easy-to-use software, user-friendly software, effective access management, network security, real-time implementation and enhanced patient access efficiency. The strategies suggested for patient data privacy and protection have been explored in the S-CI for performance assessment initiatives and various security services. Finally, we believe that the future enhancement will benefit from our roadmap of this flourishing and creative area.

References

[1] Mukhopadhyay, S. C. 2015. Wearable sensors for human activity monitoring: A review. IEEE Sensors Journal.

[2] Tripathi, R. and Agrawal, S. 2014. Comparative study of symmetric and asymmetric cryptography techniques. Int. J. Adv. Found. Res. Comput.

[3] K. L. K. 2016. Body area networks. Int. J. Res. Eng. Technol.

[4] Roman, R., Alcaraz, C., Lopez, J. and Sklavos, N. 2011. Key management systems for sensor networks in the context of the Internet of Things. Comput. Electr. Eng.

[5] Fortino, G., Di Fatta, G., Pathan, M. and Vasilakos, A. V. 2014. Cloud-assisted body area networks: state-of-the-art and future challenges. Wirel. Networks.

[6] Osterhage, W. 2011. WLAN. In Wireless Security.

[7] Zaunseder, S., Fischer, W. J., Netz, S., Poll, R. and Rabenau, M. 2007. Prolonged wearable ECG monitoring—A wavelet based approach. In Proceedings of IEEE Sensors.

[8] Li, J., He, S. and Ming, Z. 2014. Study and design of a smart home system based on intelligent gateway. Shenzhen Daxue Xuebao (Ligong Ban)/Journal Shenzhen Univ. Sci. Eng.

[9] Lele, A. 2019. Cloud computing. In Smart Innovation, Systems and Technologies.

[10] Chen, M., Gonzalez, S., Vasilakos, A., Cao, H. and Leung, V. C. M. 2011. Body area networks: A survey. Mobile Networks and Applications.

[11] Wang, J. et al. 2018. A software defined radio evaluation platform for WBAN systems. Sensors (Switzerland).

[12] Lee, J. S., Su, Y. W. and Shen, C. C. 2007. A comparative study of wireless protocols: Bluetooth, UWB, ZigBee, and Wi-Fi. In IECON Proceedings (Industrial Electronics Conference).

[13] Li, M., Lou, W. and Ren, K. 2010. Data security and privacy in wireless body area networks. IEEE Wirel. Commun.

[14] Liu, J. and Kwak, K. S. 2010. Hybrid security mechanisms for wireless body area networks. In ICUFN 2010—2nd International Conference on Ubiquitous and Future Networks.

[15] Xu, X., Zhu, P., Wen, Q., Jin, Z., Zhang, H. and He, L. 2014. A secure and efficient authentication and key agreement scheme based on ECC for telecare medicine information systems. J. Med. Syst.

[16] Barker, E., Roginsky, A., Locke, G. and Gallagher, P. 2011. Transitions: recommendation for transitioning the use of cryptographic algorithms and key lengths. NIST Spec. Publ.

[17] Katz, J. and Lindell, Y. 2014. Introduction to Modern Cryptography.

[18] Maurer, U. M. and Wolf, S. 2000. The Diffie-Hellman protocol. Des. Codes, Cryptogr.

[19] Juels, A. and Sudan, M. 2006. A fuzzy vault scheme. Des. Codes, Cryptogr.

[20] Zhang, Z., Wang, H., Vasilakos, A. V. and Fang, H. 2013. Channel information based cryptography and authentication in wireless body area networks. In BODYNETS 2013—8th International Conference on Body Area Networks.

[21] Tsouri, G. R. and Wilczewski, J. 2011. Reliable symmetric key generation for body area networks using wireless physical layer security in the presence of an on-body eavesdropper. In ACM International Conference Proceeding Series.

[22] Zhao, Z. 2014. An efficient anonymous authentication scheme for wireless body area networks using elliptic curve cryptosystem. J. Med. Syst.

[23] Maughan, T. J. D., Schertler, M. and Schneider, M. 1998. Internet Security Association and Key Management Protocol (ISAKMP).

[24] Divya, R., Sundararajan, T. V. P. and Deepak, K. R. 2015. Effect of wormhole attack in hierarchical body area network and need for strict security measures. In 6th International Conference on Computing, Communications and Networking Technologies, ICCCNT 2015.

[25] Venkatasubramanian, K. K., Banerjee, A. and Gupta, S. K. S. 2010. PSKA: Usable and secure key agreement scheme for body area networks. In IEEE Transactions on Information Technology in Biomedicine.

[26] Halperin, D. et al. 2008. Pacemakers and implantable cardiac defibrillators: Software radio attacks and zero-power defenses. In Proceedings - IEEE Symposium on Security and Privacy.

[27] Guennoun, M., Zandi, M. and El-Khatib, K. 2008. On the use of biometrics to secure wireless biosensor networks. In 2008 3rd International Conference on Information and Communication Technologies: From Theory to Applications, ICTTA.

[28] Alghoul, K., Alharthi, S., Al Osman, H. and El Saddik, A. 2017. Heart rate variability extraction from videos signals: ICA vs. EVM comparison. IEEE Access.

[29] Felisberto, F., Costa, N., Fdez-Riverola, F. and Pereira, A. 2012. Unobstructive body area networks (BAN) for efficient movement monitoring. Sensors (Switzerland).

[30] Zhang, M., Raghunathan, A. and Jha, N. K. 2013. MedMon: Securing medical devices through wireless monitoring and anomaly detection. IEEE Trans. Biomed. Circuits Syst.

[31] Hei, X., Du, X., Wu, J. and Hu, F. 2010. Defending resource depletion attacks on implantable medical devices. In GLOBECOM - IEEE Global Telecommunications Conference.

[32] Hu, C., Zhang, N., Li, H., Cheng, X. and Liao, X. 2013. Body area network security: A fuzzy attribute-based signcryption scheme. IEEE J. Sel. Areas Commun.

[33] Abidoye, A. P., Azeez, N. A., Adesina, A. O., Agbele, K. K. and Nyongesa, H. O. 2011. Using wearable sensors for remote healthcare monitoring system. J. Sens. Technol.

[34] Kumar, P. and Lee, H. J. 2012. Security issues in healthcare applications using wireless medical sensor networks: A survey. Sensors.

[35] Gebrie, M. T. and Abie, H. 2017. Risk-based adaptive authentication for internet of things in smart home eHealth. In ACM International Conference Proceeding Series.

[36] Shivashankar, H., Suresh, N., Varaprasad, G. and Jayanthi, G. 2014. Designing energy routing protocol with power consumption optimization in MANET. IEEE Trans. Emerg. Top. Comput.

[37] Report, M. W. and Services, H. 2003. HIPAA privacy rule and public health. Heal. San Fr.

[38] Kumar, R. and Nair, R. 2016. Multi-cryptosystem based privacy-preserving public auditing for regenerating code based cloud storage. Int. J. Comput. Appl., 155(10): 16–21.

[39] Allard, T. et al. 2010. Secure personal data servers: A vision paper. Proc. VLDB Endow.

[40] Al Agha, K. et al. 2009. Which wireless technology for industrial wireless sensor networks? The development of OCARI technology. IEEE Trans. Ind. Electron.

[41] Janetos, T. M., Ghobadi, C. W., Xu, S. and Walter, J. R. 2017. Overview of high-risk medical device recalls in obstetrics and gynecology from 2002 through 2016: implications for device safety. Am. J. Obstet. Gynecol.

[42] Alemdar, H. and Ersoy, C. 2010. Wireless sensor networks for healthcare: A survey. Comput. Networks.

[43] Al Ameen, M., Liu, J. and Kwak, K. 2012. Security and privacy issues in wireless sensor networks for healthcare applications. J. Med. Syst.

[44] Alamri, A., Ansari, W. S., Hassan, M. M., Hossain, M. S., Alelaiwi, A. and Hossain, M. A. 2013. A survey on sensor-cloud: Architecture, applications, and approaches. International Journal of Distributed Sensor Networks.

[45] Nadeem, F. and Qaiser, R. 2015. An early evaluation and comparison of three private cloud computing software platforms. J. Comput. Sci. Technol.

[46] Celesti, A., Celesti, F., Fazio, M., Bramanti, P. and Villari, M. 2017. Are next-generation sequencing tools ready for the cloud? Trends in Biotechnology.

[47] Araujo, J. et al. 2014. Software aging in the eucalyptus cloud computing infrastructure: Characterization and rejuvenation. In ACM Journal on Emerging Technologies in Computing Systems.

[48] Galante, G., Erpen De Bona, L. C., Mury, A. R., Schulze, B. and da Rosa Righi, R. 2016. An analysis of public clouds elasticity in the execution of scientific applications: a survey. J. Grid Comput.

[49] Zhang, K., Liang, X., Baura, M., Lu, R. and Shen, X. 2014. PHDA: A priority based health data aggregation with privacy preservation for cloud assisted WBANs Inf. Sci. (Ny).

[50] Dash, S. K., Mohapatra, S. and Pattnaik, P. K. 2010. A survey on applications of wireless sensor network using cloud computing. Int. J. Comput. Sci. Emerg. Technol.

[51] Chippendale, T., Gentile, P. A., James, M. K. and Melnic, G. 2017. Indoor and outdoor falls among older adult trauma patients: A comparison of patient characteristics, associated factors and outcomes. Geriatr. Gerontol. Int.

[52] Lounis, A., Hadjidj, A., Bouabdallah, A. and Challal, Y. 2016. Healing on the cloud: Secure cloud architecture for medical wireless sensor networks. Futur. Gener. Comput. Syst.

[53] Sayler, A. et al. 2014. Private and public key cryptography and ransomware. Manuscript. Prelim. version.

[54] Adviti, C. and Gupta, J. 2016. Review on encrypt the text by MD5 and RSA in client cloud approach. Int. J. Adv. Res.

16

Fog Robotics

A New Perspective for Cloud-based Robots

*Jaykumar Lachure** and *Rajesh Doriya*

16.1 Introduction

IoT is driving the current world by connecting daily objects and devices, simplifying our lives and shifting our data more and more to the cloud-hosted devices. Within the current world, the information created is growing at an exponential rate, which can lead to infrastructure and network congestion challenges. J. Kuffner coincided with the term Cloud Robotics, where robots have independent with unlimited processing and computing power [1]. It provides all types of services or tasks on-demand only. It includes large data storage, objects, images, libraries, trajectories and data of maps, etc., all together in one place. Cloud Robotics can remove the burden of robots as they share all the information through the cloud, which results in saving battery life, reducing cost of storage, and computation offloading at the cloud infrastructure [2, 3].

Currently, the situation is different and changing towards the speed and security of the system [4]. Current architectures cannot really inculcate the huge volume of knowledge. On seeing this, the fog network is suggested by accenting the entity nearer to wherever the information is being used or created. This approach has coincided with the fog computing system [5]. The

Department of Information Technology, National Institute of Technology Raipur, India.
Email: rajdoriya.it@nitrr.ac.in
* Corresponding author: jaykumarlachure@gmail.com

fog computing design shifts the present scenario of ancient closed system models that depend on the cloud to a totally new procedural model that moves computation to nearest edge node devices which are right up to the cloud node in steps by using robots, sensors, and actuators supporting processing capabilities and our network necessities. The points close to the edge devices which perform a part of the computation are known as fog nodes [6, 7].

As per NIST [8], Cloud Computing is a model which provides ubiquitous devices with user friendly and on-demand access to a variety of manageable/configurable computing resources. Herein, the cloud infrastructure resources can be promptly provisioned with minimal service provider interaction. The cloud infrastructure is generally deployed in four varieties: Private Cloud, Public Cloud, Hybrid Cloud and Community Cloud. The services from cloud infrastructure are extended by using three service delivery models: Software as a Service (SaaS), Platform as a Service (PaaS) and Infrastructure as a Service (IaaS).

Fog computing is the system level configuration that extends networking capabilities from cloud to end nodes of the networks. Cisco has reported that approximately 40% of IoT traffic pass through the fog nodes. Fog systems have to be open and practical for the market to succeed—the Open Fog syndicate and different bodies are hard at work on it. The following are the key capabilities of Fog that are essential to IoT:

- Low Latency
- Bandwidth Efficiency
- Security
- Scalability
- Interoperability
- Manageability
- Autonomy and Agility
- Hierarchical Organization
- Programmability
- Reliability and Robustness

Fog Computing is a kind of computational technique that uses excessive node architecture to find out the nodal computational skills to compute and initiate any sort of mechanism for the oriented computing phenomenon. It uses certain and subtle edge devices which make it a profound device to perform any sort of computational skills and aforesaid device for communication and other reported principles, like storage or communication, and which can inevitably be globed around the internet. It can be implemented in a humongous edge storage system for the indelible implementation over the requisite network and can be divided over the data plane and control plane. Control points to control the various required information and the Data plane are there to store the data between various components which can act as active data centers [10].

Security in Cloud Computing and Fog Computing plays an important role. Here, the term security means protecting the data and a set of information from unauthorized access and misuse by the blissful components of network security and other mechanism and keep is protected and safe from malicious attacks and profound hindrance. In order to provide confidentiality and integrity to the data, there exist many cryptographic algorithms. For instance, use of asymmetric cryptographic technique for providing confidentiality to data and utilizing hash functions to provide data integrity [11, 12].

16.2 Fog Computing Architecture

Fog Computing architecture [13] consists of layers or nodes which may be direct or peer to peer, centralized, and distributed or a combination of both which may rely and be implemented on dedicated hardware, software or both. Figure 16.1 shows the general architecture of Fog Computing. The main aim of Fog Computing is to distribute the computing infrastructure and services, storage and communication control. It can take the services from cloud infrastructure whenever required to achieve the desired task. It cannot choose between the Cloud server and Fog server, instead, they form a mutually beneficial system and interdependent continuum. Use of Fog architecture offers the following benefits to IoT applications and robots:

- Providing scalability to distributed applications which spatially/ geographically separated
- Lower latency delay
- Location-aware services
- Quality of Services (QoS) support
- Support for online streaming communication and processing
- Offers efficient communication system
- Provides better access control and mobility

These benefits allow the solutions to solve several challenges of many applications of robots and IoT devices to be created. The architecture of integrating fog computing, cloud computing with IoT devices and robots is like a stack of services and, in the figure, the architecture shown on the top layer of the system cloud robotic server is there and at the middle layer Fog Robotics Server along with sub-Fog Robotic Server nodes may be present and at the end layer accommodates robots and IoT devices. During this design, the fog can offer control and optimization services along with additional close

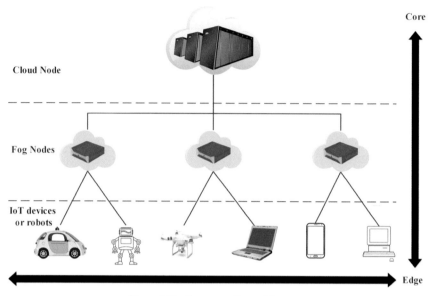

Figure 16.1: Fog computing architecture.

observation for the IoT applications, whereas the cloud can offer an open observation feature.

16.2.1 Pillars of Fog Computing

The pillars of Fog computing consist of architecture and services. Figure 16.2 shows the pillars of fog computing system with different service aspect [14].

The pillars of Fog Computing are as follows [15]:

i. *Security*: In the Fog Robotic architecture, security is not a one to size all other types of architecture. Often, it is defined as the mechanisms that can provide security to all fog node from IoT devices or Robots. An aspect of a business, target market, and use cases, along with node location itself, will create a set of requirements for fog node. However, to build a secure execution, certain fundamental parts of the architecture must be in place in order.

ii. *Scalability*: For Fog deployment, there is a need for scalability of pillar addresses the dynamic, technical, and business model. Elastic scalability is an important aspect of cloud and Fog computing. All fog computing applications cut across through elastic scalability. The location at logical edges of node and hierarchical properties of node provides additional scaling opportunities.

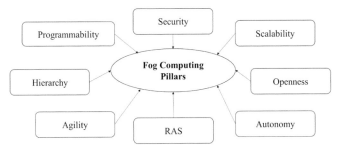

Figure 16.2: Fog computing pillars.

iii. *Openness*: For the success of an omnipresence, fog computing openness is a crucial scheme for platforms and hardware driven applications. Omnipresence solution has more impact on proprietary or single-vendor solutions which results in a negative impact on quality, system price, restricted provider diversity, and innovation. For a complete practical system, the openness pillar is important and highlighted, supported by a live provider scheme.

iv. *Autonomy*: Continue to deliver services from fog nodes, the autonomy pillar has to be enabled. It is designed functionally to face external service issues and failures. Autonomy support throughout the hierarchy in the architecture model. Decision making makes at all levels of fog node that deployed in a hierarchical way which includes device near or high order layer from fog node. In cloud computing, centralized decision making is no longer, apart fog computing have distributed decision making. For business sense, autonomy at the edge network from the local device to the peer system with data with intelligent technique is used.

v. *Reliability Availability and Serviceability*: In the Open-Fog robotic architecture, reliability, availability, and serviceability (RAS) is available throughout the success system and, on great importance. Hardware, software, and operations are the main prospects of RAS.

vi. *Agility*: In an Open-Fog deployment, the agility pillar addresses business operational decisions. It is hard to analyze the data generated by the sensors of IoT devices and robots. For the rapid, operational decisions for the sound business, the data generated at scale is get predicted once the result comes from fog node. Agility pillar focus on transforming the data generated into actionable vision. The agility also works for fog node deployment which is dynamic in nature and dedicated and also needs to give a quick response for change as per the requirement.

vii. *Hierarchy*: For all Open-Fog architectures, the system hierarchy and Computational and is not required but still, it is expressed in many deployments of fog system. For traditional cloud architectures, Open-Fog architecture is complementary. Due to which it is a part of the Open-Fog hierarchy pillar.

viii. *Programmability*: For highly adaptive deployments, the programmability pillar is important and it enables the support which includes programming support at the hardware and software layers. Programmability brings automation and dynamic operation for a cluster of fog nodes or re-tasking. The programmability helps for retasking of fog nodes which directly interfaces using general-purpose registers for computing, network security.

16.2.2 Fog Computing Architecture

Fog Computing Architecture uses a multitude of computation clients or edge node devices. They can operate in coordination with the associated cloud system to carry out a computation, storage, networked communication and optimized based on workload requirements for associated management tasks.

The necessary conditions of a Fog architecture are as follows:

- Latency ought to be reduced by storage at or around the tip device and business reading.
- By performing the computation close to the end of node reduced Network and other migration costs (including bandwidth).
- Use low latency communication to avoid exploitation communication that needs to be routed and synchronize through the backbone networks.
- All computed results that are measuring and regionally computed and then analytically to be derived to the back-end of the cloud server in a very secure manner for more analysis.

16.3 Fog Robotics Architecture

Chand Gudi et al. [4] has defined Fog Robotics as an architecture system that includes storage, control, store data for mapping, networking functions along with decentralized computing closed to the robot. Figure 16.3 shows the basic architecture of Fog Robotics (FR). It consists of Fog Robot Server (FRS) and Cloud Robot Server (CRS). FRS computed with the help of FR extended the cloud system for computation. FRS is adaptable, and it consists of processing power for computation, map data, storage data, network capability, and sharing of secure outcomes from FRS of robots to other robots with different communication techniques with a better response rate for efficient performance. Storage may be temporary or permanent along with how much size of memory needed and it depends on the necessity of the system.

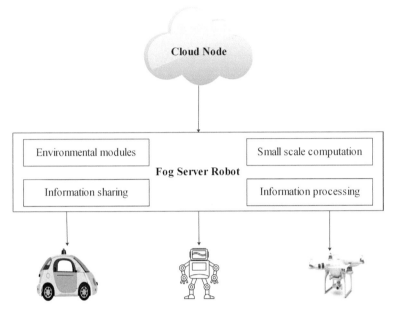

Figure 16.3: Architecture of Fog robotics.

The number of specific required IoT devices along with robots will drastically increase shortly soon which will raise security concerns and a demand for greater bandwidth among other issues. Fog robotics provides a network of robotics that provides the capability of immediate leveraging of data from the cloud with the help of a local server. It consists of a network of robots, a fog robot server, and the cloud where the robot server provides environment modules, processes information, and shares the outcomes of the robots. A robot sends a request for information to the fog robotics system. If the server can successfully respond to the incoming request, it passes that information to the concerned robot. Else, it further sends the request to the fog robot server. If this server is also unable to meet the demand, the request is finally passed to the cloud with eventually responds with the requested information to the robot. Fog robotics balances storage and computation between nearby Edge resources and distant Cloud data centers. It thus meets the quality of service and lower latency requirements [16].

16.4 Cloud Robotics v/s Fog Robotics

Fog Robotics (FR) is an extension of Fog computing (FC) [4]. Cisco first coined the FC term which recently used to solve some prominent problems related to the 5th generation communication system (5G), IoT, healthcare, agriculture, and many more domains. Low latency, storage capacity, power requirement with low real-time latency with better response time is completely diversified in the robotic field. FR gives such a service which is taken from FC. On the other hand, Cloud robotics involved cloud computing and cloud storage system. Both CR and FR are dedicated to sharing the outcomes of robots with some differences.

FR may be independent of the cloud system and it only approaches towards cloud system if it can't acquire information from FRS for computation. Table 16.1 shows a comparison between FR and CR services. CR has permanent storage where FR has temporary or transient small memory only for a dedicated application. FR response within millisecond as it is near to robot whereas CR response time is in seconds. The robot can use CR if FRS is unable to give the decision. Latency in CR is high as compare to FR and security is generally as in FR it is specific.

In Figure 16.4 shows CRS takes a long time to respond as latency is very high as compare to FRS. The average delay time for IoT devices or robots is very low if communication occurs directly without the interaction of FRS and CRS. For processing, FRS takes the data from robots and process it. If a new service needed that unable to FRS, then it goes to CRS. CRS operates and gives the result towards FRS and data also gets storage in CRS permanently for further use. As FRS directly interacts with robot or IoT nodes the delay gets reduced and response gets improved.

Table 16.1: Comparison between cloud robotics and Fog robotics.

Parameters/Aspects	Cloud Robotics	Fog Robotics
Communication latency/Jitter	High and unstable	Low and stable
Storage capacity	Large and scalable long term storage	Small or medium temporary storage
Location	Centralized system	Distributed system

16.5 Use Cases of Fog Robotics

In fog enable IoT network, the goal is to minimize the energy of the assigned tasks in the fog network where the tasks are assigned offline. With the help of fog nodes, the delay can be minimized and latency delay can be improved for offloading services. A homogeneous fog network with IoT devices or robots is considered to maximize efficient task scheduling. If few tasks are already running on the fog node then the new task can be shifted to other fog nodes within this system [17, 18]. In fog computing, there is a need for scalable design and dimensioning of the system to minimize latency. For cost optimization, the scalable design is defined with proper dimension. IoT devices and robotic applications sends the data generated from sensors and actuators directly to

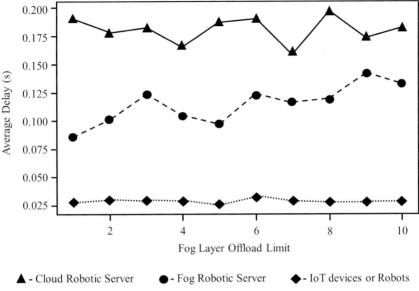

Figure 16.4: Comparison between FRS, CRS and a standalone robot.

fog networks, for receiving big data, the fog network should be scalable and with load balance. Machine learning methods are used in Fog computing to prepare the model and predict it for the IoT sensor data with minimum latency, secure communication within the homogenous network [19, 20]. A study of Fog Computing with Multi-Robots Systems (MRS), Self-Driving Cars and Weed Detection System in Agriculture has been done and being presented in the following subsections.

16.5.1 Fog Robotics for Multi-Robot Systems (MRS)

Multi-robot System (MRS) is one of the challenging application for robotics. In MRS, multiple robots are deployed to carried out a task collectively [21, 22]. When MRS is connected to the cloud, it generally uploads or share its data with the cloud infrastructure. But in Fog robotics these nodes may be imploded nearer to operate the applications. Fog nodes can be assisted in the working volume. Non-global and meager latitudinal help may be received by those for applications using more than the robot. For fog computing, a nurturing sequence is given as follows for major assisting. Robots have limited processing capabilities. However, some robotic applications require a programming solution that needs the implementation of algorithms and also require splendid computing principles processing ability. More than one or even one unit may be utilized for the service processor to support the MRS applications.

Figure 16.5 shows the MRS system. FRS to FRS-communication delay at the time of running the process to give the output of the data by communicating with other FRS system. As in the MRS, every robot sends the data to the FRS and every FRS process that data, and can communicate with each other in different mode such as peer to peer communication, Direct FRS communication, and Hybrid FRS communication. In peer to peer communication FRS interact as a client-server model, as communication is distributed any one can act as a server and client. It can exchange all the services among themselves. Direct communication of FRS, it acts as a general client-server model, where every time the client FRS requests for services to server FRS. For hybrid communication of FRS, it is maybe a combination of both peer to peer, and direct communication.

Figure 16.6 shows the delay incurred the MRS communication. In the MRS, FRS helps to reduced latency delay, and increase the response time. As multiple Robots share data to nearest FRS and FRS perform the process on data with different offload limit of FRS. Once all FRS systems communicate with each other the result is sent to every robot for taking further action as per the requirement.

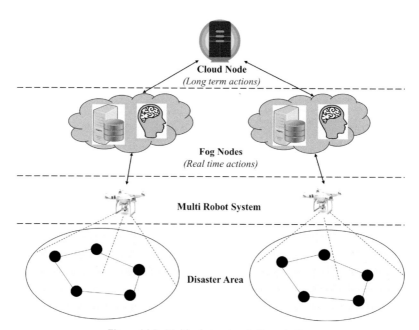

Figure 16.5: Multi robot system in Fog robotics.

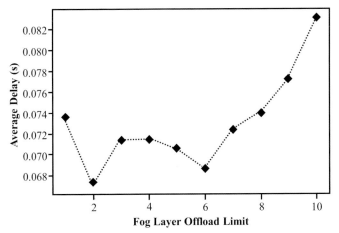

Figure 16.6: Fog server to Fog server delay in MRS.

There exists number of needful services in MRS which are as follow [23, 24]:

i. *Services for Data Storing*: They utilize bots that possess some info storage abilities, and few more than one robotic applications require gathering and keeping lump sum data sets such as moving images and HD photos. They may give non-permanent info keeping services to those apps on those nodes.

ii. *Communication Services*: Few More than one robotic applications require to talk to remote resources to finish their work. However, large-ranging and often talks may elevate issues on power utilization, load pay levels, safety, and full implementation life cycle of the bots. They may be fledged with strong 11 talking tools to construct as floodgates in between the few more than one robotic applications and the remote resources. All data to be transferred between more than one robotic applications and distant resources shall be given away through fog nodes. Those shall relay the data-sets to the distant resources and Quality of Service (QoS) with integration. That may give information diffusion and separation of help for the betterment of stream talk. The exchange between MRS and facilities that need for MRS are passed through fog nodes. Consequently, the bots shall not possess the managerial of the complete long-range talking needed on-board. The remote facilities and add Quality of Service (QoS) provisions are relay on fog nodes information. They can provide a fusion of data along with altering services as well as streaming communication in a better way. So, the result of that, the robot doesn't require to manage long communication on board.

iii. *Services for Security*: Since all the fog nodes communicated among all robots and nodes. Those fog nodes may give talking facilities, those may even integrate safe communication principles among the more than one robotic applications and the distant resource. Apart from those, they may integrate safe characteristics like authentication, control of access of bots, recalls, methods that check and find intrusion. More than one robotic applications may depend on those help to safely associate with each other and talk to different systems.

iv. *Control Services*: This mechanism of computing may be utilized for empowering service control for more than one robotic applications. Those may give complete controls to fundamental bots or half fledged controls to multiple advanced bots that possess built-in functional control and route implementations. A nice example to showcase assistance control is the allocation of work.

v. *Collision and Deadlock Avoidance Services*: More than one robotic applications may give and take certain facilities which include voluminous geography, but there are many attempts to collide among the More than one robotic applications. Among those nodes possessing large processing strength and information saving power, it is plausible to get vigilant services under control which may effectively plan works facilities to assist and prevent deadlock.

vi. *Global Reference Time Support*: Umpteen operational More than one robotic applications could not be correctly get without possessing a non-local time of the frame. That permits every bot to command and pair up with events, actionable visitation. That is just a need in a few More than one robotic applications for entrusting security, precise operations. Notwithstanding a non- chemical reference supportive time is offered in few novice hardware and networks, it is not given and backed up in most of the bots. In the following label, that may give up a 12 prudent and non-local reference supportive time to be utilized for More than one robotic applications.

vii. *Coordination of Services and Synchronizing*: Applications of MRS have to synchronize and robots' actions are coordinated. The coordination and synchronization of the services are required as some of the underlying tasks is at the same time done whereas others are obsessed on the fortunate completion of others, to boost the productivity, parallel processes, and safety of those tasks, synchronization, and coordination services are needed and fog nodes will help these services.

viii. *Integration of MRS with services of others system*: An MRS application system may need to figure out alternative applications and devices, with remote services and operational space among them. Fog computing will offer communication, the ability of processing, and security to support the mixing of different nodes or robots. The mixing of MRS applications with alternative systems with fog systems easily facilitated. The MRS system with cloud computing services easily gets facilitate like detector network.

ix. *Data Caching Services*: A retrieval of knowledge sets from different systems needed when the MRS system needed. The different systems may consist of FRS, cloud services, fog-services, etc. with remote storage facilities for the operation performed that needed by MRS. The fog nodes store the retrieved knowledge for potential future reference. However, the retrieval of data will take unreasonable and unacceptable time. As counting on the dimensions of such knowledge sets may be large, that will long time to retrieve and with high traffic on that network used. Fog computing used to retrieve the expected required knowledge sets before to the correct fog nodes with provided knowledge caching services. Therefore, the operations of the MRS get enhancing the retrieval method furthermore.

x. *Keeping Eye services*: Most of the MRS applications need services, and it to watch that it collaborates with robots, the operating atmosphere, their actions, and the progress of the task. Some watching services are needed to accomplish the needed tasks. In most of MRS applications, the task can't get success and faithfully execute while not have watching services. Fog computing is the middle platform between the cloud server and MRS elements. Fog computing is a central platform to the MRS system and alternative systems like IoT devices such as sensing elements and sensor networks. The MRS applications utilize the watching services which will be provided by abstract groups.

xi. *Movement Supports*: In the MRS system, few robots are autonomous and can move from one space to a different as they work in that region. Fog nodes are connected across the full operational region in the MRS system. It will be attainable to produce services for managing the quality of robots. Services with hand-off and replacement, location pursuit is provided to make sure that obstructive free operations of the bots, along with continuous property and error-free.

xii. *Support for Scalability*: As the MRS grows, the complexness of the operations and coordination additionally grow within it. It becomes hard to maintain the efficiency of the operations. Observance and management services while not sacrificing performance. Quantifiable performance for massive-scale MRS applications is supported by fog computing, that has different robots distributed over large geographical areas. Fog nodes are organized through data structure to efficiently support totally to different functions. For instance, with this structure, stratified management is often used for management services. Generally, data structure distribution in fog nodes will enhance efficiency, quantifying, and performance for any large-scale IoT systems as well as large-scale MRS.

16.5.1.1 Relationship between Fog Nodes and Cloud Centralized Node in MRS System

In MRS system, Fog computing having 'n' nodes, and it may communicate peer-to-peer or direct, and hybrid communication among themselves. These nodes directly communicate with the cloud system. A centralized node is cloud server and all major operations like data storage, the security of data, computation, communication, authentication and security. Consider all fog or edge nodes are connected to one centralized cloud node. These nodes can map into graph structure to identify and the centrality metrics that varying from node to node in complex networks. It is a powerful tool in network analysis, with the help of this tool it is easy to analyze the communication among the nodes with or without a centralized node.

Over the decade, different algorithms proposed to measure and analyze the nodes and their role in network with or without a centralized node. A large number of centrality indices and corresponding algorithms have been proposed to analyze and understand the roles of nodes in networks. In a typical communication network, it consists of fog nodes, IoT devices, robots, and a centralized cloud system. Among these nodes and IoT devices along with robots are communicated with centrality indices and closeness centrality. However, communication between fog networks among themselves along with devices uses the shortest path and excluded the longest path. These two measures (current flow, closeness centrality) having drawbacks, and to remove it, the method was introduced and which proved to be accurate and exact the information centrality. For better discriminating power than between centrality and closeness centrality, it also counts all possible paths between nodes [25].

Consider a connected undirected weighted network of consist of fog nodes, IoT devices, and robots along with cloud server. The graph is given by $G = (V, T, w)$ where V is the set of nodes, $T \subseteq V \times V$ is the set of edges, and $w: T \to \mathbb{R}_+$ is the edge weight function. Consider w_{max} to denote the maximum edge weight. Let $n = |V|$ denote the number of nodes and $m = |T|$ denote the number of edges. For a pair of adjacent nodes a and b, we write $a \sim b$ to denote $(a, b`) \in T$. $L = D - A$. It is the Laplacian matrix of G is the symmetric matrix, where D is the degree diagonal matrix and A is the weighted adjacency matrix of the graph.

Let the ith standard basis vector for e_i, and $b_{a,b} = e_a - e_b$. Let fix's an arbitrary orientation for all edges in G. For each edge $e \in E$, we define $b_e = b_{a,b}$, where a and b are front end and back end of e, respectively. For verifying it is very easy such that $L = \sum_{e \in T} w(e) b_e b_e^\top$, where $w(e) b_e b_e^\top$ is the Laplacian of e. L is positive partial-definite and singular. The pseudoinverse of $L^\dagger$ is $(hL + \frac{1}{n} J^{-1} - \frac{1}{n} J)$, where J is the matrix with all entries are being ones.

The path distance called residence distance for given network $G = (V, T, w)$, is given as hope between two nodes a, b is $\mathcal{R}_{ab} = b_{a,b}^\top L^\dagger b_{a,b}$. The path distance $\mathcal{R}_b$ of a node b is the sum of path distances between b and all nodes in b, that is, $\mathcal{R}_b = \sum_{a \in b} \mathcal{R}_{ab}$, which can be expressed in terms of the entries of $L^\dagger$ as

$$\mathcal{R}_v = n L_{bb}^\dagger + L^\dagger \tag{16.1}$$

Let the submatrix of Laplacian L is given as L_b, and which is obtained from L by removing the row and column of corresponding nodes to node b. For a connected graph G, L_b is invertible for any node v, and the resistance distance $\mathcal{R}_{uv}$ between v and another node u is equal to $h L_{b\ uu}^{-1}$. Thus, we have

$$\mathcal{R}_b = L_b^{-1} \tag{16.2}$$

To measure the efficiency for node b, the path distance $\mathcal{R}_b$ can be used in transmitting information to other nodes. Stephenson and Zelen introduced to measure the importance of nodes in social networks and it is closely related to information. The information I_{ab} transmitted between a and b is defined as

$$I_{ab} = \frac{1}{B^{-1}(a,a) + B^{-1}(b,b) - 2B^{-1}(a,b)},$$

where $B = J + L$. The information centrality I_b of node b is the harmonic mean (HM) of I_{ab} over all nodes a.

Information centrality I_b of a node $b \in B$ for a connected graph $G = (V, T, w)$, is defined as

$$I_b = \frac{n}{\sum_{a \in B} 1/I_{ab}},$$

It was shown as

$$I_b = \frac{n}{\mathcal{R}_b}, \tag{16.3}$$

Let includes ϵ-approximation and super-modular function. Consider $a, b \geq 0$ be two non-negative scalars. ϵ-approximation is consider for a of b if $\exp(-\epsilon) a \leq b \leq \exp(\epsilon) a$. Hereafter, $a \approx_\epsilon b$ t represented that a is an ϵ-approximation of b.

Consider P be a finite set, and 2^P be the set of all possible subsets of P. A super-modular function is given as set function on P is $f: 2^P \to \mathbb{R}$. For any subsets $S \subset X \subset P$ and any element $a \in P/X$, we say function $f(\cdot)$ is super-modular if it satisfies $f(P) - f(X \cup \{a\}) \leq f(S) - f(S \cup \{a\})$. If $-f(\cdot)$ is super-modular function then $f(\cdot)$ is sub-modular. A set function $f: 2^P \to \mathbb{R}$ is called monotonic decreasing for any subsets $S \subset X \subset P, f(S) > f(X)$ which holds.

Suppose that two nodes a and b are connected through edge e, then $L(S \cup \{e\})b = L(S)a + w(e)E_{aa}$, where E_{aa} is a square matrix which have entries at the ath diagonal is being one, and all other being zeros. By (2), it suffices to prove that

$$L(X)_b^{-1} - hL(X)_b + w(e)E_{aa}^{-1} \leq L(S)_b^{-1} - hL(S)_b + w(e)^* \ E_{aa}^{-1}.$$

As, X is a super-set of S, $L(X)_a = L(S)_a + D$, where D is a diagonal matrix having non-negative values. For simplicity, in the following proof, consider notation a M to denote matrix $L(S)_b$. Then, it is to prove that

$$hM + D^{-1} - M^{-1} \leq hM + D + w(e)E_{aa}^{-1} - hM + w(e)E_{aa}^{-1}$$

Define function $f(t)$, $t \in [0,\infty)$, as

$$f(t) = hM + D + tE_{aa}^{-1} - hM + tE_{aa}^{-1}$$

For, $f(t)$ takes the minimum value at $t = 0$ then the above inequality problem holds. For showing that $f(t)$ is an increasing function by solving and proving $\dfrac{df(t)}{dt} \geq 0$. By applying the derivative formula on matrix

$$\frac{d}{dt}A(t)^{-1} = -A(t)^{-1}\frac{d}{dt}A(t)A(t)^{-1}$$

Differentiate function $f(t)$ w.r.t dt as

$$\frac{df(t)}{dt} = -hM + D + tE_{aa}^{-1}\ E_{aa}\ hM + D + tE_{aa}^{-1} + hM + tE_{aa}^{-1}\ E_{aa}\ hM + tE_{aa}^{-1}$$

$$= -E_{aa}\ hM + D + tE_{aa}^{-2} + E_{aa}\ hM + tE_{aa}^{-2}$$
$$= -hhM + D + tE_{aa\ aa}^{-2} + hhM + tE_{aa\ aa}^{-2}.$$

Let $N = M + tE_{aa}$, and let Q be a matrix with exactly one positive diagonal entry as non-negative diagonal matrix $Q_{hh} > 0$ and all other entries being zeros. We now prove that $N_{ij}^{-1} \geq hN + Q_{ij}^{-1}$ for $1 \leq i,j \leq n-1$. Using Sherman-Morrison formula,

$$N^{-1} - hN + Q^{-1} = \frac{Q_{hh}N^{-1}e_h e_h^\top N^{-1}}{1 + Q_{hh}e_h^\top N^{-1}e_h}.$$

As, every entry of N^{-1} is positive, it is the same with every entry of $N^{-1}\ e_h\ e_h^\top N^{-1}$ and it is an M-matrix. In addition, N^{-1} is positive definite, the denominator $1 + Q_{hh}\ e_h^\top N^{-1}e_h$ is also positive. Therefore, $N^{-1} - hN + Q^{-1}$ is also a positive matrix, as the entries are greater than zero.

For above process, by applying repeatedly, it concluded that $N^{-1} \geq hN + P^{-1}$ is a positive matrix. Thus,

$$\frac{df(t)}{dt} = -hhN + P^{-2}{}_{aa} + hN^{-2}{}_{aa} \geq 0,$$

This relationship shows the information centrally working node with all other nodes in network.

16.5.2 Self-Driven Cars

Self-driven cars are a very sophisticated structure which requires a considerable amount of real-time processing with zero expected error [26]. Figure 16.7 shows an elementary structure of a Self-Driven Car. There is no room left for any marginal error. Operation accuracy every millisecond of drive time is very critical to everything due to its real-time nature. The Self-driven vehicle involves huge computations requirements. According to Intel [27], it is estimated by 2020 each self-driving vehicle data more than 4K GB per day which is equivalent to the amount of data generated by 3,000 internet users where average internet user produces 1.5 GB per day. Following that math, a million of self-driven cars will generate as much data as 3 billion people. In order to have this calculation, the data transfer rate considered by Intel is ~ 20–40 MB/sec for video cameras, ~ 10–100 KB for Sonar, ~ 10–70 MB/sec for Lidar, ~ 50 KB/sec for GPS and ~ 10–100 KM/sec for Radar.

Herein this calculation, bitwise precision has been kept to insure safety and quality operations. This quality of operation comes with the expense of big data generated by the self-driving cars with the real-time service requirements.

Indeed, the workload of serf-driven cars will require nothing less than the world's most advanced network architecture. A new communications ecosystem Self-Driven Car's inter and intra-system communications necessitates the development and enhancement of need to use the cloud and which services are more efficiently conducted without the cloud, at the node and network level.

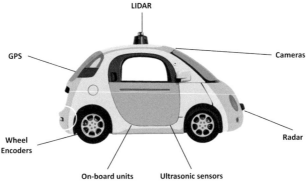

Figure 16.7: Self driven car.

Vehicle to Cloud technologies adhering to the Open Fog Architecture [15] enables self-driven cars processes while providing various services that assist the self-driven cars driving process. This can help vehicles on roads drive cooperatively with one another and to be aware of road hazards. Fog also includes higher-level mobile fog nodes in the vehicles that coordinate the functions of the lower-level processors that manage things such as power-train control, sensing, collision avoidance, navigation, entertainment, and so on. Fog nodes are also widespread in roadside units, intensive computational devices, secured and reliable large storage are kept within the range of autonomous vehicles. Above that, regional fog nodes coordinate the operation of roadside fog nodes, optimizing the smart highway for all drivers. And when the fog infrastructure communicates with the cloud, it is to ensure that everything is safe and efficient across the entire smart transportation system. The fog architecture was designed to easily enable Vehicle to Everything communication and services. Each vehicle is a mobile fog node that communicates with the infrastructure, other vehicles, the cloud, and outside entities, such as pedestrians and bikers.

16.5.3 Weed Detection in Agriculture

Agricultural is the main key to the economy and it has primary importance in all aspects. Agriculture has concerns which includes various types of crop, vegetables, rice, fruits, corn, wheats, aquatics, hydroponics, etc. Apart from this, the agriculture has also spanned to meat and dairy production in a big scale. In many geographical regions, agriculture process can be optimized and the returns can be maximized by converting them to large corporate farms. Many farms have already started using new revolutionary technology to effectively manage the various processes of farming. In order to ensure quality in farming products, many farms have started doing proper report of soil testing, water resources, right crop, and proper crop management services that apply the correct herbicides and pesticides and maximize uses of land fertility, and water, etc. [28].

In efforts to maximized yield and production. Besides, smaller farms that having few lands less than 2 acres (< 2 acre) will also play a challenging role in increasing the supply of food for our global population grows. To maximize the elective use of their resources these smaller farms also have an equal need. An old tradition and common themes exist across this segment of the farm. They are not aware of new technology and methods. Cloud computing is a new technology for the farmer which leads to a lack of reliable or cost elective connections to the cloud. For real-time electives of herbicide and pesticide usage, environmental factors including but not limited to water and soil, and animal health having complexity [29]. For a larger farm concern to

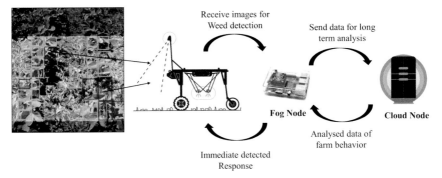

Figure 16.8: Scenario of weed detection.

this segment may have dedicated IT staff and that of small farmers do not have a dedicated IT staff. So, even if the farmer uses cloud infrastructure and connects with the services, it is hard to clarify how they could capitalize on that investment as they are pooling natural resources as they do today.

16.5.3.1 Visualization of Fog Architecture

Fog Robotics is a concept which needs to be visualized first before you start working on it. We have implemented a model reflecting how exactly a fog layer looks like and it's working based on the current sensor data. In this model, we have implemented the three different layers of fog architecture using the components as Arduino as the edge layer or the end layer, Raspberry Pi as the fog layer and adafruit.io as the cloud layer. We are capturing the IR sensor data and sending the complete data to the fog layer wherein we are putting a threshold value to send only a few values to the cloud layer for the analysis. This model can be further enhanced by using end users as robots [30].

16.5.3.2 Weed Detection System

On-farm, weed is a crucial and unwanted part of the agricultural system [31]. For removing weed detection there is a need for a vision guidance system for automated weed detection using a robot or IoT system. The overall scenario of week detection system is illustrated in Figure 16.9. The image processing technique is used to separate the weed from the plant. In a vision-based system, the detection of inter-row spacing between weeds and crops can be done by using many image processing techniques. Once plant and weed get detected in the image then the frame wise current pose and orientation can be obtained using Hough transform. To predict the changes in pose and orientation from frame to frame this dynamic model will be used for the evolution of values over time. This vision system detects the weed and plant and separates it [32, 33]. Once the model is deployed in IoT device or at FRS. IoT device or

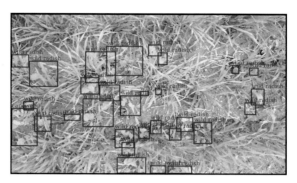

Figure 16.9: Weed detection through FRS.

robotic system will successfully detect and calculates the pose and orientation of the crop boundaries. The robot will capture the image and this image goes to the FRS system, this image gets feed to model and detect the plant and weed separately. We shall begin while studying and considering a small patch land that is under our study and shall assign bots to several robots which will help us for detecting weeds in the field of land.

Algorithm 1 depicts the working of Weed Detection Process. The first and foremost step is the using the line follower robotics which shall divide the

Algorithm 1: Weed Detection Process

Procedure WDP (image) → Fog server takes the images from robots
    Image Acquisition
    Image Segmentation
    Grayscale values
    ROI selection
    if *ROI = whole image* **then**
        Edge Detection
        if *Edge Detect ≥ threshold* **then**
            Hough Transformation
        else *Image Segmentation*
            Boundaries Detection
            Bag of Word Method → for assigning labels
    if *Boundary found* **then**
        Result sent to robots for navigation
    else *Boundary not found*
        Go to Image Segmentation Step and repeat

---

piece of land into the coordinate systems of *x* and *y* and using that coordinate system it will make the use of detecting the weed crop which is analogous to detecting the chaff from grain. It will use the subtle coordinate system and the coordinate axes to detect the weed. The line follower robots shall be used under this case study. After which image processing techniques shall be used which will analyze and detect the weed as per the given stipulated features of weed that how it is different from the crops. The first image sends to the FRS system where image acquisition, image segmentation, Hough transformation, and another image-building phenomenon through which weed is detected and by using Bag of Word method and the result send to the robot through Fog node network.

As shown in Figure 16.9, once the result acquired by a robot than by specific scrutiny and other mechanism and weed is detected and fertilizer is spread all over.

16.6 Challenges of Fog Robotics

Everything faces challenges and so as Fog computing too [34]. It includes major challenges in load balancing and its distribution of resources between the cloud and the edges, various APIs, SDN communications. There are a few more examples of the same.

i. *Instilling Dynamic analytics*: In fog systems, the resource management capable environment should determine dynamically which tasks should be inhibited to minimize the latency and maximize the throughput. Other factors such as privacy laws of the country must be taken care of.

ii. *Models and architectures*: A lot of Streams like Apache Storm, do not give large scalability and edibility for foggy and even IoT systems as their configurational architecture are entirely based on non-dynamic configurations. They need the ability to append and delete dynamic resources as those nodes which do processing are movable devices that often join and leave the network.

iii. *Security, reliability, and fault tolerance*: Forcing security in a foggy environment is a keyhole challenge because of the reason that they possess multiple service givers and users, and the distributed resources as well. Designating and enforcing authorization with authentication can work out well with multiple fog nodes whose computing capacities are different. A potential solution is a public key infrastructure. Fog architecture generally covers the failure of individual sensors, networks, service platforms, and applications. To enhance this, they could standardize the applications, such as the SCTP, which deal with reliability in events and packets in sensor wireless networks.

iv. *Power consumption*: They comprise of many nodes. Therefore, the computational calculation is distributed and is less efficient than the centralized systems of clouds. They use effective and efficient communications protocols and channels such as sampling techniques, CoAP, and effective filtering techniques.

16.7 Conclusion

Cloud Computing technology has opened the door to many interdisciplinary research. Cloud Robotics is one such field where robots can make the use of cloud infrastructure to share/upload its data to cloud. It also facilitates the availability of online run time functionality and computation offloading. But there exist many applications where there is no need to send all the data to the cloud rather some of the processing can be done at an intermediate node. This intermediating node can result in reducing latency, energy efficient low cost hardware system at user's end. Due to these advantages, there are many potential applications of robotics field that can be leveraged. In this article, we have explored the potential of Fog Robotics architecture. Fog Robotics architecture has been compared with Cloud Robotics architecture along with a standalone robot where we found that Fog-enabled robots exhibit low latency delay than the Cloud-enabled robots. Three use case studies of Fog Robotics with Multi-Robotic System (MRS), Self-driven Cars and Weed Detection in Agriculture has also been presented.

References

[1] Kuffner, J. 2010. Cloud-enabled humanoid robots.
[2] Doriya, R., Chakraborty, P. and Nandi, G. C. 2012. 'Robot-Cloud': A framework to assist heterogeneous low cost robots. doi: 10.1109/ICCICT.2012.6398208.
[3] Doriya, R., Chakraborty, P. and Nandi, G. C. 2012. Robotic services in cloud computing paradigm. doi: 10.1109/ISCOS.2012.24.
[4] Gudi, S. L. K. C., Ojha, S., Johnston, B., Clark, J. and Williams, M.-A. 2018. Fog robotics for efficient, fluent and robust human-robot interaction. In 2018 IEEE 17th International Symposium on Network Computing and Applications (NCA), pp. 1–5.
[5] Dastjerdi, A. V., Gupta, H., Calheiros, R. N., Ghosh, S. K. and Buyya, R. 2016. Fog computing: Principles, architectures, and applications. In Internet of Things, Elsevier, pp. 61–75.
[6] Xiao, Y. and Zhu, C. 2017. Vehicular fog computing: Vision and challenges. In 2017 IEEE International Conference on Pervasive Computing and Communications Workshops (PerCom Workshops), pp. 6–9.
[7] Perera, C., Qin, Y., Estrella, J. C., Reiff-Marganiec, S. and Vasilakos, A. V. 2017. Fog computing for sustainable smart cities: A survey. ACM Comput. Surv., 50(3): 1–43.
[8] Mell, P., Grance, T. and others. 2011. The NIST definition of cloud computing.
[9] Chiang, M. and Zhang, T. 2016. Fog and IoT: An overview of research opportunities. IEEE Internet Things J., 3(6): 854–864.

[10] Bonomi, F. 2011. Connected vehicles, the internet of things, and fog computing. In The Eighth ACM International Workshop on Vehicular Inter-Networking (VANET), Las Vegas, USA, pp. 13–15.

[11] Nandhini, C. and Doriya, R. 2017. Towards secured cloud-based robotic services. In 2017 International Conference on Signal Processing and Communication (ICSPC), pp. 165–170.

[12] Nandhini, C., Murmu, A. and Doriya, R. 2017. Study and analysis of cloud-based robotics framework. In 2017 International Conference on Current Trends in Computer, Electrical, Electronics and Communication (CTCEEC), pp. 800–8111.

[13] Byers, C. C. 2017. Architectural imperatives for fog computing: Use cases, requirements, and architectural techniques for fog-enabled IoT networks. IEEE Commun. Mag., 55(8): 14–20.

[14] [Online] www.openfogconsortium.org, "No Title."

[15] Consortium, O. and Others. 2017. OpenFog reference architecture for fog computing. Archit. Work. Gr., pp. 1–162.

[16] Bonomi, F., Milito, R., Zhu, J. and Addepalli, S. 2012. Fog computing and its role in the internet of things. In Proceedings of the First Edition of the MCC Workshop on Mobile Cloud Computing, pp. 13–16.

[17] Zhang, G., Shen, F., Liu, Z., Yang, Y., Wang, K. and Zhou, M.-T. 2018. FEMTO: Fair and energy-minimized task offloading for fog-enabled IoT networks. IEEE Internet Things J., 6(3): 4388–4400.

[18] Yang, Y., Wang, K., Zhang, G., Chen, X., Luo, X. and Zhou, M.-T. 2018. MEETS: Maximal energy efficient task scheduling in homogeneous fog networks. IEEE Internet Things J., 5(5): 4076–4087.

[19] Martinez, I., Jarray, A. and Hafid, A. S. 2020. Scalable design and dimensioning of fog-computing infrastructure to support latency sensitive IoT applications. IEEE Internet Things J.

[20] Patman, J., Alfarhood, M., Islam, S., Lemus, M., Calyam, P. and Palaniappan, K. 2018. Predictive analytics for fog computing using machine learning and GENI. In IEEE INFOCOM 2018-IEEE Conference on Computer Communications Workshops (INFOCOM WKSHPS), pp. 790–795.

[21] Doriya, R., Mishra, S. and Gupta, S. 2015. A brief survey and analysis of multi-robot communication and coordination. doi: 10.1109/CCAA.2015.7148524.

[22] Parker, L. E., Rus, D. and Sukhatme, G. S. 2016. Multiple mobile robot systems. In Springer Handbook of Robotics, Springer, pp. 1335–1384.

[23] Mohamed, N., Al-Jaroodi, J. and Jawhar, I. 2018. Utilizing fog computing for multi-robot systems. In 2018 Second IEEE International Conference on Robotic Computing (IRC), pp. 102–105.

[24] Mohamed, N., Al-Jaroodi, J. and Jawhar, I. 2018. Fog-enabled multi-robot systems. In 2018 IEEE 2nd International Conference on Fog and Edge Computing (ICFEC), pp. 1–10.

[25] Shan, L., Yi, Y. and Zhang, Z. 2018. Improving information centrality of a node in complex networks by adding edges. arXiv Prepr. arXiv1804.06540.

[26] Doriya, R., Singh, A. K. and Chkraborty, P. 2016. A cloud-based solution of dynamic traffic routing problem for autonomous robots. Int. J. Control Theory Appl., 9(42): 315–322.

[27] Canavan, L. 2017. Without fog, autonomous cars are going nowhere. IoT Agenda.

[28] TongKe, F. 2013. Smart agriculture based on cloud computing and IOT. J. Converg. Inf. Technol., 8(2): 210–216.

[29] Ray, P. P. 2017. Internet of things for smart agriculture: Technologies, practices and future direction. J. Ambient Intell. Smart Environ., 9(4): 395–420.

[30] Ferrández-Pastor, F.-J., Garc\'\ia-Chamizo, J.-M., Hidalgo, M. N. and Mora-Mart\'\inez, J. 2017. User-centered design of agriculture automation systems using internet of things paradigm. In International Conference on Ubiquitous Computing and Ambient Intelligence, pp. 56–66.

[31] Liu, B. and Bruch, R. 2020. Weed detection for selective spraying: a review. Curr. Robot. Reports, 1(1): 19–26.

[32] Billingsley, J. and Schoenfisch, M. 1995. Vision-guidance of agricultural vehicles. Auton. Robots, 2(1): 65–76.

[33] Bak, T. 2001. Vision-GPS fusion for guidance of an autonomous vehicle in row crops. Aalborg University, Department of Control Engineering.

[34] Gudi, S. L. K. C., Johnston, B. and Williams, M.-A. 2019. Fog robotics: a summary, challenges and future scope. arXiv Prepr. arXiv1908.04935.

Index